More Critical Praise for *And Then I Danced*

"Mark Segal has for decades been a pathfinder for LGBT journalists of all stripes. We're indebted to him for his years of radical activism, helping to foster a movement for change that has had a dramatic and positive impact for millions."
—Michelangelo Signorile, author of *It's Not Over: Getting Beyond Tolerance, Defeating Homophobia, & Winning True Equality*

"Mark Segal's ideas run from the alpha to the omega. Sometimes I think there's got to be more than one Mark Segal: he has done way too much for one lifetime. I highly recommend this book. If you can't get to meet Mark in person, this is the next best thing!"
—Michael T. Luongo, editor of *Gay Travels in the Muslim World*

"Before there was Ellen, Will, Grace, Rosie, Andy, and Anderson, Mark Segal was the _____
that forced _____
still alive, _____
Read all a _____

"Mark Se _____
cess has n _____
pioneers. _____

"Mark Se _____
communit _____
indisputab _____
leaving a p _____
it is impor _____

AND THEN I DANCED

TRAVELING THE ROAD TO LGBT EQUALITY

A MEMOIR BY

MARK SEGAL

OPEN
LENS
GREAT NECK LIBRARY

Published by Akashic Books
©2015 Mark Segal

Hardcover ISBN: 978-1-61775-410-4
Paperback ISBN: 978-1-61775-399-2
Library of Congress Control Number: 2015902762

First printing

Open Lens
c/o Akashic Books
Twitter: @AkashicBooks
Facebook: AkashicBooks
E-mail: info@akashicbooks.com
Website: www.akashicbooks.com

To Jason Villemez, who each day tells me there is more I can do and encourages me to dream and follow that vision; my parents Marty and Shirley Segal, who encouraged their son to be who he was; and Fannie Weinstein, suffragette and civil rights supporter, who taught her grandson well.

Acknowledgments

As a newspaper publisher, my knowledge of book publishing was nonexistent. A project of this scale does not get done without those people who have the expertise and believe in it to the point that they encourage you to make yourself vulnerable. Marva Allen, my copublisher, is a legend in the African American literary community who was one of the first women to break that glass ceiling. Upon our first meeting she told me simply, "You have a story to share and we will get this done." She soon introduced me to her colleagues Marie Brown and Regina Brooks at Open Lens, and to the folks at Akashic Books, which hosts their imprint. Again at first meeting they gave me the encouragement I needed since the endeavor frightened me. After all, up until this project, I only wrote a 500-word weekly column, not an entire book. Thanks too to my actress friend Sheryl Lee Ralph, who introduced me to my future publisher.

After the first draft, we invited the talented editor Michael Denneny (*The Mayor of Castro Street: The Life and Times of Harvey Milk* and *The Band Played On*) to work on the project. He took it on and explained to me that this was history that had to be recorded. He also took a book that was full of flashbacks and showed me how to put it in a mostly chronological order. I believe his special sense of history and enthusiasm for this book made me fully realize that it had to be completed.

I must thank my close friends and family, who were aware of the manuscript and kept it quiet knowing that I wanted to be able to abandon it at any time, and understood that they would read it only when it was published. Also, Richard Aregood, former Pulitzer Prize editorial writer for the *Philadelphia Daily News*, who helped me shape the early version of this book.

I have a new sense of appreciation for LGBT historians who assisted with getting me the hard facts needed to underscore issues in the book, especially Sean Strub, author of *Body Counts* and founder of *POZ* magazine, who read my chapter on AIDS to assure its accuracy.

Thanks to my family at *PGN*, who allowed me the time away from the office to do my various projects and who fill me with pride by delivering award-winning journalism each week.

Many writers forget the work our editors do, and my editors had a special task in teaching me to put my passion into words, and then into a weekly column. To Al Patrick, Pattie Tihey, Sarah Blazucki, and Jen Colletta—thank you.

Finally, thank you to those who lived this history with me and are still with us, and to those gone pioneers and friends who inspired and worked with me. To my sisters and brothers in Gay Liberation Front New York who were my teachers, especially Jerry Hoose, who in true GLF fashion debated with me many parts of this book. (Jerry lost his battle with cancer before it was completed but his spirit lives in these pages). To my Gay Youth New York family, who allowed me to learn to lead. To my friends in LGBT media, who fight each day to inform our community. And to my friends in mainstream media, who taught an activist how to become a publisher.

Table of Contents

Introduction

The rights that the LGBT community have gained and continue to gain, from marriage equality to employment nondiscrimination, are the result of decades of hard work from individuals who in the early days, most of the time, lived off the kindness of friends. In the 1960s, being a gay activist was not a profession; it was an unpaid job for those dedicated to LGBT equality. When the newly energized gay movement sprouted from the Stonewall riots of June 1969, there was no organizational support with deep pockets, bailing people out of jail. Those of us in the riot didn't have any best practices or contingency plans to fall back on. The only gay person I knew who was receiving a modest stipend was Reverend Troy Perry, who was building the gay-friendly Metropolitan Community Church.

Thanks to the early activists, today the LGBT community is represented in every segment of American society: from Fortune 500 CEOs, to leaders in education, labor, public safety, and politics, including at the White House. The Obama administration has appointed out LGBT individuals in almost every capacity at the highest levels of government.

We were able to get here because of the tireless work of pioneers such as Frank Kameny, Barbara Gittings, Harry Hay, Del Martin and Phyllis Lyon, Randy Wicker, Reverend Troy Perry, Martha Shelley, Marty Robinson, many of my brothers and sisters in New York's Gay Liberation Front, and so many others, including a man named Henry Gerber, who in 1925 created the first LGBT organization in the nation in Chicago.

Since we had no funds, we had to be creative in our efforts to change individuals' minds about who we were. This is my story but it is also an American story, one that illuminates and documents the historic LGBT struggle for equality. In most cases, I've kept to a chronological narrative, but sometimes, as is typical for me, I go off and explore issues that deserve further discussion and attention.

Chapter 1

The Boy from the Projects

I was an outsider from the beginning. When I was born in 1951 to Martin and Shirley Segal, my father was the proprietor of a store in South Philly, one of those neighborhood groceries that were once common throughout the big cities; in New York they are called bodegas. His proprietorship was short-lived. Against the backdrop of row homes and big Catholic churches, my father's store was condemned by eminent domain to be replaced by a housing project. My parents, with two little boys and no work, were provided for by the city. At some point, we moved to nearby Wilson Park. There, as a member of the only Jewish family in a South Philadelphia housing project, I got an expert lesson in isolation. Kids who lived there said that we were from the other side of the tracks, and it was a reality since the housing project was sandwiched in on one side by an expressway and on the other by the 25th Street railroad bridge. We were, literally, across the street and an underpass away from a middle-class, mostly Catholic neighborhood.

We were poor, which in the Jewish community is almost a sin against God, or in our case a sin against the rest of the family. To them, living in a housing project was almost unimaginable. Our relatives either turned up their noses at us or pitied us. We were the lowest rung of the family. I was ashamed of my address, 2333 South Bambrey Terrace, of wearing the same clothes until

they wore out, of our lack of money, and of every other charac-
teristic of being poor.

Our new neighbors were hardly welcoming. I still remember
the first few days of kindergarten when Irish and Italian kids
would say to me, "You killed our Christ," or the one that always
stumped me, "You're a devil with horns." Somehow I became a
deformed six-year-old murderer. For a while I'd subconsciously
touch the top of my head, waiting for the horns to grow, and I
wondered, *How could I possibly comb my hair with horns?*

The only support system I had were my parents, whom I
adored and who adored me. They followed the Jewish tradition, knowing that their central obligation as parents was to
love their children and to tell them they're the greatest people
in the world. They did that well. I knew I was loved and I knew
I was smart. I also knew that I could face the world armed with
those two gifts. After all, what else did I have? They gave me the
strength to persevere.

My father taught me to be quietly modest, although I occasionally (note: always) broke that rule. I knew my father had
been in the war, that he had a Purple Heart, and that his plane
had been shot down over the Pacific. That's all I knew until
he died and I went through his papers. He was a war hero who
would only say to us, "I have a fake knee, it's platinum and it's
more expensive than gold. When I die, dig it out and cash it in."
Neither he nor my mother would talk much about those times
or about their grandparents, my great-grandparents, who died
in the Holocaust.

One time my mother went to my grade school to defend
me because the teachers had demanded that I sing "Onward,
Christian Soldiers." In those days there was still prayer in public
schools, and they had us sing Christian songs. I didn't know why
I didn't want to sing that song, I just didn't. My teachers couldn't,

or more appropriately were unable to, force me to utter a word. Hence, my mother's first of many trips to the school. Of course, that made everyone in Edgar Allen Poe Elementary—students, teachers, and principals—hate my guts. The compromise on the hymn was that I was to stand and be silent while everyone else bellowed out that they were "marching off to war." So I knew discrimination from a very young age—from my affluent extended family, from the people around me in school, and even from the poor people in the project where I lived, who had their own noneconomic reasons not to like me. My refusal to sing "Onward, Christian Soldiers" was my first political action, my first defiance of conformity and the status quo.

Kids growing up in Wilson Park knew to make friends only with other kids in the neighborhood, not the kids across the tracks. My friends included my neighbor Barbara Myers, the only girl who would communicate with me. She was a slim blonde with buckteeth, glasses, and an unfortunate early case of acne, which never seemed to go away. This made her a fellow outcast, so we had a mutual bond. Mrs. Myers didn't take to the idea of her daughter having a Jew for a friend, but since I was the only one Barbara had, she tolerated me. Barbara eventually became my first sexual relation—well, I'm not sure that's what you'd call it.

Sexuality to my generation arrived in the form of the Sears, Roebuck catalog. That book showcased almost any item that was necessary for the household, including clothing. Every boy waited for the new edition to arrive, and when it did, the first page he turned to was the one with women's lingerie. Let's get this straight: they weren't drag queens in the making searching for an outfit, but normal prepubescent boys looking for their first sexual thrill, and they found it from the various models posing in bras and panties. That didn't really work for me. Actually, the only reaction it stirred in me was to make commentary on color choices. I would think, *Gee, she might look decent if that dress was another color.* What really worked for me was the men's fashion section. My eyes were glued to the men in underwear.

There was no name for it, at least none that I knew, but somehow it seemed wrong that I was looking at the men in the catalog. After all, men were supposed to be eyeing and sizing up women. I decided to try it. And thus, my first foray into heteronormativity began. Let's call it an experiment.

Somehow, kids in the neighborhood saw Barbara and me as a couple. Puppy love, they thought. We were friends, and for me that friendship might be used to discover this mystery that I couldn't quite solve.

Barbara's parents had one of those above-ground pools in their backyard. It was made of thin aluminum and had a flimsy plastic liner that you hoped didn't get punctured during the first swim. It was about four feet deep and six feet in diameter, and of course it was a calming sea blue. One afternoon while in the pool together, my hand started to feel its way around Barbara. I closed my eyes as my hand traveled down her body. Feeling the top half didn't do a thing for me, so I continued in search of that thrill that had been so well advertised to be at the bottom half. As my hand reached the most important part, it spoke loudly to my brain: *Something is missing here.* With that, I did what any other kid would do: I investigated. I put my head underwater, opened my eyes, and watched as my hand slipped into the bottom of Barbara's two-piece swimsuit. She didn't stop me. When I actually saw my hand there, it scared me so much that my mouth opened in shock and I swallowed so much water I almost drowned—a watery death filled with screams of "Yek!"

To say my experiment was unsuccessful would be an understatement. The thrill that other boys experienced with the scantily clad women in the catalog was, for me, false advertising. Years later, Barbara and I both had a good laugh about our little test. It was her experiment as well and the end result was that she liked boys. Guess we both had the same feelings.

It seems that every time you turn on the news or watch a talk show you hear about someone who was brought up in a public housing project and became a gazillionaire. While I'm not a gazillionaire, I'm well off, and I'm now proud of my roots going back to the Wilson Park housing project, 2333 South Bambrey Terrace.

Almost every politician talks about lifting people out of poverty. As someone who has been there, I can tell you most of them just don't get it. They've never experienced the daily grind of poverty. Their romanticized solution is nothing more than solving a numbers and jobs game. To those of us who have been there, poverty is a culture, one that envelops your entire being, from the constant hunger and degradation, to the fear, despair, and hopelessness that never go away. Even if you get out and get a good job, even if you become a gazillionaire, you still worry, even if irrationally, about being there again. Poverty never leaves you. We poor, those of us who have gotten out, strive every day never to be there again. I for sure never want to go back to Bambrey Terrace.

Our two-story brick row home was constructed as cheaply as the city could get away with. There was no basement. The kitchen was a dark cubbyhole with a slanted ceiling that supported the stairs to the second floor. A bulb swinging on a single cord from the ceiling was the only lighting. There was a closet where washcloths and other sundry items were stored just off the kitchen. When I was growing up, that closet gave me the creeps.

Our dining table and four chairs took up virtually the entire room. It was a typical Formica table with aluminum chairs that had cushioned backs and seats. Next to the dining area was our living room, which consisted of a couch and matching end tables, a chair, and a television atop a faded reddish-brown Oriental-style carpet. On the second floor were two bedrooms, my parents' and the room I shared with my brother. The family all used the same bathroom. Each of the bedrooms had a closet without a door, which my parents covered with curtains. I worried at night about who might be behind those curtains. Every night I prepared myself for Dracula and Abraham Lincoln to come lumbering out. Everyone can appreciate Dracula, the scary Bela Lugosi, but old Honest Abe? As a boy, for some reason the likeness of Abraham Lincoln frightened me.

Children are children even if you're poor. You still ask for the things you want, the things you see that other children have. To this day the moment of my life I feel most guilty about came after I asked my parents to buy me something they couldn't afford. In our house when you wanted something you went to my father. One day, while asking Dad for something, I don't even remember what, he exploded like I'd never seen before. He tried to explain to me why he couldn't get it for me, and then he began to cry. I can't remember what he actually said but I know what it was about. He was crying because he couldn't do better for his kids and felt like a failure. He tried to make me understand the "why" as he talked and cried, but it was way over my head. Finally, he told my mother he was going to take a walk. Ashamed of the pain I caused him, I also ran out of the house.

My mom was Edith Bunker from *All in the Family*—the Jewish version. Fragile, soft spoken, and wouldn't say a word against anyone. She was the most delicate, loving, decent human being I've ever known on this earth, but when it came to Dad she could be strong-minded. She loved that man no matter what. She followed us both out of the house that day and found me sitting on a park bench. "Mark," she leaned over and tried to explain, her words still resonating today, "Dad means well. It's just hard for him to make ends meet. We have to help him. He's a good man." Then she put on her best smile and said, "Let's take a walk and see what we can find."

Getting out of the projects was a treat, especially with Mom holding my hand. Passing Vare Junior High School we headed to Point Breeze Avenue, which in the 1950s was lined with cheap mom-and-pop shops.

After several blocks of walking my mother took me to a variety store, or what was once called a five-and-dime. She looked around and found the engine and caboose of a red plastic train set. They were wrapped in a see-through cellophane bag and were cheap. She asked me if I'd like them, and I screamed with delight. Mom handed the bag to me, and I held on tight. It was my prized possession. We then began our walk back to the projects, taking the same route past the beat-up school, with its overgrown weeds and unkempt ball field. As we entered Wilson Park she asked if I liked my toy. I reached into the bag and my train was gone. I said nothing. Seeing my reaction, she took the bag and found the hole in the bottom through which my toy had fallen out. She just started to cry. Watching my mother cry after all that had occurred that day, I wanted to cry and yell as well, but instead I got sick to my stomach. I just stood there in silence, awash in guilt. I had lost the toy and made my Mom cry. She quickly pulled herself together and we went home. It was never spoken about again, but it still makes me emotional.

The bright light of those dark years was my grandmother, Fannie Weinstein. Grandmom, all four feet seven inches of her, was a smart-dressing former suffragette. In the winter she vacationed in Miami but in the summer she stayed in Atlantic City, and each year I was her guest for two magical weeks. Grandmom was sort of the queen bee of the Jewish ladies' circuit of Atlantic City. And she was proud of her grandson. She made sure that when I was with her I was dressed properly. Each night we'd walk the boardwalk going from one rolling chair to another. She'd delight in bragging about me. How bright, how handsome, and how oh so charming I was. Each year, the two weeks were topped off with a dinner party. Never were the same guests present twice.

Grandmom celebrated diversity before it was fashionable, and the aim of those parties was to introduce me to a variety of people. So avant-garde it all was, it reminded me of one of the first books I had read, *Auntie Mame,* about a boy growing up with his eccentric aunt and her madcap adventures. Her zest for life was captured by her saying, *Live, live, live,* and the famous line, *Life is a banquet, and most poor sons of bitches are starving to death!* It became my motto in life. When Rosalind Russell struts across the screen in the film version, I saw my grandmother, my very own Auntie Mame.

Those parties, as I look back at them, were attended only by women, except for my Uncle Stan, who lived with my grand-mother and me. It was not unusual for there to be African American or Latino women among these eclectic folks, but one year I was introduced to Mrs. Goldman and her friend. When I looked at Mrs. Goldman, I thought that something was different about her. She was dressed in a skirt and wore a man's jacket and even walked like a man. Her friend, on the other hand, was dressed in a stylish woman's outfit. I remember that they sat very close together on the sofa. Grandmom asked Mrs. Gold-man to tell me about her job. She was a prison warden. How stereotypical that job would be for a lesbian, but back then the only question I had for Grandmom after everyone else left was, "Why were they so strange?" Grandmom smiled and told me that there are all types of people in the world, and one should never judge a person on what they look like on the outside. Mrs. Goldman was a good person, and that was all that counted.

To my delight it wasn't just in the summer that I'd see Grandmom. Sometimes she'd show up out of nowhere and take me to a movie, a speech, the art museum, or, as I remember most fondly, my first civil rights demonstration.

That day when she picked me up, she looked at my mother and said, "I have a very important place to take Mark—we'll be back by dinner." She grabbed my hand and we began to walk. When I asked her where we were going, she said to City Hall.

When we got to City Hall, we saw hundreds of people gathered, mostly black men and women. Grandmom walked up to someone and he handed her a stick with a sign on it. With the picket sign in one hand and me in the other, she marched us around City Hall, alongside everyone else. It all seemed to be some sort of game to me, but Grandmom explained it was about the issue of fairness.

After the march she introduced me to the man who had organized it. His name was Cecil B. Moore, a Philadelphia attorney, president of the local NAACP and a civil rights activist who, along with the Reverend Leon Sullivan and Sam Evans, were the major organizers for the African American community in Philadelphia at that time. He chatted with Grandmom, and it was obvious that they had known each other. At some point he leaned down and looked at me but said to her: "Your grandson certainly is skinny!" Then he laughed and walked away. Some twelve years later, the Democratic Party of Philadelphia honored Cecil B. Moore by nominating and electing him to the city council.

On my return to Philadelphia in the early seventies, one of my first tasks was to lobby for the introduction of nondiscrimination legislation into the city council to protect gay men and lesbian women. It was my job to go to each councilmember and ask if they would cosponsor the legislation or vote for it. At that point Cecil B. Moore was an elder statesman, having led the fight to integrate Girard College and the trade unions; he was always known to be outspoken and confrontational and was clearly unfazed by what people thought of his opinions. He often said whatever he wanted, sometimes just to get a reaction.

When I walked into his office for our designated appointment, he had his feet propped up on his desk and was smoking a cigar. He looked at me and said, "What do you want?" I went into a speech I had put together on why gays and lesbians needed protection from discrimination. About halfway through, he stopped me and said, "Just wait there." And, with what looked like an angry face, he added, "Are you asking me to support a bill for fags and dykes?" I was staring at him in disbelief, wondering if this was the same man my grandmother had asked me to march with, and then he broke into a big laugh and said, "You can count on me."

By the time I was nine years old, I knew that being poor sucked and that I had to get out. That desire to lift myself out of poverty's debilitating grasp led me to me my first newspaper job. There was a company contracted by the *Philadelphia Inquirer* to sell subscriptions to suburbanites. Their plan was simple: take inner-city schoolkids to the suburbs, have them go door to door and read a prepared text. "Hi, ma'am, my name is Mark Segal. I'm in a school contest to win a trip to Cape Canaveral to further my science education. You can help me win by subscribing to the *Philadelphia Inquirer*." Who would not buy from a poor, skinny, yet charming nine-year-old at their door?

Stereotypical as it is for a Jew (though believe me, I didn't care an ounce about stereotypes), I was the best salesman on our team. Those trips to the suburbs gave me my first view of how the other half lived, and put some money in my pocket. The car would pick us up in the projects around six p.m. each weekday.

We'd head to a fast food place for dinner with our team leader (we paid our own way), then spend about an hour or so going from door to door before returning home by eight or nine p.m. Often we'd go to a New Jersey development, mostly single-family homes with a bit of land around them. Those yards! Each house was similar but, to me, large with very nice furniture, and the swimming pools made me realize what my family didn't have. That experience taught me to dream. The money I made allowed me to buy some of the things I wanted; and brought the realization that there must be even better jobs out there for me. The job also taught me about anti-Semitism, from incidents with my coworkers. At that young age I knew life was going to be a fight if I wanted to succeed, but it was one in which I was willing to engage since my parents had promised me it was worth the effort, no matter how hard it might be. My parents never lied.

In my teens, Dad's luck turned a little. He had been driving a cab and made enough so we could move to Mount Airy, a much better neighborhood, well away from the projects. It was a middle-class community, the model of an integrated neighborhood, populated by Jews, Christians, and African Americans. At Germantown High School, I simultaneously got my first taste of organizing and learned an important lesson.

One teacher in my senior year had never taught high school

before, and couldn't handle the students. Most of us were a bit unruly, and even when we weren't misbehaving, we simply found it impossible to understand his teaching. His last resort at keeping control was to tell us that we were all going to fail his class. His class was a requirement to graduate, so I took up a petition. It was the first time I had ever done anything like that. This was the middle of the counterculture era, 1969. The inspiration for my campaign came from the rancor of the antiwar and civil rights movements that I watched nightly on the television news. One of the many items I listed in the petition as a reason for our lobbying was that he was teaching Communism. All the white kids signed, but the black kids refused and were angered by the focus on Communism. Finally, one of the black kids explained it to me. In the South, when the police were pushing around the civil rights workers, they justified it by claiming they were Communists. So I took that item off the petition and even today I still think about what an unfair and cheap shot it was. Once we did it, however, everyone signed. We all passed the class and graduated. It was my first organizing success, and I learned a valuable lesson in compromise and listening.

While other kids were collecting eight-millimeter stag films, my collection was of old J.C. Penney, Montgomery Ward, and Sears, Roebuck catalogs. I didn't think there were any stag films or porn for people like me. One day at a farmers market in Berlin, New Jersey, I stumbled upon an old magazine stall and began flipping through various periodicals. I found a magazine with men modeling in what today would be called Speedos, and in jock straps, some wearing strategically placed loincloths, attempting to emulate the look of a Greek god. Ashamed to take it to the cashier, I put the periodical inside another magazine and purchased that one instead. Telling the clerk that I didn't need a bag and holding it tight like my freedom depended on it, I exited the store posthaste.

I didn't want to kiss the girls. I'd look at the guys in my class and feel far more attracted to them. There was no doubt in my mind about this, but I didn't know the word for who I was or what I was feeling. I knew, however, that I was okay with it. Now, I wasn't going to tell anybody, not in the 1960s.

I did have a few friends in Mount Airy. Randy Miller became my closest friend and my first real crush, which was an obstacle in our friendship, since he wasn't gay. I never told him how I felt about him. This experience taught me that there is more to a relationship than physicality . . . The way I felt about him, the way I desired him, wasn't just for sex because I wouldn't trade the emotional connection of our friendship for that alone. I realized that any real relationship had to include emotional connection.

When I was younger, maybe five or six years old, my cousin Norman was sixteen. His father discovered that he was gay, gave him a major beating, and threw him out of the house. Cousin Norman was the family member whom nobody mentioned. One day, I was in the backseat of my parents' Studebaker while they were discussing him and I somehow picked up on the fact that he was a guy who liked guys—a *fegeleh*. It was rarely brought up in the family and this clued me in to the dynamic that silence was preferred on this topic. Talk or no talk, I knew that whatever it all meant, I too was a *fegeleh*. And I knew never to speak about it.

As a teenager, I read in *TV Guide* one afternoon that on his PBS talk show, David Susskind was going to interview "real live homosexuals." A new word different from *fegeleh*, somehow I knew it also referred to me. I just knew it. In the fifties and sixties, those words were rarely used, but if you were found to be a homosexual, you were a sinner in religious circles; you were a criminal in legal situations; you were insane in the psychiatric community; and you were unemployable by city, state, and federal governments. Pretty much a life of condemnation awaited you. If people found out the word *homosexual* applied to you, chances were you would lose your job, your family, be subjected to electrical shocks, and lose everything else you valued, so most remained inside a closet within a closet. I didn't know all of this as a kid, but I knew it was a dangerous subject to discuss. This would all change later on, but in the early sixties there weren't many places to turn if such a life was yours.

My parents had given me a nine-inch portable black-and-white television set for my bar mitzvah. It was all the rage back then, an itty-bitty set with big round batteries. The David Susskind show came on at late at night and I remember taking my TV up to my room, making my bedcovers into a tent, and watching the show. There was a man from the Mattachine Society in New York talking about gay people. I thought to myself, *There are homosexuals in New York. There are people like me.* Then and there I knew I would move to New York.

It was awhile before I took action, but that night a plan began to form in my head. I was going to be with people like me. For a long while I had no idea how I'd do it, but it eventually came to me. Radio Corporation of America (RCA) had a technical institute that taught high school students how to be television cameramen. That was my ticket. It broke my father's heart since he really wanted me to go to college, and Mom always said I'd make a great lawyer. But the only thing that mattered to me then was to be with my own kind and there were none of us in Philadelphia, at least none that I knew. In New York I would become part of a new breed of gay men who didn't slide easily into the popular and unfortunate stereotypes of the times—and that would work to my advantage.

On May 10, 1969, the day after grades were finalized, I moved to New York on the pretense that I would start technical school in September. My parents drove me up, dropped me off, and I got a room at the YMCA. I dressed up in my best clothes and set off for a gay evening, probably expecting that my gay brothers and sisters would line up to embrace me and welcome me into their community. The problem was, I had no idea where to go. There were certainly no neon signs pointing to the gay area. It seemed the place to start my search was Greenwich Village, which according to the network news was the counter-cultural hub of the 1960s. Getting off the subway in the Village, I had an unhappy, lonely feeling. Leaving the security of home, finding myself in a strange place with no prospects of a job and little money, was a bit daunting. Yet my search was on. It didn't begin very well, though, and that first night I returned to my tiny four-dollar sweatbox room, exhausted and unsuccessful in finding my people.

After a few days of looking around, I came across a Village dance bar, the Stonewall, a mob-owned dive. The search was over. As it turned out, two boys who I'd met at the YMCA from Saint Cloud, Minnesota, were there that night as well.

That first week, remembering the Susskind show with real live homosexuals, I also looked up *Mattachine Society* in the telephone book and went to their office. I had no idea what to expect. All I knew about them from the television show was that they worked on keeping gay people from getting fired. I walked out of the office about fifteen minutes later with a guy named Marty Robinson, who would later become one of the most unsung heroes of the gay movement. Marty was young and evidently frustrated in his dealings with Mattachine. He said, "You don't want to be involved with these old people. They don't understand gay rights as it's happening today. Look what's happening in the black community. Look at the fight for women's rights. Look at the fight against the Vietnam War."

It was 1969 and Mattachine had become old. They were men in suits. We were men in jeans and T-shirts. So he told me that he and others were going to start a new gay rights movement, one more in tune with the times. Marty was creating an organization called the Action Group and I became an inaugural member. We didn't know exactly what we were going to do or what actions we might pursue, but none of that mattered. Others at that time were also creating gay groups to spark public consciousness, similar to the groups feminists were establishing. It deserves to be said right here and right now that the feminist movement was pivotal in helping to shape the new movement for gay rights.

Groups across New York worked independently of each other, but all with the same goal of defining ourselves rather than accepting the labels that society had branded us with. We were on the ground floor of the struggle for equality, and though some might have seen it as a sexual revolution, we saw it as defining ourselves. Years later a friend would remark, "Mark was so involved with the sexual revolution that he didn't have time to participate." The Action Group would hold meetings walking down Christopher Street—our outdoor office, so to speak. We didn't have a headquarters.

Then, just a little over a month after I arrived, on June 28, 1969, Stonewall happened.

Chapter 2
Stonewall

Many in the LGBT community think of the Stonewall vets, as some call us, like heroes. For me it started out as a frightening event.

I was in the back of the bar near the dance floor, where the younger people usually hung out. The lights in the room blinked—a signal that there would be a raid—then turned all the way up. Stonewall was filled that night with the usual clientele: drag queens, hustlers, older men who liked younger guys, and stragglers like me—the boy next door who didn't know what he was searching for and felt he had little to offer. That all changed when the police raided the bar. As they always did, they walked in like they owned the place, cocky, assured that they could do and say whatever they wanted and push people around with impunity. We had no idea why they came in, whether or not they'd been paid, wanted more payoffs, or simply wanted to harass the fags that night. One of the policemen came up to me and asked for my ID. I was eighteen, which was the legal drinking age in New York in those days. I rustled through my wallet, very frightened, and quickly handed him my ID. I was no help in their search for underage drinkers. I was relieved to be among the first to get out of the bar.

As a crowd began to assemble, I ran into Marty Robinson and he asked what was going on.

"It's just another raid," I told him, full of nonchalant sophistication. We walked up and down Christopher Street, and fifteen minutes later we heard loud banging and screaming. The screams were not of fear, but resistance. That was the beginning of the Stonewall riots. It was not the biggest riot ever—it has been tremendously blown out of proportion—but it was still a riot, although one pretty much contained to across the street on Sheridan Square and Seventh Avenue. There were probably only a couple hundred participants; anyone with a decent job or family ran away from that bar as fast as they could to avoid being arrested. Those who remained were the drag queens, hustlers, and runaways.

People had begun to congregate at the door after they left the bar. One of the cops had said something derogatory under his breath and the mood shifted. The crowd began taunting the police. Every time someone came out of the bar, the crowd yelled. A drag queen shouted at the cops: "What's the matter, aren't you getting any at home? I can give you something you'd really love." The cops started to get rough, pushing and shoving. In response the crowd got angry. The cops took refuge inside. The drag queens, loud and boisterous, were throwing everything that wasn't fastened down to the street and a few things that were, like parking meters. Whoever assumes that a swishy queen can't fight should have seen them, makeup dripping and gowns askew, fighting for their home and fiercely proving that no one would take it away from them.

More and more police cars arrived. Some rioters began firebombing the place while others fanned out, breaking shop windows on Christopher Street and looting the displays; somebody put a dress on the statue of General Phil Sheridan. There was an odd, celebratory feel to it, the notion that we were finally fighting back and that it felt good. Bodies ricocheted off one another, but there was no fighting in the street. All the anger was directed at the policemen inside the bar. People were actually laughing and dancing out there. According to some accounts, though I did not actually see this, drag queens formed a Rockettes-style chorus line singing, *"We are the Stonewall girls / We wear our hair in curls / We wear no underwear / To show our pubic hair."* That song and dance later became popular with a gay youth group I was part of, and months after Stonewall, Mark Horn, Jeff Hochhauser, Michael Knowles, Tony Russomanno, and I would dance our way to the Silver Dollar restaurant at the bottom of Christopher Street. We were going to be the first graduating class of gay activists in this country—indeed, most of us are still involved, and we're in touch with each other to this day.

Marty Robinson, after seeing what was happening, disappeared and then reappeared with chalk. Most people don't realize that Stonewall was not simply a one-night occurrence. Marty immediately understood that the Stonewall raid presented a "moment" that could be the catalyst to organize the movement and bring together all the separate groups. He was the one person who saw it then and there as a pivotal point in history. At his direction several of us wrote on walls and on the ground up and down Christopher Street: *Meet at Stonewall tomorrow night.* How did Marty know that this night could create something that would change our community forever?

The nights following the Stonewall raid consisted primarily of loosely organized speeches. Various LGBT factions were coming together publicly for the first time, protesting the oppressive treatment of the community. Up until that moment, LGBT people had simply accepted oppression and inequality as their lot in life. That all changed. There was a spirit of rebellion in the air. More than just merely begging to be treated equally, it was time to stand up, stand out, and demand an end to fearful deference.

Stonewall would become a four-night event and the most visible symbol of a movement. We united for the first time: lesbian separatists, gay men in fairy communes, people who had been part of other civil rights movements but never thought about one of their own, young gay radicals, hustlers, drag queens, and many like me who knew there was something out there for us, but didn't know what it was. It found us. So, to the NYPD, thank you. Thank you for creating a unified LGBT community and thank you for becoming the focal point for years of oppression that many of us had to suffer growing up. You represented all those groups and individuals that wanted to keep us in our place.

The Action Group eventually joined with other organizations to become the Gay Liberation Front, or GLF. In that first year Marty helped create the new gay movement, along with people like Martha Shelley, Allen Young, Karla Jay, Jim Fouratt, Barbara Love, John O'Brien, Lois Hart, Ralph Hall, Jim Owles, Perry Brass, Bob Kohler, Susan Silverman, Jerry Hoose, Steven Dansky, John Lauritsen, Dan Smith, Ron Auerbacher, Nikos Diaman, Suzanne Bevier, Carl Miller, Earl Galvin, Michael Brown, Arthur Evans, and of course Sylvia Rivera.

I'd like to believe that the GLF put us gay youth in a good position to succeed, since many of us have done so in different ways. Mark Horn has had an incredible career in advertising and public relations at top firms; Jeff Hochhauser went on to his dream of becoming a playwright and teaching theater; Michael Knowles is in theater management; and Tony Russomanno, who for a while in those early days was my partner, continued on his path in broadcasting, winning multiple Emmy and Peabody awards as a news reporter and television anchor.

* * *

Over the last few years, LGBT history has become a passion of mine, and sometimes it seems that the younger generation doesn't really care about it. The Gay Liberation Front has mostly been ignored in the history books, even though it helped forge the foundation upon which our community is built.

Stonewall was a fire in the belly of the equality movement. Even so, accounts of it are full of myth and misinformation, and much of that will inevitably remain so, since there are differing accounts from those active in the movement. That's the nature of memory, I suppose. Regardless of the diverging stories, and no matter how intense the fighting was, Stonewall represented, absolutely, the first time that the LGBT community successfully fought back and forged an organized movement and community. All of us at Stonewall had one thing in common: the oppression of growing up in a world which demanded our silence about who we were and insisted that we simply accept the punishment that society levied for our choices. That silence ended with Stonewall, and those who created the Gay Liberation Front organized and launched a sustainable movement.

But Stonewall was not the first uprising. LGBT history is written, like most history, by the victors, those with the means and those with connections or power. Two similar uprisings before Stonewall have almost been written out of our history: San Francisco's Compton Cafeteria riot in 1966 and the Dewey's sit-in in Philadelphia in 1965. Drag queens and street kids who played a huge role in both events never documented those riots, thus they have been widely eliminated by the white upper middle class, many of whom were ashamed of those elements of our community. But Stonewall, Compton, and Dewey's all have one thing in common: drag queens and street kids. For some historians, drag queens are not the ideal representatives of the LGBT community. Oppression within oppression was and is still of concern. Even recently, with the transgender issue finally being taken seriously, there is still a backlash from the community about including them in the general gay movement.

It has been over forty years since the Gay Liberation Front first took trans seriously, but the gay men who wore those shirts with the polo players or alligator emblems didn't want trans people as the representation of their community. Their revisionist history has been accepted into popular culture because they were the ones with connections to publishers, the influence, as well as the money and time to sit back and write about what "really" happened.

The riot of 1966 in San Francisco grew out of police harassment of drag queens at Compton's Cafeteria. It all started with the staff at Compton's telling the drag queens to settle down. It was the drag queens who, night after night, went there and bought drinks, sustaining the business. It was, in a sense, their home. The management's job, according to their deal with the police, was to keep the queens in order. One night, like Stonewall, the queens decided they didn't want to be controlled any longer.

And even before Compton's there were the Dewey's restaurant sit-ins in Philadelphia in April 1965. The restaurant management decided not to serve people who demonstrated "improper behavior." The reality was that they didn't want to serve homosexuals, especially those who didn't wear the acceptable clothing. Meaning drag queens. A spontaneous sit-in occurred and over the next week the Janus Society, an early gay rights organization, had picketers on site handing out flyers. Most were people who had little to lose, the street kids and drag queens once again. Those LGBT people with the little animals on their polo shirts were in short supply.

Both Compton's and Dewey's point to the fact that in the

mid-1960s the fight for black civil rights was beginning to influence the more disenfranchised in the gay community. The
major difference with those two early events is that from the
Stonewall riots grew a new movement, one that still lives today.
Nonetheless, they deserve to be remembered.

The biggest fallacy of Stonewall is when people say, "Of course
they were upset, Judy Garland was being buried that day." That
trivializes what happened and our years of oppression, and is
just culturally wrong. Many of us in Stonewall who stayed on
Christopher Street and didn't run from the riot that day were
people my age. Judy Garland was from the past generation, an
old star. Diana Ross, the Beatles, even Barbra Streisand were
the icons of our generation. Garland meant a little something
to us, as she did for many groups—"Somewhere Over the Rainbow"—but that was it. And, honestly, that song was wishful
thinking, an anthem for the older generation. In that bar, we
were going to smash that rainbow. We didn't have to go over
anything or travel anywhere to get what we wanted. The riot
was about the police doing what they constantly did: indiscrimi-
nately harassing us. The police represented every institution of
America that night: religion, media, medical, legal, and even
our families, most of whom had been keeping us in our place.
We were tired of it. And as far as we knew, Judy Garland had
nothing to do with it.

While I didn't know it at that moment, I was fighting back
against feelings that had been suppressed for so many years. No
more J.C. Penney catalogs for me. It was time for the real thing.
As the riot was happening all around me, the idea of a circus
came to mind, and then it hit me: we can shout who we are and
not be ashamed, we can demand respect. It was at that point
that Marty Robinson's words hit a chord. We were fighting for

our rights just as women, African Americans, and others had done throughout history.

After my Grandmom had taken me to my first civil rights demonstration at thirteen, I'd watch the news every night, waiting to see the latest update on what was happening. My television viewing and newspaper reading included following the Freedom Riders in the South. The sit-ins and marches had a big impact on me. The images of Birmingham, of Bull Connor with his German shepherds snapping, of the fire hoses blasting people marching for desegregation moved me. They led me to ask how one human could possibly treat another in that manner. I realized, too, the brilliance of Martin Luther King Jr., the Atlanta pastor and face of the movement, in his strategic use of Bull Connor and Birmingham to showcase the hatred behind segregation. What's more, Bayard Rustin, MLK's contemporary in the fight for equality and his chief of staff for the March on Washington, was a gay man, vocal on the rights of gay people. The FBI and others tried to use Rustin's "homosexuality" against him, and some of the organizers of the march wanted to drop him, but MLK stood tall in supporting him. It wouldn't be until I interviewed Coretta Scott King in 1986 and she reaffirmed her husband's support of "gay rights" that I got to personally offer my gratitude. It was an unknown fact to many, including those of us in Gay Liberation Front, which would become the only university I ever attended.

Gay Liberation Front, in all likelihood, was the most dysfunctional LGBT organization that ever existed, which shouldn't be very surprising. Born from the ashes of the Stonewall riots, it brought together for the first time the various elements and fractions of the community, to organize, to strategize, and to fight back. Before Stonewall we were polite; after Stonewall we demanded our equality. To that point we had no understanding of who we were as a people, we only had what society told us we were, and at that time a lot of us in New York were attempting to redefine ourselves. There were many individuals who began to set up collectives, lesbian separatist groups, discussion groups, even communes, and everything in between.

In addition to redefining ourselves, we also realized from the beginning that we were focused on building a community, since we couldn't count on any part of society to provide the basic services we needed. We had to create those institutions where they had never existed before. We were trying to establish our goals and figure out what kind of organization we would be. Since we were oppressed by the system, we didn't want to use any of their old tools in our meetings.

Therefore, there was no leadership at GLF, no permanent chair, only the occasional use of *Robert's Rules of Order*. Decisions were made by consensus, and in order to reach that point some meetings went late into the evening. It was total chaos. It worked, but at times it was almost comedic.

At one meeting a woman spoke about how men were trying to control women in the organization. Her example was that the men with beards in the group did not understand how through the ages facial hair had been used to symbolize the dominant male of a community, i.e., the leader. So men with beards at Gay Liberation Front were supporting the oppression of women. The following week several men, in order to show solidarity, came to the meeting with their beards shaved. That upset some of the other men, who saw beards as fashion or a symbol of who they were, accepting their masculinity. That in turn upset the fairies who wanted men to accept their feminine side. And around it went.

We debated everything, with the exception of creating

community—we were all agreed on that goal, and worked to form groups to help us achieve it. There was no debate when I advocated for a gay youth group and little debate when Sylvia Rivera created Street Transvestite Action Revolutionaries (STAR), one of the first-ever trans organizations. There was no debate on health alerts, and the only conflict about opening a community center related to money, not the idea. This is part of why 1969 is often cited as the start of the new gay rights movement. Gay Liberation Front led our struggle from a mere movement trying to change laws into one of harvesting community.

We were so radical that even Harvey Milk, the "Mayor of Castro Street" who lived in New York before he became the first elected openly gay member of San Francisco's Board of Supervisors in 1977 and was assassinated in 1978, stayed clear of us.

Little known fact about Harvey: His former partner and later a friend of mine was Craig Rodwell, founder of the Oscar Wilde Bookshop. He was also the founder of what today is Gay Pride Day, but what Craig then called the Christopher Street Gay Liberation Day. Milk was so closeted in 1970 that he wouldn't involve himself with the event or any other gay movement. He only did so after moving away from his New York family to San Francisco in 1972. It says something about San Francisco circa 1978 that an openly gay man would be assassinated in what was considered the nation's most gay-friendly city. (For those who appreciate LGBT history, the first openly gay or lesbian elected official anywhere in the country was Nancy Wechsler, voted to the city council in Ann Arbor in 1972, then Elaine Noble to the state house in Massachusetts in 1974. It would not be until 1987, when Barney Frank came out, that we would have an out member of Congress, and 2012 when we finally had an out member of the US Senate, Tammy Baldwin.)

Like all caucuses, committees, cells, or communes, each

group within the Gay Liberation Front had its mission. While I didn't form the first youth group, I organized the first one intended to be a foundation on which a community could then be built. We were going to reach out beyond the areas where LGBT youth were thought to be. We took on the serious issues of bullied, battered, homeless, and suicidal gay youth. We created safe spaces and safe activities. And not only were we there to offer our support to one of the most endangered segments of our community, we were there to nurture future activists. We were in some ways the first graduating class of gay liberation. Donn Teal wrote in *The Gay Militants*: "As GLF had given birth to organizations for transvestites and transsexuals and for Third World people, so did it sire Gay Youth." Published in 1971, this was the first LGBT history of those early years.

Our flyers clearly stated that our goals were both political and social. We even surprised our older comrades in the Gay Liberation Front with our media outreach directed at gay youth. We went on radio talk shows and even TV shows. We spoke at high schools. One of my favorite items of that time was a copy of the *Spider Press*, the newspaper of Oceanside High School, and there on the cover is a picture of Gay Youth members Tony Russomanno and Mark Segal with the headline, "Gay Activist Lecture; They Are Not Neurotic." This was October 23, 1970.

At one time or another I was chairman, president, or sometimes just the leader. My steadfast vice president, Mark Horn, whose title never changed, would smirk at my various titles. Tony Russomanno helped us in our goal of becoming the first national gay youth organization by starting our Detroit chapter—and we called ourselves, simply, Gay Youth. We soon had chapters in San Francisco, Chicago, Tampa, Ann Arbor, and even my hometown of Philadelphia. Our Philly chapter started by Tommi Avicolli Mecca, now a housing activist in San Francisco, intended "to act as a basic introduction to Gay Liberation Front." In Stephan L. Cohen's book *The Gay Liberation Youth Movement in New York,* our "demands" in various national LGBT organizational meetings, to summarize, were: ending ageism in all its forms, ending age-of-consent laws, ending abuse by parents, ending repression by schools and religious institutions, and, most importantly, an equal voice at the table for LGBT organizations.

I hosted movie nights in my five-story walk-up apartment on 12th Street and Avenue C, which was a three-room tenement decorated with donations and furnishings from the street; the bathtub was in the kitchen. It had a nice living room where we would plug in the borrowed projector and show films on the wall, before leaving to take a walk across town to Christopher Street. These movie nights grew too popular for the apartment so we moved them to Alternate U, where we held our dances. Gay Youth did all of this with no real funding, with the exception of what came from our pockets or what we received from the small Gay Liberation Front treasury.

As Marc Stein writes in his book *Rethinking the Gay and Lesbian Movement,* "Interest was so great among young people that in 1970 GLF-NY established a Gay Youth caucus . . . Led by Mark Segal, Gay Youth soon was functioning as an autonomous organization with affiliated groups elsewhere in the United States and Canada." For me, Gay Youth was a lesson in both creating lifelong friendships and leadership. It also helped me prove to myself that my career as an activist was real—as long as I had no expectations of a salary.

The most contested topic at any Gay Liberation Front meeting was sexism, but we debated many subjects. At times the debates became personal and it was not unusual to hear people being labeled capitalist pigs, fascist, racist, sexist, and for good measure I'd even toss in the label ageist on occasion.

Somehow even the simple act of a kiss took on political overtones. Perry Brass tells this story: "Someone explained to me that these were 'political kisses,' to show that we were out and proud, especially at a GLF meeting. At my first meeting we broke into discussion groups after the 'business' part of the meeting was over. My discussion group of six people included Pete Wilson, a good-looking young man who also had a program on WBAI radio. Pete had a wonderful voice, and a remarkably sparkling, outgoing personality. I was drawn to him, and I remembered a lot of what he said, talking about how important it was for us to throw off old habits and fears. I certainly had enough of the old habits and fears, growing up in an extremely repressive atmosphere. I noticed, though, there was a distinct coolness to Pete. He was not someone to hug and smooch with other people. But he was very political and could talk an excellent political line.

"Several weeks after this first meeting, I went to Carnegie Hall for an afternoon concert. After it was over, while walking down from the balcony, I spotted Pete in the stairway. He approached me in the midst of a throng of people, and kissed me. He had never kissed me before at a meeting, or any place. I was embarrassed for a second; I was not used to kissing outside. We talked a bit, and I hid any concerns I had about being kissed in the stairway of Carnegie Hall. At the next GLF meeting, on seeing him, I walked up to Pete and kissed him.

"'Why did you do that?' he asked.

"I shrugged. It seemed the right thing to do. 'You kissed me at Carnegie Hall,' I said.

"'Oh, that was a political kiss,' he explained. 'You don't have to do that here.'"

Some topics weren't discussed, such as gays in the military or marriage, but we still had members who went off by themselves and dealt with those issues without the endorsement of the organization. Working with elected officials became a major effort of Marty Robinson and Jim Owles. Gay Liberation Front's support for the Black Panthers, and our numerous demonstrations outside the Women's House of Detention which then was in our neighborhood on Greenwich off Christopher, caused a rift. We'd often join the demonstrations and march and shout, *"Hey hey, ho ho, the house of D has to go!"* And our contingent would then shout, *"Ho ho, hey hey, gay is just as good as straight!"* Ultimately, these types of issues caused Jim and Marty and a few others to break away from Gay Liberation Front and create Gay Activist Alliance. The last straw for them was the support given to the Black Panthers.

Many of us felt religion was a fundamental element in our repression. When Reverend Troy Perry held a meeting in New York at the Summit Hotel on Lexington Avenue to organize a branch of his fledgling LGBT church, Metropolitan Community Church (MCC), we picketed. Yes, one gay organization picketing another. After his meeting, however, Troy came out to speak to us. He took me aside and explained that while we were effective at reaching some members of the community, we had little possibility of reaching those who were religious. His church gave people a place to go where they could be both religious and a member of the LGBT community. His point was pragmatic and started a friendship between us that lasts to this day.

The same holds true for my sisters and brothers in Gay Liberation Front. Being one of the youngest in the group, I was allowed certain liberties, and for that reason I was and am on good terms with most of our surviving members. They were my teachers, and all that I have accomplished has its roots in what I learned in GLF.

* * *

After GLF's incredible first year, many thought we should celebrate Stonewall and our achievements. Chief among them was Craig Rodwell, so he organized what is now commonly known as a gay pride parade. As I've already mentioned, its name then was Christopher Street Gay Liberation Day. I was one of the many who volunteered to be a marshal those first few years. One of the original posters from the event hangs in a place of honor in my den.

It was Sunday, June 28, 1970. No one knew what would happen since we intended to march up to Central Park without a permit. We held self-defense/martial arts classes at Alternate U where we learned how to protect ourselves, since we had no idea who or what would greet us. After all, we were going to march through the middle of Manhattan from the Village to Central Park. That march was one of the great products of Stonewall.

GLF changed the world in one year. Think that's an overstatement? Here are the facts: before Stonewall, the movement for LGBT equality consisted of one large national public demonstration each year on July 4 in front of Independence Hall in Philadelphia, and of course the Compton's and Dewey's events and a couple of small regional pickets. But the picket line at Independence Hall lasted from 1965 till 1969. No more than fifty to one hundred people attended. That was the preeminent LGBT demonstration of its day, and the picketers came from across the nation, though mostly from the East Coast. In a few major cities there were organizations like One Inc. (Los Angeles), Mattachine (Washington and New York), Daughters of Bilitis and Janus Society (Philadelphia), and a handful of others. That was it.

But Gay Liberation Front, along with its brother and sister organizations, wanted to create something more than just a march for equality. Before Stonewall, these few brave organizations, and the people on those picket lines outside Independence Hall each July 4, all that existed were bars, secret gay hook-up venues, and private parties.

In 1969, the Mattachine Society in New York would not allow anyone under eighteen into their offices, afraid that the police would raid them. So we organized our youth, welcomed them to our meetings, set up a suicide hot line, a speakers' bureau that went to high schools, and, when the *Village Voice* would not publish the word "gay," we marched on them. The laws were wrong; we were not!

That Sunday morning we gathered on Christopher Street. By the time we reached 23rd Street, the crowd still reached all the way back to Christopher Street. Estimates were everywhere from 5,000 to 15,000 people. We had taken the movement from a brave crew of a hundred people willing to march in public at those Independence Hall pickets to what was now a march of many thousands. That first year of Gay Liberation Front was one of the most pivotal years in the struggle for LGBT equality. As my friend Jerry Hoose used to say about that year, "We went from the shadows to sunlight."

And in 1972, when the gay pride march was officially launched, the *New York Times* reported on June 26, "The message of the march, according to Mark Segal, the grand marshal, was simply, 'We're proud to be gay.'" Well, I wasn't the grand marshal, and I wouldn't return to that march again until Stonewall 25—and then again in 2004, when Frank Kameny, Jim Kepner, Jack Nichols, some of my brothers and sisters from Gay Liberation Front, and I, among others, were put on two giant floats and recognized as pioneers of the struggle for LGBT equality.

* * *

New York City was for me the center of everything, especially the East Village, where I lived. At that time, it was not the trendy neighborhood it is today; rather, it was one of the most dangerous in the city and therefore affordable to me. Many of my new friends were connected to the outer fringes of show business: James, a dancer from Ohio, and his sister Kelly, who was dating one of the doormen at Stonewall. Mark "10 1/2" Stevens, who found a career in straight porn films even though he was gay and, as my parents might say, a nice Jewish boy. And then there was my roommate, Rosemary Gimple, and her friend Jeff Hochhauser.

Rosemary and Jeff had written a musical called *Graduation* that was being performed at New York Theater Ensemble. They enlisted me as their stage manager despite knowing that my only previous theatrical experience was in high school where I had one line in our school version of *The Man Who Came to Dinner*. (I was to appear at a pivotal point in the plot and shout, "Stop, I'm the FBI and this is a raid!" When I walked onstage my friends in the audience applauded and I froze.)

Graduation was the story of a teenage boy coming of age and accepting himself. It was, I believe, the first gay-themed musical on the New York stage and it led to my second and last job in the theater, managing a show down the street for Andy Warhol "superstar" Jackie Curtis. All I can remember is a song titled "White Shoulders" and what we would today call a transgender actress, Holly Woodlawn, whom everyone adored. Nearby was La Mama, which seemed to always have a show featuring a drag queen. Sometimes that drag queen was Harvey Fierstein, who went on to win many Tonys on Broadway and be inducted into the American Theater Hall of Fame.

The off-off-Broadway community was flourishing. On nights when you weren't working, you could get yourself invited to see these other offerings. One night for me it was a reading of an unfinished show titled *Small Craft Warnings*, which I knew nothing about. As I watched the first act, I grew increasingly agitated and annoyed. The self-pity of the gay character was precisely what my activism was trying to end. At that point, gays in the media had only three variations: pitiful, villainous, or suicidal, and this was going down that same old path. So with my newfound activism and left-leaning language, I stood up and shouted, "Bullshit! This is oppressive to gay men!" As I continued to go on about gay liberation, a small man made his way down the aisle to my row. He told me he was the playwright and that I should get the hell out of the theater. He was Tennessee Williams, who claimed fame following his blockbusters *The Glass Menagerie* and *A Streetcar Named Desire*. The show, when it officially opened, received poor reviews and closed quickly.

On another night Jackie Curtis invited me to a party at Andy Warhol's Factory right off of Union Square. The Factory was the hip hangout for socialites, drag queens, bohemians, intellectuals, and Hollywood types. I remember walking upstairs and winding up in a large, dimly lit loft with lots of people and not much food or drink. By the time we got there Jackie was already stoned. My fifteen minutes with Warhol were spent watching him walk aimlessly around the loft holding a jar of Hellmann's mayonnaise. Warhol, who lived as an openly gay man even before the gay rights movement, said a few unmemorable, indecipherable words and was off. Later on at the party, someone speculated about what he used the mayonnaise for; I'll spare you the details. There were many solitary people who ambled around without agenda, as well as groups of people who huddled tightly together like pickles.

The off-Broadway theater crowd hung out at Phebe's, which served the best burgers in the city. One night I met a guy who claimed to be a Broadway producer. Why would a Broadway producer be slumming on East 4th Street with the off-off-Broadway crowd? He invited me to stand with him in the wings and see his latest show in previews. The show was called *The Love Suicide at Schofield Barracks* and it closed after five performances. My friend Rosemary told me that the guy then tried the movie business. His name was Robert Weinstein. He made the right move.

Another friend, Charlie Briggs, was the assistant stage manager for the Broadway musical production of *Purlie*, starring Cleavon Little, Melba Moore, and a former Philadelphian named Sherman Helmsley whose TV audiences would get to know him as George Jefferson on the TV sitcom *The Jeffersons*. Little and Moore, who went on to have a major music career, won Tony Awards for their performances in *Purlie*. On my visits to the show, Helmsley and I would often compare notes on our home city. There has been much speculation about his sexuality since his death in 2012. While he certainly took a keen interest in our talks and my gay activism, there is nothing more that I can add to that discussion.

On another occasion Rosemary wanted to go to the theater to see a revival of an old musical, *No, No, Nanette*. She got us orchestra tickets in the next-to-last row for the final preview before its opening night at the 46th Street Theater. While I was reading the playbill before the show, Rosemary tapped me on my shoulder. She pointed across the aisle at two of our fellow theatergoers, Senator Ted Kennedy and his wife.

Rosemary, always a little amused at my dealings in activism, said with a smirk, "Why don't you ask him about gay rights?"

I smiled, got up from my seat, and made my way to Senator Kennedy. He was sitting up front in an aisle seat. I tapped him on the back, which startled him. A life lesson: never sneak up on a man who has seen two of his brothers assassinated. He turned in surprise and I introduced myself, after which I asked him his position on gay rights. He looked a little bewildered—after all, the gay movement was still relatively new at this point. I watched each word as it tiptoed off his tongue.

"What?" he said.

I asked again, this time using the h-word instead of *gay*, and he replied, "I've never been asked that before, but I'm for all civil rights." I thanked him and made my way back up the aisle to my seat.

Along with *No, No, Nanette*, I got to see the original productions of *Company* and *Follies*, which resulted in a passion for the words and music of Stephen Sondheim, one of the only sophisticated elements of my quite makeshift life.

A few days later Rosemary's friend Keely Stahl somehow arranged tickets and backstage passes for us to attend a Beach Boys concert in Central Park. Rosemary suggested that I ask them to do a gay rights fundraising concert, but I only got blank stares from them when I explained what I wanted. Keely said they were too stoned to understand me. We left in utter amusement and wonderment of how they performed in such a state.

There was also a new and unusual kind of performance space called the Continental Baths in the basement of the Ansonia Hotel on the Upper West Side, which was actually a men's bathhouse. I had heard about this crazy lady called Bette Midler who sang up a storm there, so I decided to check it out. The bathhouse was a place for gay men to meet discreetly, but this was the early seventies and gay life was starting to bloom and smash out of the closets and businesses wanted to cater to this crowd, so they added entertainment to the mix of faux exercise, swimming pool, and anonymous sex. When I first saw the divine Miss M., she was singing by the pool accompanied by her pianist, Barry Manilow. Bette did indeed sing her heart out and she drew a much larger crowd than the space could hold. Crammed to the gills, people actually fell into the pool trying to watch her perform.

Bette glorified the camp humor in the gay community. In the middle of her performance she'd look down a hallway and call out, "Hey, boys, there's a girl out here working," or, "Come out, come out, wherever you are . . . I know you're in those damn rooms doing who knows what." She was so good that I had to have a recording of her performance, and I did the unspeakable: I took a tape recorder to the baths.

Not everyone walked around in towels, although most did, and it has been reported that even Manilow sometimes did so, though I don't believe that was the case. But Bette certainly brought in people who were there only to see her and who were not necessarily gay at all. Ah well.

After the success of the first two gay pride marches, it was decided that we needed something more than just speeches. We needed a feel-good moment as reprieve from all our internal fights; a moment to identify ourselves beyond turmoil. So Bette Midler's friend Vito Russo approached her and she agreed to sing at our third gay pride event. Susan Silverman, an early Gay Liberation Front member, recently reminded me that someone suggested that Gay Youth be in charge of Bette's security—and I got to be her bodyguard. What the hell did we know about security for a woman who at the time was becoming a national show-biz wonder? I vividly recall how she greeted us on the stairway to the stage that day. She looked up at me, since she was so short, and said: "Yeah, this is my security." She laughed, walked up the steps, and added, "Okay, boys, let's get this show on the road."

* * *

I was still young and poor, with no prospects but hope for the future, and New York was a wonderland; it allowed me to grow. From an emotionally battered kid I morphed quickly into a person with his own identity. The excitement never ended, and there was something new happening almost every day. While worrying about the police or FBI listening in on our phone conversations or planting someone in our meetings (we learned later that J. Edgar Hoover and his FBI actually did this), my group of friends expanded to include porn stars, drag queens, actors, playwrights, musicians, and even the prince of a small country. Then there were the eclectic spiritual beings of various varieties. I helped a friend open a short-lived witchcraft store at 119 Christopher Street. I wanted to explore every aspect of what I didn't have growing up. And thanks to Grandmom I was open to diversity.

My favorite book and movie growing up, as I've said, was *Auntie Mame*. It always reminded me of my grandmother Fannie. Somehow I discovered that *Auntie Mame* was based on a real-life woman named Marion Tanner who lived in New York. It became my mission to find her, and I did. She lived on the West Side and was running a boarding house. When I rang her bell, she invited me in and we sat at her kitchen table. She wasn't at all glamorous. She looked like she had been cleaning the house, which was exactly what I'd interrupted. When I asked her about the book, she delivered a cryptic line: "The book is like a plane: sometimes it's on the ground and other times it's in midair." She gave no details and wouldn't talk about her nephew Patrick Dennis, who wrote the book. I left that house realizing that I already knew Auntie Mame and she wasn't the lady I had just met. Her name was Fannie Weinstein and she was my grandmother.

Most evenings had me picking up my friend Doug Carver at

his place at 11th Street between avenues A and B and walking over to Christopher Street in the West Village to attend meetings, hand out flyers, or just hang out at the Silver Dollar near the pier. We'd walk up and down that street all night meeting our friends and popping into bar after bar like the reopened Stonewall or the 9th Circle to see who was there. The scene was now very sociable, like when Grandmom would take me chair to chair on the Atlantic City boardwalk each summer.

Yet activism was not glamorous. Revolutions are work-intensive and that kept me living on a can of SpaghettiOs and potato salad for dinner most nights. We only bought clothes, usually at thrift stores, when the ones we had were worn thin.

To support myself—barely, since we were creating a revolution and had little time to make money—I had a litany of jobs. The one that kept me going was, like my father, driving a cab. Dover was my garage, and even today I have my hack license hanging on my office wall. My other part-time job was as a waiter at John Britt's Hippodrome, literally a rundown gay dive bar on Avenue A between 10th and 11th Streets. My most vivid memories of working there were from Monday nights when I got to be a bartender, since few people came in and John had no one else who would work just for tips. Only one customer stands out in my memory. Almost every Monday he'd sit at my bar, and often he was the only customer. We'd talk, but not about his business, which I'd learned many weeks into our relationship was dance and ballet. Robert Joffrey, of Joffrey Ballet fame, who was born Abdullah Jaffa Bey Khan to an Afghani father and Italian mother, never talked shop, thank goodness. In all honesty, the only thing about ballet that I actually like are the men in tights. It takes me back to those J.C. Penney catalogs.

As an organizer in the LGBT community, I was willing to drop any and everything just to be involved. This meant that I didn't always show up for my shift at Dover to get my cab. New drivers like me sometimes demanded the better cabs that often went to the longtime drivers, and that didn't sit well with the veterans. This led to a confrontation with three older drivers, all well built and intimidating, who cornered me one day and suggested that the garage didn't need faggots making demands.

Since I couldn't live on the money from the Hippodrome alone, some GLF friends suggested a solution: sign up for welfare. For a guy from a working-class family who had escaped the projects and envisioned never being a part of that world again, this seemed out of the question. But when the rent was due and the landlord threatened eviction, I realized my friends had a convincing case.

According to them, the state was giving us welfare as restitution for the despicable treatment gays suffered. Since it was society that was oppressing us as citizens, why shouldn't we use their tools to fight back? When I researched how to sign up, it surprised me to learn that all one had to do in 1970 was walk in a welfare office and tell them you were "homosexual" and, because of that, you could not keep a job and therefore needed public assistance.

In desperate straits I made the journey and filled out the paperwork. As I waited for my turn to meet with the social worker, I wondered how hard the qualifying questioning would be and expected to be tossed out on my butt. When I finally got my turn, a bland man in a brown suit looked over my paperwork and muttered, "Homosexual." He stamped the paper and said, "You'll have to do counseling," and directed me to another window to finalize my acceptance. That was it, with no further questions. As I got out of my seat, my anger rose. What it all meant was that the state of New York classified homosexuality as a mental illness and we, as a group, were incapable of working.

Was I using the system or was I validating their belief system? Regardless, it angered me. We were both wrong—and this act was somehow further impetus for me to help bring about change.

Back on Christopher Street, welfare somehow gave me cred with my fellow Gay Liberation Front members, which made it a little easier to swallow.

My life now had a purpose: in a very short span of time I had gone from quiet high school student to gay revolutionary with a minor in theater on the side. Meanwhile, my parents still thought I was in school. And I was—at a place called GLF University.

It seemed there was a demonstration almost every week. Leafleting was constant as we grew GLF. There was no Internet, no cell phones—just feet. We handed out papers on the street as people made their way to a club or restaurant or we pasted them onto poles and buildings along Christopher, Greenwich, Seventh Avenue, and other areas of the Village.

Then came a call from my father.

Chapter 3

Mom, Don't Worry, I'll Be Arrested Today

In 1971, hearing my father's voice on the other end when picking up the phone was unusual. Calls from home always, always started with Mom's greeting. So I knew this was no ordinary call. My father never made demands, he requested, and allowed one's good sense to respond. This meant that he just gave me the facts: Mom had advanced kidney disease and needed a transplant, and an extra hand around the house might be useful at this time. Dad made the point that he wasn't asking me to stop anything I was involved with. Most fathers, after finding out their son was spending his days fighting for LGBT equality, would have taken those words back, but not my father; he rejoiced in them. In many ways my parents soon became activists themselves.

After a visit to the library to research my mom's illness, it struck me hard that what she had was tough to beat. Transplants in 1971 were 50/50 odds at best. The thought of losing Mom frightened me more than anything else that had been tossed my way.

Living, truly living, only began for me in 1969 when New York beckoned. Now I was returning, back to the place where I thought there would be nothing for me. I had a vibrant life in New York; Gay Liberation Front had become my family. We were brothers and sisters, and being one of the youngest in the group, I was often treated like a son. These were the people who brought about my understanding of why I'd felt as I did all my life. Now I had to leave; yet with my GLF University education under my belt, the tools of revolution were in my hands and in my heart.

Then it hit me: I'd been part of the movement and helped to create the Gay Youth organization in New York, so why not do the same in Philadelphia? In retrospect the timing might have been ideal, because soon after my departure from New York, the GLF organization imploded—but not before it gave birth to the next stage in community growing.

After selling his United cab 441, Dad had become a door-to-door salesman. He sold everything from encyclopedias to education courses to Jesus. Literally. His final big job was selling 3-D pictures of Jesus Christ in cheap plastic frames. Watching this short Jewish man hawking this tacky picture to a housewife was amazing. He started off by quoting a passage from the Bible, then he'd talk about Our Lord and the importance of having Him in not only our hearts but also our homes. If the pitch wasn't going well he'd drop to his knee and say, "Let's pray," and begin reciting the Lord's Prayer. That was often a closer.

After Dad decided it was getting too hard to do the door-to-door thing he began a new business buying and selling leather belts. These were slightly defective belts called "seconds" with a nick or some other minor flaw. He started selling them at flea markets for a dollar. He offered to bring me into the business, and though it seemed strange—after all, I was supposedly in an RCA technical repair program—what else could I do? Besides, the belt business was profitable. He was bringing in decent money from working just two days a week.

Times should have been good. But Mom wasn't. Dad never accepted that she was as sick as she was. The only change in their lives now was that there was no more bickering about money that they didn't have. Instead, Dad treated Mom like she was a queen, whereas in the past she had only been treated as a princess. Whatever Mom wanted, she got, but she rarely wanted anything—she would never take advantage of any situation or anyone.

Mom was a trouper, like her own mom. She never complained. When her condition deteriorated and she finally had to go on dialysis, her only complaint was that she'd have to quit her job. She was a floor manager at the E.J. Korvette store in Cedarbrook Mall, an early version of Kmart.

So my new life consisted of working with Dad and taking Mom to dialysis. She was often cheerful on the way to her treatment, but when I'd pick her up she was always exhausted and cold. One day while taking her to the hospital during a snowstorm, the car got stuck on a patch of ice. In a panic, knowing she needed her treatment, I jumped out of the car and flagged the first person who passed by, demanding they assist me in pushing the car out of its rut. For my mom I'd give the world.

In the evenings I began attending the local chapter of Gay Activist Alliance, which proved to be a little tame for me. The one exception was that after the general meeting, run strictly by *Robert's Rules*, with a parliamentarian to boot, there was always a topic for discussion. Many quite interesting. At one of the first meetings I attended, a Dr. Dennis Rubini, who became one of the first in the country to teach LGBT history, at Temple University, was giving a talk on the food supplements he ate to create a more healthy body and save the environment. When a questioner asked him how he could survive with just the supplements, Dennis exploded and yelled about the genocide of cows to feed a capitalist society, and summed it all up with, "Anyone who eats meat, fish, fowl, or processed food is a pig." Thereby trashing nearly the entire audience. Ah, I had now found my people. I was home again.

The Gay Activist Alliance's major objective was to get a nondiscrimination bill introduced into the city council. At the time I joined, they were still unable to find a sponsor for the bill from any of the seventeen members on the council. My entrance from New York's Gay Liberation Front gave me great credibility, and though it was arrogant of me to think that I would create a movement in Philadelphia where there already was one, and one that had been the vanguard for the nation in the past, I would try. What I wanted to do was redefine what that movement should look like and what it should achieve.

Not long after joining I was voted in as the political chair. My platform was built on the promise that, if elected, I'd get the bill introduced. This would be a complete change in my life, going from revolutionary to an elected chairman working with the city council.

I started to meet with city council members, even if they didn't want to meet with me. Standing outside their offices, sitting on the steps of their favorite restaurants, or hanging out at the city Democratic headquarters was par for the course. They'd see me and sigh and I'd say, always with a smile, "You'll break down one day and talk to me." As time went on I'd start to joke with them: "Will this be my lucky day?" "Hey, I'm really a nice guy."

Finally they began to smile and chat with me, first on the street, then having actual meetings in their offices. This was a big deal in those days. Politicians did not meet with "homosexuals." The City Hall press began to notice me as well and started to run news items on my work. Zack Stalberg, the future editor of the *Philadelphia Daily News*, saw something in me that I hadn't noticed as yet—dogged determination—as did show-biz gossip columnists Larry Fields and Stu Bykofsky. Somehow, what I was doing was fodder for good copy at the *Daily News* which, after all, was a tabloid newspaper. In an attempt to be more cutting edge than its sister publications the *Philadelphia Inquirer* and the *Evening Bulletin*, they hyped it up a bit. Those were the days of a big city having at least three daily newspapers.

As more and more people would talk to me, my profile began to grow. Producing a daily column is not an easy job, especially if it's local gossip where you need to keep readers interested. So Larry Fields took almost anything I pitched to him, and as luck would have it, appearing in his celebrity news column miraculously made one a "celebrity." It's basically the same path to fame that Paris Hilton and the Kardashians used, minus the sex. Despite these superficial methods, celebrityhood opened doors. Those media mentions led to a radio talk show appearance to discuss nondiscrimination, which in turn led to a feature article and then to a TV interview. The cycle was then repeated. I soon had my city council sponsors and the bill was about to be introduced.

This first victory plowed the way for me on all other legislative and government successes to come. Our nondiscrimination legislation now had a number, Bill 1275. To become a law in the city it first needed to be read at a city council session. During council, most of the time, the clerk would read the bill number and title, which in our case was "a bill to amend the Philadelphia Fair Practice Ordinance," and just move on. The audience in the chamber would have no idea what each piece of legislation really entailed. On the designated morning I went with my friend Harry Langhorne, president of Gay Activists Alliance, and sat in with the audience to watch the council. They were saluting the Boys Club of America for who knows what good deed this time and the North Philadelphia Catholic High School, which had just won a debate championship. The gallery was full of people from the various local Boys Club chapters and from archdioceses—students, a priest, and some nuns. Harry and I went around telling them that a bill was about to be introduced that supported Cesar Chavez and the California migrant lettuce pickers. We were going to stand and applaud when it was introduced and we would appreciate if they'd join us in the celebration. As we took our seats, Bill 1275 was introduced. Harry stood up and applauded on cue, then I stood and applauded. Like clockwork the remainder of the gallery stood up and applauded, and then everyone on the council joined in on the excitement. The following day, the headline in the *Philadelphia Daily News* was "Gay Rights Bill Introduced, Priest and Nuns Applaud."

All lightheartedness aside, these early successes were meaningful. The bill got introduced, but we couldn't move it out of committee since George X. Schwartz, the city council president, was a major homophobe. This led me to take various actions against the council. One of the most memorable, and one that brought me a lasting friendship, was a simple act of disruption. During a council meeting, we climbed over the railing separating the council chambers from the gallery and began to take over the chambers. Schwartz ran out as I approached. I sat in his chair, which was on a perch above the council, almost like a throne. Trying to do my best George X. Schwartz imitation, I plucked a cigar out of my pocket and stuck it in my mouth as I put my feet up on his desk. I took his gavel and brought order to the room. Just when I was about to do a pretend vote on Bill 1275, the sergeant-at-arms was called in along with the police. The sergeant, a very tall and big man, wrapped his arms around me in a bear hug and picked me up. While carrying me out of the chambers he gave me a friendly lecture. Rather than have me arrested, he deposited me outside the chamber in the middle of a group of visiting nuns. "*The Wizard of Oz,*" he said, and walked away laughing. That sergeant-at-arms is now Congressman Bob Brady, the ranking member of the US House Committee on Administration and Philadelphia Democratic City Committee chairman. A close friend of Vice President Joe Biden, he's sometimes called the "Mayor of Capitol Hill." His grace and good humor at that encounter led to a lasting friendship, a shopping partner in his wife Debbie, and a gay ally who knows the political ropes. He was the first politico to try and teach me "how to get business done."

It was now December and the council was winding down for the year. If the bill didn't pass by the end of the session we'd have to start the entire process over again. People were all abuzz with their gift shopping and holiday planning. In the middle of City Hall there was a Christmas tree, decorated in ribbon and ornamentation with a star on top. I decided to chain myself to it and announced that I'd go on a hunger strike until the city gave a hearing on the gay rights legislation. The press loved it, especially when I was asked why I was chained to the Christmas tree. "I'm the Christmas fairy," I replied.

That headline didn't move George Schwartz, but it did, surprisingly, move one Mayor Frank Rizzo, who sent an aide out to the courtyard to ask if I'd meet with him in his office. The reality was that I had no exit strategy on this action, so hell yes. It was another strange but lucky day in my life, one in which an invitation came from a mayor who'd once called San Francisco "the land of fruits and nuts"!

Later I heard from Marty Weinberg, Rizzo's chief adviser, that when he said he wanted to meet me, his staff had cautioned against it. He overruled them and said, "I like the kid, he has balls." The meeting went well and Rizzo explained that although he couldn't tell the council what to do, he could request that the Human Relations Commission hold the hearings. I left Rizzo's office with a victory and with the knowledge that I would not have to spend the night chained to the city's Christmas tree. Truth is, the reason behind his generosity was that Rizzo was in a feud with Schwartz. They were simply using me as a pawn. Though in reality, we were all using each other. We got two days of hearings out of it that led to two days of media coverage. We also got the final report issued by the Human Relations Commission, which stated, "There is obviously overwhelming discrimination aimed at members of the gay and lesbian community, and we urge council to pass legislation."

This embarrassed Council President George Schwartz (later to be indicted in the infamous Abscam case that cited bribery, extortion, and conspiracy, fictionalized in the film *American Hustle*) so much that he decided to declare where he stood on the issue. He'd hold his own hearing in the council that he would personally chair. We finally got the hearings we wanted, but it was Council President Schwartz's "big top." Schwartz called in all the anti-LGBT troops he could influence to speak out against the legislation, including Philadelphia Cardinal John Krol regaled in all his clerical drag—purple robe, cape, rings, and shoes. All he needed was a tiara.

But Schwartz saved his best for me. As I read my prepared statement, every so often I would look up to gauge the reaction. At the councilman's table, Schwartz looked like a caged lion ready to pounce. The second my statement was completed, when the chair usually asks if any of the other members of the council have any questions, Schwartz said, "I have some questions for you."

In my head I said, *Let the circus begin.* And it did.

In front of a gallery full of spectators and a complete press pool, Schwartz started out by explaining that he didn't understand people like me. *Who are you people? What do we expect from people like him? What is a homosexual?* Then he finally looked directly at me and loudly asked, "Mr. Segal, what do you do it with?" The look on my face and the silence in the chambers made him grow angrier and even more despicable. "I mean," he shouted, "what do you do it with?" I could only stare at him, and in a rage he yelled, "Do you do it with parakeets?"

My reaction was one of shock, downright anger, and a pain that I still cannot explain. I'm not sure what I said in response. Perhaps it was a mere diplomatic brush-off, or more likely I just got up and walked out silently. In the hall, the press crowded around me wanting my reaction. Instead I just nodded and walked out of the building in disgust. Inside the chambers, Schwartz immediately ended the hearings, having what he thought was his pound of flesh.

But a strange thing happened. My friends at the *Philadelphia Daily News* were outraged by Schwartz's behavior, and in the following day's edition they ran an editorial with the headline, "Shut Up, George." They included a picture of Schwartz with that cigar pose that I had imitated. He had never been treated this way by the media before. And his downward political slide began.

That hearing taught me a few lessons. First, being a victim of a bully in front of an entire city and handling it with grace wins a lot of friends; and second, it reinforced my belief that as long as non-LGBT society only thought of our community as a sexual one, we wouldn't get very far in the fight for equality. My silence and unwillingness to talk about sexual practices taught me that sex had nothing to do with nondiscrimination. Most important was that I became a darling of the local press. While it was great for my ego, it was better for the LGBT community since up until then, most people still had no idea who a gay man really was. They'd continued to believe all the longstanding derogatory myths about gay people. Now, with all of this press coverage, they saw one live and could finally identify.

The hope of bringing a new kind of activism back to Philly was at last realized. Not only did I bring a radical movement with me, but I was able to map the next step in LGBT liberation: speak up. To put it simply, Oscar Wilde had been correct that homosexuality was "the love that dare not speak its name," but it was time to change that. And that was the most controversial decision I'd ever make. Since I was using myself as the guinea pig, it would unleash toward me a hatred not only from homophobes but from my own community, which often chews up and spits out its young, then stomps the spit wad into the ground.

The Schwartz fiasco set in motion the path for the next act, the Gay Raiders. I had seen the light. I knew how to get there. Despite the backlash, other people's fear and my ego were not going to stand in my way. Why should they? I had nothing to lose. After all, I had already been there, since my childhood and Wilson Park.

As the vanguard of the new gay rights movement, New York was in turmoil. Gay Liberation Front had died after the birth of Gay Activist Alliance, which would soon make way for the first organization in America that could truly be called Gay Inc., the National Gay Task Force (NGTF), today known as the National LGBTQ Task Force. It was the first organization to have a well-paid executive director, Bruce Voeller, and a full-time staff. They set themselves apart from those of us who were activists. NGTF was also to become the first organization to attempt to market the LGBT community and raised what we thought at that time was big bucks. As far as they were concerned, the day of the sit-in, picket, and other activism was over. It was time for lobbying and legislation. To them we were the radicals, harbingers of shame who needed to be swept under the rug.

In a sense the new guys were taking us back to the days of the Independence Hall demonstration where, to put a good look on "homosexuals," the marchers were told that the men must wear suits and ties and the women must wear dresses. The divide in the community was vicious. People like me from Gay Liberation Front had made a movement for LGBT equality a reality; now the guys with the alligators and polo emblems on their shirts wanted us to leave the stage.

The solution to the problem of invisibility as a people was clear. The general public had no idea who we were since what they were fed about us from the media, with only a few exceptions, was negative. Since, for the most part, we were all in the closet, who was there to refute it? Most non-gays didn't know us. All the public knew were the sins religion gave us, the crimes the law pressed on us, and all the torture the medical and psychiatric profession tried on us to stop us from our "evil ways." There was only one answer: to show people who we really were by using the very media that vilified us, and the time for that was immediately. What you wore was not at all the issue for acceptance. We could conform by wearing a suit and tie forever but still miss the mark on what equality required. People had to—they absolutely had to—get to know you as a person.

So in 1972, Philadelphia became my own test lab. It started with a simple plan. The effort to pass nondiscrimination legislation taught me that using myself as a focal point had resulted in the public seeing and getting to know an actual gay man. It was not about the legislation, since passing legislation would not change minds; it was about using that legislation as a platform to communicate with the public. It had gotten me on a number of television and radio talk shows. At that point many called me a local celebrity. Harvey Milk wouldn't receive that notoriety in San Francisco for several years. That "celebrity" status could help to accomplish our long-term goal, but it also needed to be nurtured and cultivated in the right way. Each piece of news had to be one step up from the last.

A plan was drawn up to use what we called *zaps*. A zap is a disruption. Sort of. They were to be nonviolent protests that put us in a light that was not stereotypical. They were upbeat and of course had a point to communicate. We wanted the public to start talking about us. Talk can eventually lead to education. Education usually leads to less fear and more understanding of the unknown. The word *zap*, and using it as a noun for the action, is attributed to my old friend Marty Robinson. The basic rule in the equality struggle—from its inception back in 1895 with Dr. Magnus Hirschfeld, the German physician and sexologist who stomped for sexual minorities, through the 1960s liberation movement in the US, until this very day—is that progress is based on one word and one word only: education.

Our organizational role, we felt as gay men and women, was exactly that: to educate society. Ask any gay person how easy it was to come out to their parents. Today it's still hard. Those who have come out to their parents usually started with an education process. In some ways, just the act of coming out is a form of gay activism since it is the desire to no longer live a double life but live one's truth. Parents, in turn, often educate their friends and so the process begins.

There's an old saying in the gay community: if every one of us was out of the closet, there'd be no need for a gay rights movement since others would learn that we are their brothers, sisters, uncles, aunts, cousins, and even mothers and fathers.

Back then we were everywhere, but at the same time, we were invisible. The Gay Raiders were about to change that.

Our plan called for a zap or press opportunity every six weeks. A zap followed by the initial press, then the talk show circuit, and by the time that was dying down, another event or zap. The goal was to keep us right up there in the public's face and to create conversation.

When 99 percent of your community is in the closet, and you're one of the few being out, proud, and front and center, you're not a popular person. Up to this point, our gay meeting places like clubs, bars, private residences, and cafés were either secret or not publicized. These were safe places where we could be ourselves, and the feeling from that 99 percent was that I was putting a spotlight on those places and possibly on them. The line that activists like me heard most often was, "You'll ruin it for all of us."

The press knew me from GAA, but I was now striking out on my own with few supporters; it had to be made clear that the Gay Raiders were different and separate and it had to be big enough to get everyone's attention. So, we thought, why not zap the city's icon of independence: the Liberty Bell. The plan was simple. Back then, the bell was on the first floor of Independence Hall and you could easily walk in and even touch it.

We of course leaked what we were about to do to specific press people whom we could count on not giving the plan away. At the prescribed time we appeared. I already had handcuffs on one arm, with the other end waiting to be attached to part of the bell. As I entered Independence Hall there was a cluster of flashes and it dawned on us that the plan had been more widely leaked. Like Keystone Cops, the incompetent fictional characters of silent movies, we were off, with the police trying to catch me before I did the deed and the press in hot pursuit. It truly felt like a Buster Keaton movie: me running from one room to the next, jumping over rope lines and crashing into walls, taking two steps at a time to the second floor and doing a circle around the room, then back down the stairs and another trip around those chairs once occupied by Ben Franklin and John Hancock. Finally, I climbed the stairs to the second floor again and quickly sat down and handcuffed myself to the rail directly above the bell. Then, on cue, as soon as the TV camera lights were on, I began yelling, "Independence for gay people! We want nondiscrimination!"

This went on for about ten minutes until they cut me loose and gave me a ride to jail—a nickel ride. That's when you're cuffed with your hands behind your back, tossed into a police wagon, and the wagon takes off at high speed, hitting every pothole it can and making turns on a dime. The objective is to cause as much bruising as possible without the police laying a hand on you.

Next up was the United Way. Why them? They didn't fund any gay organizations. We found a large bike brace and one morning, when the staff of United Way turned up for work, they discovered it was impossible to enter since I was chained by my neck to their front doors. Any time anyone came near me someone would yell, "Don't touch him, you could break his neck!" It worked better than a bomb, and guess what happened? The next year they funded their first LGBT organization.

Then, according to plan, six weeks later it was time for another zap.

This led to my first interaction with a president, Richard M. Nixon. On November 1, 1972, we disrupted a Republican fundraiser for Nixon's committee to reelect the president, known to some of us as CREP. Clark MacGregor, chairman of the reelection committee, was speaking when I produced a roll of paper that when unraveled read, *Gay Power*. Again I was wrestled to the floor and took another nickel ride in the police wagon, but this one had a happy ending: the next morning, the White House condemned the disruption.

By that point we had staged a few zaps that had been downright serious and, for me, dangerous. It was time to lighten things up a little. So why not throw a party? How 'bout free morning coffee and donuts to all City Hall workers? There was only one catch: the guest of honor didn't know he was the guest of honor. Enter District Attorney Arlen Specter, later to become a US senator, and who will forever be linked to the fiasco involving Anita Hill and Supreme Court Justice Clarence Thomas. Prior to that, he was a lawyer for the Warren Commission that investigated the assassination of President John F. Kennedy. He was the one who came up with the single-bullet theory.

Back in those early days of the battle for gay rights, Arlen was district attorney of Philadelphia. He had not taken a stand on the gay rights bill that was before city council. Efforts to set up a meeting went unanswered. So we had to be a little creative. One crisp Monday morning, a caterer delivered two large coffeemakers and dozens of donuts to Arlen's office. His staff thought that he had ordered the special treat, and Arlen thought his staff had arranged it. At the same time, in the City Hall courtyard and in the corridors of the building, members of the Gay Raiders were handing out flyers that read, *District Attorney Arlen Specter invites you to a reception in honor of gay rights legislation in city council. Please join him at ten a.m. in his office, room 666.* (That really was his office number.)

At ten a.m., we, along with hundreds of city workers and a huge collection of newspeople, arrived at his office. We walked in and there was Arlen's staff trying not to look too surprised at a reception held in their office that their boss was hosting, about legislation he had not endorsed. Arlen remained in his inner office. At first, the media took pictures of me handing out coffee and donuts to City Hall staffers, and we weren't sure if Arlen would even come out of his private office. Finally, the door opened and there he was, all smiles. He walked over, shook my hand, helped me hand out coffee, and we then went back into his private office. His first comment to me was, "Mark Segal, who else would cater a disruption? Did you think I'd allow you to have all the media attention to yourself?" And then he flashed that big smile.

The *Philadelphia Inquirer* the following day (October 10, 1973) had a large picture of the event and reported: *District Attorney Arlen Specter shakes hands with Mark Segal, leader of the Gay Raiders, who parked outside the district attorney's office until he emerged and granted them an interview. The Raiders handed out free donuts and coffee while waiting for Specter.*

Arlen eventually went to the National District Attorneys Association and asked them to get on board and support non-discrimination legislation. Now, here's what most people never knew: in Arlen's Republican years in the US Senate, when it was hard to support LGBT rights, he was always behind the curtain ready to vote yes on gay rights if it was needed to assure passage. Only Human Rights Campaign and I were aware of that. I'll never forget the 1996 vote on the Employment Nondiscrimination Act, when he broke ranks with the GOP and the bill failed by only one vote. He later supported the repeal of "Don't Ask, Don't Tell" and the repeal of the Defense of Marriage Act.

A few years later, while I was waiting in a room with others to officially endorse Arlen, someone asked him about his single-bullet theory. Since I was standing next to him, he used me as the John F. Kennedy stand-in and showed where the bullets entered and exited Kennedy's body. That was an eerie feeling.

* * *

The Gay Raiders' zaps produced the desired effect: Philadelphians were talking about gay issues. We were everywhere, including the cover of the Sunday *Inquirer* magazine. This was not happening in other cities.

The zaps were sometimes downright dangerous. For example, a zap of Dr. David Reuben, author of the book *Everything You Always Wanted to Know about Sex but Were Afraid to Ask*, in which he belittled, embellished, and stereotyped LGBT people, became violent. When we staged a sit-in at one of his lectures in June 1974, the police moved in with their clubs. Although it was a nonviolent protest, Bernie Boyle got his head bashed with one of those clubs.

I had little funds, since my activism kept me from helping Dad with the business, and my parents were supporting me. It took me years to realize the contribution my parents made to the struggle for gay rights. Never did they complain, they only offered words of encouragement.

My partner at the time, Phillip, spent weekends at the house, most of which were filled with making plans for the next zap or demonstration or other issues to be dealt with. One Saturday afternoon we were watching TV and a teenage dance show came on the air. It was Ed Hurst's show in Atlantic City, *Summertime on the Pier*. Watching the dancers made us wonder: *What would happen if a gay couple joined in?* That is how the campaign against the networks began, and once again events swept me up faster than I had planned.

Sage Powell, a friend from Gay Activist Alliance, agreed to go to Atlantic City to be my dance partner on the show. The following Saturday, with very little organizing, a group of us set out. The show was little more than a gimmick to get people to buy tickets to Steel Pier. Teenage dance television shows were born in Philly; *American Bandstand*, the granddaddy of them all, was wildly popular.

We bought our tickets and made our way to the ballroom. The show was already on the air—like *Bandstand*, it was a live show. We watched for a while to get our bearings and then, when a song we knew was being played, Sage and I made our way to the floor. We must have danced for three minutes before we heard Ed Hurst yelling from the stage, over the microphone, "Get them off! Get them off the floor!"

Security was called in and we were royally thrown off the pier. We got in the car and laughed all the way home. Sage, who is African American, said we got kicked off the show because we were an interracial couple, not because we were both men. I'm not sure if we even made it on camera, but it didn't matter, we knew what the next step would be: a demonstration.

Gay Activist Alliance protected our honor by picketing the TV station and demanding an apology. They refused to apologize. And thank God they wouldn't. It led us to the next step: the Gay Raiders decided to disrupt the evening news. It was only logical, right? The ABC affiliate in Philadelphia was, and still is, the local news ratings king. Almost every household tuned in to *Action News* on ABC.

Despite how quickly they seemed to happen, zaps were not usually pulled out of thin air. It was a major process. Once the target was settled on, we went to work on planning. Success depended on planning, execution, and security. A good zap couldn't happen in a few hours. But this time, little planning would be needed since we already knew the station well. Being a "celebrity" means being invited onto the talk shows, and their studios were no exception. I'd been there before.

We knew there was a security guard at the front desk and, once in the building, we knew where the studio was. We even had a hideout where we planned to wait until the show was on the air. All we needed was to create a diversion at the front door. Therefore, we had researched and practiced a trick learned from movie stuntmen. A guy on fire running around would surely do the job. So we employed this to our advantage. As the guard went one way, we went the other, into the building. We waited until the show was on and was reporting the top news story of the night. Their format was the same each evening, and we decided we'd treat the city to a newly written script. As the anchorman said, "But the top story tonight . . ." we became the big story as we burst onto the live set. There were the anchorman, Larry Kane, weatherman Jim O'Brien, and sportscaster Joe Pellegrino.

Larry has written about this in his autobiography, and his version seems to be a little embellished. He writes of blood on the walls. The only fluid that I recall being exchanged was the sportscaster's makeup smearing my jacket as I yelled at him, "Hey, watch it, your makeup is getting on my shirt!" We were pushed to the ground and wrapped in cables until the police arrived and treated us to another nickel ride. This time I had friends to knock against. We got released without bail somehow, and we went to our respective homes to sleep. It was nearing four a.m.

The entire front page of the next day's *Daily News* was devoted to the zap, and the story was picked up by almost every other news media outlet. The phone never stopped ringing. By the end of the day it was obvious that we had perfected the solution to invisibility. *Action News* had its format, now the Gay Raiders had ours. We were a force that could not be controlled. We had a laser beam on the networks. We'd hit them, and we'd hit them hard. No live or even taped show was immune to us, and we started reinventing ways to get into the studios.

First up was a syndicated variety show, *The Mike Douglas Show*, one of those mindless afternoon entertainment programs. I chained myself to the camera while crooner Tony Bennett and the first lady of the American stage, Helen Hayes, were getting their feet read by a professional foot reader. I started to do gay chants like, *"Two, four, six, eight, gay is just as good as straight,"* and almost anything else I could think of until they stopped taping. They brought the police in and before they could cut the handcuff I told them that until we had some form of agreement, I'd keep coming back. They agreed to have a gay spokesperson on the show, but not me. We settled on Reverend Troy Perry of Metropolitan Community Church, the man I had picketed against in my Gay Liberation Front days. His appearance was the first time an afternoon audience in America heard from a gay member of the clergy. Troy is an artful speaker and he made me and many others who saw that nationally syndicated show proud.

Next up was the *Today* show. To familiarize ourselves with the studio we took several tours offered by NBC. They were quite educational. We gained entrance to 30 Rockefeller Center in the early-morning hours and just waited in a closet. While the news was being read live I appeared on camera walking across the studio. I believe the director thought this was somehow part of the show. The news anchor actually got up out of his chair and, as some people described it, looked like he was trying to climb the walls. My first thought was to comfort the guy, but I was there for a reason and had to stay on mission. In mid-sentence I'm tackled and again wrapped in camera cables, then taken out to the hall with a security guard. As we're walking away, me expecting to head off to jail once again, it was a relief to know that Morty Manford of the New York GAA was ready to bail us all out. Before anything else could happen, a woman yelled at the guard and told him to stop. Barbara Walters, the doyen of the morning news network crowd, with pen and pad in hand, walked over and asked me why we were protesting the show. My explanation was that it wasn't just the *Today* show but all of network TV that censors us on their news, stereotypes us on their entertainment shows, and keeps us invisible by not having LGBT people on their programs. In the middle of this exchange a producer came out and told her to get back in the studio since she was about to go on air. She firmly replied that this was a story and she wasn't going back in until she had it.

Years later, in January 2012, the *Today* show celebrated its sixtieth anniversary. To honor the occasion, Running Press published Stephen Battaglio's *From Yesterday to TODAY: Six Decades of America's Favorite Morning Show*. The book goes through the highlights of the sixty years and I'm proud that the zap was included. NBC, to secure my participation in the book, gave me a DVD of my zap, and it was the first time I got to see it in over forty years. But there is another connection with the *Today* show that few know.

I had many friends in the media. Edie Huggins, who had various programs on WCAU through the years, was one of the first African American women to host her own talk show. She called me to explain that the station wanted to do a pilot with a new staff member in order to determine if he had what it took to host a show. Would I do the station a favor and shoot a pilot with him? Then she added, "He is very pleasing to the eye." His name was Matt Lauer. When I met Edie at the station, she explained that the show would be done in two sections. One with me "playing" the angry gay radical, then the second, me being my pragmatic self. They wanted to test Matt Lauer on how he would handle each scenario. He was only given my name and position as a gay activist. I arrived on the set; we were introduced, shook hands, and began the taping.

Matt opened the show then introduced his guest, me, and asked his first question. To my amazement he had done some research and asked me about the slow progress of nondiscrimination legislation. I wanted to get into real dialogue, but with my assignment in mind I replied, "It hasn't moved because the legislative pigs in Harrisburg want to keep gay people in their place." He kept going without a bat of his eyelashes: calm, cool, and polite; it almost made me angry. After ten minutes of this he segued into a fake commercial break. Then we began part two of the pilot. This time he asked a question about AIDS and how the mayor was handling it. While the question surprised me, since I was not used to local reporters doing proper research, my shift in demeanor surprised him. It's a pleasure to meet a reporter who understands the issues and can appreciate all the areas that AIDS encompasses. Again we went on until another fake commercial, and then it was over. As soon as we heard we were done, everyone including Matt broke down in laughter. The pilot was picked up. Matt, you owe me.

Next up in my war against the media was what I thought would be the mother lode, Los Angeles. By this point the campaign against the networks was getting major press coverage as we zapped the networks from coast to coast. Along the way, *Variety*, the show-business bible, had an article on how the Gay Raiders had cost the networks over $750,000 in tape delays and lost revenue, a figure that in today's dollars totals over three million.

Johnny Carson, king of late-night TV, was our next target. We expected this zap would be our largest audience to date and make the networks cave. This time we entered as audience members. During Carson's monologue, which I knew they did in one take and couldn't cut away from, I left my seat and walked to the camera and did my old handcuffs trick. Carson, the true pro, just kept up his monologue as his staff came over trying to cover my mouth. They gagged me and told me if I agreed to be quiet they would meet with us and try to negotiate a settlement. I nodded my head in agreement since I couldn't speak. At commercial they cut me loose and then there were police in the studio. They had no intention of negotiating anything. A producer simply said that to get me out of there.

When the police deposited me and my partner on the Carson zap, Mike Walters (a volunteer for the LA Gay Community Services Center), at the Burbank jail after our zap of the *Tonight Show*, we were fingerprinted, photographed, and put in a holding cell. There were six cells that opened to a communal area where there was a table and chairs. There were only four other prisoners in the cell when we arrived and after all the official paper shuffling was done, we joined them. At first the conversation was basic. Where are you from, how old are you? The other prisoners seemed to be friendly and not dangerous—this was Burbank after all. It was all going well until one of the guys asked two men who looked like brothers why they were in the jail. The taller of the two said, "We killed a faggot. I hate those faggots." They then asked me why we were there. Not giving them a second glance I headed back to my cell and closed the door, and remained there until my old friend Troy Perry of Metropolitan Community Church bailed me out. I sometimes wonder if the Burbank police staged that, and what would have happened if those two men knew the real reason we were in that jail with them. The *Tonight Show* did a good job of editing me out and they refused to meet with us, but *Variety* published an article on March 14, 1973, titled "A Segal Lock or How Taping Can Turn into Gay Time for Carson." As the story reported, "He then ran down the aisle to the rail that separates the audience from the stage and handcuffed himself. Guards followed and, when they told him to unlock the cuffs, were told he didn't have the key. Segal was quoted as saying he had mailed it to Philadelphia."

During this campaign against the networks in Los Angeles, it seemed that every hour was accounted for. Morris Knight and Troy Perry kept me entertained with parties and events almost every night. My living quarters most nights were in the Gay Community Services Center, then on Wilshire Boulevard, or on someone's couch. One evening Troy took me along to a recently opened Jewish temple where they were to dedicate their new Torah. On another Morris visited a campaign cocktail party for a homophobic candidate for city council, telling me en route that the woman had no idea she was about to enter a party of gay men. He then told me he was giving me the honor of confronting the candidate. I'm not quite sure what I said but the next issue of the *Advocate* headlined the event as, "Candidate Flees Gay Party."

On yet another occasion Morris took me to a fundraiser in the Hollywood Hills at the home of Terence O'Brien. Terry was the chairperson of the board of the Gay Community Services Center and had gotten his parents' permission to hold a fundraiser in their home. As I walked around the tastefully decorated place, several items caught my eye. The first was sitting on the fireplace mantle. Slowly approaching the statuette and looking at it closely to see if it was indeed what it seemed, I picked it up. Within an instant Terry appeared out of nowhere, took hold of the statuette, and said, "My father doesn't let anyone touch the Oscar, it belonged to a very close friend of his." As I glanced to the corner of the room I could see Morris smiling. I walked over to him and asked who Terry's father was. Morris looked coyly at me. "Pat, of course." He was talking about the actor Pat

O'Brien, who it seemed always played a priest or mob character. This brought a big smile to my face since it immediately made me remember him from one of my favorite old movies, *Some Like It Hot.*

Feeling a little foolish and not knowing Hollywood protocol, I just sat down to ponder the wonders of Los Angeles. Again Terry scolded me, this time saying, "Nobody is allowed to sit in that chair." Abraham Lincoln, my childhood scare, had used it when he was a statesman in Illinois. I was completely out of my cultural league, but I took it as another lesson and an opportunity to observe a different group of people.

My LA adventures even saw me at one of movie star Rock Hudson's "boy parties" where I felt even more out of place than in a TV studio. There were all these guys in skimpy bathing suits. All seemed to have great chests, short hair, many blond, and all were overly handsome. Hudson, himself exceptionally good looking, had a drink in his hand and seemed to be enjoying the view. Somehow the sight of me wearing old jeans and a T-shirt and my long hair down to my shoulders didn't seem to please him, so we made a fast exit.

The following week I had passes to almost every show at ABC, which became our prime target and would be used as an example. We called Av Westin, the vice president of program development, and requested a meeting before the passes were to be used. Troy and Morris had identified a group of media experts to join us. That was the first meeting between a national network and the LGBT community. While Westin agreed to change entertainment policy, he was honest in explaining that the news divisions of the networks operated separately and he could not assist with our negotiations with them.

NBC and CBS quickly agreed to change programming in their entertainment divisions to be more sensitive to stereotypes and said they would consider adding LGBT characters. The campaign against the networks was almost a success, but we still had to tackle the news departments in New York. It was time to return to the East Coast. Troy Perry had to buy my ticket since I didn't have a dime.

Once home, the brainstorming began. What could we do that would make the news divisions do what the entertainment divisions had done? We decided to follow the same formula and knew what had to happen. And that's the way it was.

Chapter 4
Walter

Walter Cronkite, the most trusted man in America, and his CBS viewership of over sixty million people, would be the target that would fundamentally change the LGBT community's national invisibility, though that never occurred to me at the time. To me it was just another zap, just another visit to jail, and just another long line of interviews about the zap. It was almost like I was going off to work, minus the salary.

It all started thanks to comedian Redd Foxx and his show *Sanford and Son*. Our campaign against the networks had already produced a lot of disruptions. We had gained a national reputation for putting broadcast media on notice. Either meet with us to discuss our grievances or suffer the consequences, the zaps.

Sanford and Son was about to get me on the zap trail again. They broadcast a show in which, for some strange reason, Redd Foxx's son had to pretend to be gay. In order to do this he used every stereotype known to mankind. Swish, limp wrist, high-pitched voice, over-the-top and colorful clothing, the works. We caught wind of this and tried to meet with network executives before the airing, but the network felt they were covered by the agreements we made in Los Angeles. Their explanation was that the script had already been in preparation and it would be the last one.

Once the show aired, several activists from around the country urged me to take action since the media had been my area of expertise. GLAAD, the nation's leading LGBT media advocacy organization, would not be founded until 1985, eleven years later. Until then, as disorganized as we were, there were only the Gay Raiders. There was also a feeling that the agreement the networks had made was not being taken seriously. They were testing our resolve. We needed to show them that the airwaves were in the public trust and not a place to continue to oppress the LGBT community.

Morty Manford, then president of Gay Activist Alliance in New York, called and suggested that I do something in New York again, to get the giants of network television to take notice. He also promised that once I decided on what my zap would be, he'd take care of finding me a lawyer. Both Troy Perry and Morris Knight also chimed in and felt that my kind of action was necessary to make the networks know that we were serious in changing their attitudes toward us. Even Frank Kameny, the first LGBT activist to sue the government in order to keep his government job—not to mention the organizer of those Independence Hall demonstrations back in the mid-1960s—was urging me on and giving advice.

The decision was obvious to me: expose their vulnerability with a zap. I'd go back to that first news zap, only this time it would be on live *national* TV. This would be big, and Morty and his offer for bail and a lawyer were absolutely necessary because we had no funds and no support system and I didn't want to spend the rest of my life behind bars. Harry Langhorne, a close friend from GAA and member of the Gay Raiders, became my rock-steady coconspirator in this endeavor. We were not able to gain access by a tour as we had in NBC—there was no audience, and this was a closed set in a closed building. What could we do?

For some time, my friend Tommi Avicolli Mecca had been president of the gay organization at Temple University, and he was kind enough to allow the Gay Raiders, without the university's knowledge, to use part of their budget to print materials and cover other small expenses. Tommi was a Gay Raider who also sat in on planning meetings. In one gathering at the Temple Gay Student Alliance office, Tommi, Phillip, Harry, and I discussed how to gain entrance to that secure studio. As we were debating, a student dropped by and grabbed a book he had left in the office. "I'm off to RFT," he said. What was RFT?

Tommi responded, "Radio, Film, Television."

"They teach television production here?"

Tommi nodded, and then came my request: "Tommi, I don't care how you do it, but get me a sheet of their stationary."

I had it the next day. We drafted a letter to the producer of the *CBS Evening News* explaining that we were in the RFT program at Temple University and we'd like to view a broadcast from the control room in order to see firsthand how professionals use the equipment that we were just beginning to learn how to operate. It actually worked. We received a letter suggesting a visit two weeks later, on December 11, 1973.

As we entered the control room to the *CBS Evening News* we were introduced to the staff. During that time it was Harry's job to scout the lay of the land, and as I went out to the studio he was to create any diversion necessary to allow me to get on air. Before our arrival at CBS we had timed the show and knew approximately when the commercial breaks would occur. We believed that once the show was being broadcast, everyone would be so involved that they wouldn't notice anything we did until it was too late. We also wanted to time the zap just as Walter was coming back from commercial so that if we were tuned out, CBS would have to explain to the viewers what had happened. No cutting to commercials and denying it.

The usual format for the *CBS Evening News* was to go live at six p.m. to about 60 percent of the nation. In those days there were no twenty-four-hour news channels. People got their TV news from one of three networks, and the *CBS Evening News with Walter Cronkite* was the untouchable leader for eighteen years. The audience of millions of people who saw that show and their first openly gay person on national television would not be equaled until April 1997 when Ellen DeGeneres came out on her prime-time show on ABC. *Will and Grace*, considered the first network show with an out character, finally moved past those earlier milestones in 2000.

Their usual pattern called for CBS to later rebroadcast the six p.m. show to the remainder of the country or, if breaking news warranted, they would broadcast it live again. At about fourteen minutes into the program, as Walter Cronkite was reporting to the American public about security procedures for Henry Kissinger and Richard Nixon, I knew this was the moment, and for the first time while doing a zap my heart started beating very fast. I wasn't scared but somehow I knew that after this event things would change forever. I rushed onto the set, holding up my sign and yelling the message printed on it, "*Gays protest CBS prejudice!*" The *CBS Evening News* broke down right in front of Walter. I stepped between him and the camera, thereby shutting him out of the picture to show only that sign. As millions watched, I sat on his desk and held the sign right into the camera lens so that everyone could clearly see the words. *Gays Protest CBS Prejudice.*

Noted historian Doug Brinkley's best-selling 2012 biography and *Washington Post* "book of the year," *Cronkite*, best captures the scene:

The days of lax security at CBS News abruptly ended on December 11, 1973, when twenty-three-year-old Mark Allan Segal, a demonstrator from an organization called the Gay Raiders, with accomplice Harry Langhorne at his side, interrupted a Cronkite broadcast, causing the screen to go black for a few seconds. Cronkite was delivering a story about Henry Kissinger in the Middle East when, about fourteen minutes into the first "feed," Segal leapt in front of the camera carrying a yellow sign that read, "Gays Protest CBS Prejudice." More than thirty million Americans were watching . . . "I sat on Cronkite's desk directly in front of him and held up the sign," Segal recalled. "The network went black while they took me out of the studio."

On the surface, Cronkite was unfazed by the disruption. Technicians tackled Segal, wrapped him in cable wire, and ushered him out of camera view. Once back on live TV, Cronkite matter-of-factly described what had happened without an iota of irritation. "Well," the anchorman said, "a rather interesting development in the studio here—a protest demonstration right in the middle of the CBS News studio." He told viewers, "The young man identified as a member of something called Gay Raiders, an organization protesting alleged defamation of homosexuals on entertainment programs."

Segal had a legitimate complaint. Television—both news and entertainment divisions—treated gay people as pariahs, lepers from Sodom and Gomorrah. It stereotyped them as suicidal nut jobs, flaming fairies, and psychopathic villains. Part of the Gay Raiders' strategy was to bring public attention to the Big Three networks' discrimination policies. What better way to garner publicity for the cause than waving a banner on the CBS Evening News? "So I did it," Segal recalled. "The police were called, and I was taken to a holding tank."

But both Segal and Langhorne were charged with second-degree criminal trespassing as a result of their disruption of the CBS Evening News. It turned out that Segal had previously raided the Tonight Show, the Today show, and the Mike Douglas Show. At Segal's trial on April 23, 1974, Cronkite, who had accepted a subpoena, took his place on the witness stand. CBS lawyers objected each time Segal's attorney asked the anchorman a question. When the court recessed to cue up a tape of Segal's disruption of the Evening News, Segal felt a tap on his back—it was Cronkite, holding a fresh pad of yellow lined paper, ready to take notes with a sharp pencil.

"Why," Cronkite asked the activist with genuine curiosity, "did you do that?"

"Your news program censors," Segal pleaded. "If I can prove it, would you do something to change it?" Segal went on to rattle off three specific examples of CBS Evening News censorship, including a CBS report on the second rejection of a New York city council gay rights bill.

"Yes," Cronkite said. "I wrote that story myself."

"Well, why haven't you reported on the other twenty-three cities that have passed gay rights bills?" Segal asked. "Why do you cover five thousand women walking down Fifth Avenue in New York City when they proclaim International Women's Day on the network news, and you don't cover fifty thousand gays and lesbians walking down that same avenue proclaiming Gay Pride Day? That's censorship."

Segal's argument impressed Cronkite. The logic was difficult to deny. Why hadn't CBS News covered the gay pride parade? Was it indeed being homophobic? Why had the network largely avoided coverage of the Stonewall riots of 1969? At the end of the trial, Segal was fined $450, deeming the penalty "the happiest check I ever wrote." Not only did the activist receive considerable media attention, but Cronkite asked to meet privately with him to better understand how CBS might cover gay pride events. Cronkite, moreover, even went so far as to introduce Segal as a "constructive viewer" to top brass at CBS. It had a telling effect. "Walter Cronkite was my friend and mentor," Segal recalled. "After that incident, CBS News agreed to look into the 'possibility' that they were censoring or had a bias in reporting news. Walter showed a map on the Evening News of the US and pointed out cities that had passed gay rights legislation. Network news was never the same after that."

Before long, Cronkite ran gay rights segments on the CBS News broadcast with almost drumbeat regularity. "Part of the new morality of the '60s and '70s is a new attitude toward homosexuality," he told millions of viewers. "The homosexual men and women have organized to fight for acceptance and respectability. They've succeeded in winning equal rights under the law in many communities. But in the nation's biggest city, the fight goes on."

Not only did Cronkite speak out about gay rights, but he also became a reliable friend to the LGBTQ community. To gays, he was the counterweight to Anita Bryant, a leading gay rights opponent in the 1970s: he was a heterosexual willing to grant homosexuals their liberties.

During the 1980s, Cronkite criticized the Reagan administration for its handling of the HIV/AIDS epidemic and later criticized President Clinton's "Don't Ask, Don't Tell" policy regarding gays' nondisclosure of status while in the military. When Cronkite did an eight-part TV documentary *about his storied CBS career—Cronkite Remembers—he boasted about being a champion of LGBTQ issues. And he ended up hosting a huge AIDS benefit in Philadelphia organized by Segal, with singer Elton John as headliner.*

Here's what's not in Brinkley's book: Within moments a handful of technicians came over and wrestled me harshly to the floor and wrapped me in wires. They were angry and rough. It's my belief they were acting out of loyalty to Cronkite. I was beaten and bruised. For a while I remained outside the studio with two guards while they decided what to do with me. I remember thinking in a daze about the stagehands and technicians. Were any of them gay? How did they feel about what I had just done? Did they hate me?

We were then ushered to an office on the first floor of the building under armed CBS guard, and told that we were not free to go. We were a little confused since at no point did they tell us that we were under arrest. Finally the door opened. In walked the anchor of the local *CBS Evening News* with a camera crew and several guys in suits. They told us that it would help to be interviewed. Who it would help or for what reason they didn't say. Nor would they answer any of our questions. It didn't matter. Our goal was to get the word out to the public and this was one way of doing so. We were proud to assist and would suffer any consequences later.

We were also not aware of how big a deal this all was. Later we discovered that the CBS switchboard was so overloaded that it was brought down, and many of those calls came from other media, so the network knew it had a story and they also had an exclusive story that they could keep for their own broadcast. After the interview, security guards led us down a hall, at the end of which stood a group of New York's finest. A police wagon had been brought to a back door and CBS did all it could to shelter us from being photographed while going from the door to the police wagon. We were their exclusive. When we got to the doors, escorted by the men in suits and the armed guards, all hell broke lose. Every news organization in New York was there. As the CBS guards handed us over to the NYPD, reporters kept yelling questions and flashing pictures.

While we were being transported off to jail, Walter Cronkite was doing his second live news broadcast of the evening. He reported on the disruption of his earlier show "by a group calling itself Gay Raiders and protesting CBS bigotry toward the homosexual community." In commenting on the zap during his own show, Walter was not aware that it was the first time the *CBS Evening News* had ever reported on a gay demonstration.

The next morning the story was on the front page of nearly every newspaper in the country. America wanted to know more about this man who dared hurt their Uncle Walter. It was beyond my comprehension. Requests for interviews started to come in as soon as we were out on bail. A couple of publishers asked me to write a book about my zaps, another wanted a memoir. A memoir? At twenty-three? Others felt they could somehow market me, make me a celebrity du jour, but I had no interest in any of it. My purpose in all of this was gay equality.

As the face of the Gay Raiders, I was invited to more on-air talk shows. News magazines and newspapers called for interviews. At times I felt the country simply could not comprehend a gay man who was not only open, but outrageous, proud, pushy, and also happy and fabulously full of life and humor. Offers came and all I asked for was transportation, a hotel if necessary, and meals. This was not for money; even though I had none; I was still living off the grace of my parents. I became the penniless darling of the media, and the first openly gay person to make the talk show circuit. There were other prominent activists out there like Frank Kameny, Barbara Gittings, and Harry Hay, but none of them had captured national attention as I had by disrupting Walter Cronkite's newscast. My intention was to sell gay liberation like a product, by educating the nation about LGBT people.

The hosts of the shows would introduce me as this radical controversial homosexual, and then I'd do my darndest to be a polite and gracious guest. If it was my plan to show America who gay people were, then I had to play the part, which, luckily, mirrored who I really was. Morty Manford, as promised, had arranged for a lawyer. Not just any lawyer, but Hal Weiner, who had been the attorney to incorporate the GAA. While I zapped people in person, Hal zapped them with the law. In my first meeting with Hal, he looked at me sternly and said with what felt like true annoyance: "Do you know you could get ten years in prison for this?" He waited until it sunk in, then started laughing and added, "You won't get ten minutes."

The morning after the zap, Hal called the CBS lawyers and asked to come in to subpoena Walter Cronkite. The CBS lawyer laughed and told Hal that Walter was too busy and then hung up. Hal did a little research and learned that at that time, New York law allowed a subpoena to be copied and then used as a legal subpoena. So he called the CBS lawyers back and said, "Before you hang up, I'd like to let you know about the subpoena powers here in New York." After he explained the law, the CBS lawyer asked, "What the hell does that have to do with us?" Hal then said: "I've just made one hundred copies of the subpoena and tomorrow at eleven a.m. I'm coming in to CBS, and you will have Walter available for me to subpoena him in person. If not, I'm giving fifty subpoenas to members of the Gay Activists Alliance and fifty to Hell's Angels, and I will offer a thousand-dollar reward to the first to serve Walter." Needless to say, Walter was served the next morning at eleven a.m.

While preparing for the trial, the Gay Raiders even appeared in a *Life* magazine feature called "A Day in the Life of America." Nothing like a couple of gays not making a living.

Most gay people at the time were still not supportive of our efforts. Many believed that we should be quiet, conformist, and stay in the closet. Some were ashamed of me and tried to suppress our work. As the nation's best-known out gay man I was doing national television shows with rips in my socks and holes in my shoes. Harry Langhorne, who stood lookout during the Cronkite zap, had to ask his mother for financial help. A distant relative of Lady Astor finally paid our out-of-pocket legal expenses when Morty, Morris, Troy, and even Frank Kameny, who was having his own problems making a living, were unable to get financial assistance for the defense.

I've kept a few of the notes I received at that time to remind me of where we were. One states: *While we admire your intentions, we do not admire your methods.* Another, from a wealthy friend who loaned me $150, which I thought he understood would be paid back whenever I had the funds, said, *I've never run into such a dishonest person before.* But there were those of support as well: a group of lesbian feminists from Miami sent what they could, and we did receive small donations but not enough to either live on or pay legal bills.

Today, activism is a multimillion-dollar business, with huge budgets and all kinds of wealthy backers. At that time, not one major celebrity or corporation embraced our community, much less the radical Gay Raiders.

At our trial most reporters were surprised to see Cronkite listed as a defense witness. A tape of the zap played, and Walter witnessed his open jaw during the incident. Hal asked him his reaction and Cronkite said, "Not very professional on my part," which gave everyone in the court a laugh.

As for Walter and me, we became friends. As Brinkley wrote in his book and made public for the first time, Cronkite kept his promise, but all the while he never admitted that CBS News was biased on the subject. Not while introducing me to key CBS News staffers—including Marlene Adler, his chief of staff who over the years kept us connected—not after reporting on those cities that had passed gay rights legislation, not when reporting on gay pride. It actually became a running joke between us.

Chapter 5

After Cronkite

Sixty million homes. That's how many people saw the broadcast. There was a burning-bright spotlight on the LGBT community and on me personally. The public just wanted answers. Some wanted me strung up for hurting good old Uncle Walter, and many members of my own community thought I had gone too far. But we had succeeded in our attempt to capture the public interest and we were ready to start a discussion. Percentage-wise, Walter's newscast was a juggernaut; his ratings then were higher than most shows on prime-time television today.

When Harry Langhorne and I had been released on bail and left the police station, only Morty and Hal Weiner, our attorney, were there to greet us. We talked strategy with them, then drove back to Philly. It was my turn to take Mom to dialysis that afternoon. At home she was waiting at the door. She gave me a hug and asked if I was treated okay. It had all become so normal for us. Mom would ask about the police treatment, about the cell, and about next steps. It was like any other mother asking her son, *How was your day at the office?* She was the caring mother to the hilt, no matter how sick she got. I assured her I was all right, then she insisted on cooking breakfast for Phillip, Harry, and me. The phone was ringing off the hook but we ignored it for as long as possible. Once we started to answer, it was call after call of requests for interviews for newspapers, magazines, and radio and television talk shows.

The next two years I was fully engaged with appearances on talk shows, other interviews, and making speeches across the country. I'd fly out to Chicago to do a television show, then to Los Angeles for a speech after the taping, and then do a radio show while waiting in the hotel to leave for my flight to yet another city. We still did the occasional zap, but getting publicity every six weeks via a stunt was no longer necessary; publicity was following me.

At the time, the king of the television talk shows was Phil Donahue. His syndicated show was first taped in Dayton, Ohio, before moving to Chicago and then New York. It's ironic to say that he was the Oprah Winfrey of his day, since many give him credit for inventing the genre and ultimately it was Oprah who dethroned him as talk show champion.

Somewhere along the way, I was invited onto the *Phil Donohue Show*. Before the show he came into the makeup room to explain to me that his audience was conservative. This didn't bother me because I'd known that he had done one other program on the subject of "homosexuals," during which he was sympathetic and respectful. While his other "homosexual" guest had tried to win the audience over with simple facts, my attitude would be very different. Per my Gay Liberation Front training, respect was demanded. This conservative audience was about to be challenged by a gay man, and one who would tell them that all they had learned about the LGBT community was wrong. My reply to Donahue was, "Do you think they're ready for me?" He seemed to enjoy that.

Like most talk shows, after the guests on *Donahue* were introduced, the host would begin with an introductory question or two. The real meat of his show, however, was the audience's questions, where Donahue would run up and down the aisles with his microphone.

For my first question, Donahue wanted to understand why we'd done the various zaps on network television. The answer in this case was simple. "Phil, would I be here today discussing this issue if we hadn't done those zaps?" It was true. "Thanks to those zaps, more televison and radio talk shows are now debating this subject, and so those acts far exceeded any expectations we had."

When that softball question was over he went to a lady in the audience who held up a Bible and wanted to quote from it. Donahue persuaded her not to open the Bible but invited her to say what was on her mind. She looked at me and told me I was going to hell and that God intended for me to die. "Says Leviticus," she bellowed, *"Man who lays with man is an abomination!"* She was just going on and on until Phil interrupted her and asked if she'd like to hear my response.

"Madam, from what you say it seems you don't respect religion," was my reply.

She said, "I'm a true Christian."

I stared her down. "A true Christian respects the rights of other religions. My religion accepts who I am. Are you inferring that Judaism is a false religion? If you'd like to talk religion we can do so, but I'll also quote other parts of the Bible you seem to have forgotten."

She exploded and just started tossing out various biblical verses at me.

"You don't know your Bible well," I said. That sentence would become a trademark comment from me in religious discussions. I continued, "You use your Bible like you were ordering from a restaurant menu. I call that *Bible a la carte*. You choose what parts of the Bible you wish to obey and what others to ignore." Then I looked her over and explained that all she was wearing that day made her an abomination according to that same Leviticus chapter, which condemns wearing clothing of two different fabrics. Polyester-cotton blend, anyone? I followed that up by asking the audience a quick succession of questions about shellfish, metals, pig skin, and all the rest, then asked, "Do all of you obey your husbands? While I know none of you would commit adultery, I'm sure you're aware that in cases of adultery your husband has the right to kill you. So, if I'm going to hell, you're all joining me. As the Good Book says, *He who has not sinned should throw the first stone.* Is there anyone in this audience who has not sinned?"

As total silence fell over the room, I directed my next comment back to the lady with the Bible. "Oh, and one more thing. Remember the Ten Commandments? Gluttony. How many of you are joining me in hell now?" No LGBT person had ever challenged an entire TV audience in that manner before. This kept the Bible-toting crowd focused on issues like discrimination, hate crimes, and entrapment. It was this formula that I'd use whenever I found myself in Bible Belt communities. Take it head on, then move to the real issues at hand.

The end of the show was a chance for Donahue to express his own thoughts and bring about peace in the studio. He started out by saying the obvious: "Don't think there has ever been a discussion like this on television before." And with what seemed to be a smirk on his face he added, "Some of our affiliates might not air this show, but we learned a lot about religious freedom and gay and lesbian people today."

Backstage he gushed and looked at his production team and said, "That's what makes good TV," asking to reschedule me as soon as possible. That would take awhile since I had other media obligations piled up, along with speaking engagements, surveys that we had initiated, my position as GAA political chair, and our work on a nondiscrimination bill. Additionally, I had to attend various legal trials due to the zaps, and I still had my duties at home. But eventually it did happen.

For my second appearance, Phil Donohue asked my parents and my partner Phillip to join me. When I told my parents about this request, Dad jumped at the chance, while Mom felt slightly apprehensive. On the flight over, she remained silent as Dad chatted about our engagement to the stewardesses and fellow passengers; I wondered how things would go.

It was late at night when we landed, and a car picked us up at the airport and drove us to our hotel. Early the next morning we were taken to the studio and led into the green room. About twenty minutes before taping, Phil appeared in the room with his makeup bib on. *Hollywood Squares* was playing on a television in the background, and as Phil noticed us, he looked at me and said, "That's the show I'd love to do." At this point Joan Rivers was on screen making a joke about something and Phil commented, "She's got raw talent." He looked around at my parents and added, referring to *Hollywood Squares*, "I don't think I can do that." In quick order he then told us the run of the show we were about to tape. He treated me like we were old friends and realized that my parents had never done anything like this. He calmed their fears by chatting with them. My mother was almost instantly won over by his charm, while my father decided that this was his opportunity to be comedian Henny Youngman. He asked Donahue about stage setup, timing, and the line of questions. My father, the short, very pudgy cab driver from Philly, whose most exciting event in life to this point had been a full house at the weekly cousin's club card game, was all in. My father had gone Hollywood and showed no sign of nerves. In fact, he was overly excited, which in turn made me nervous.

The first part of the show was just me with Phil and the audience. We discussed the pioneering work I had just begun with Pennsylvania's Governor Milton Shapp in order to find ways to end discrimination, as well as my other exploits as an activist. For the second half of the show Phil brought my parents and Phillip back onstage. No sooner had he introduced them when my father went into his routine: "You know Mark lives at home with us, and on weekends Phillip joins him. We enjoy each other's company, but I know Phillip loves Sunday morning best of all. On Sundays, this nice Catholic boy comes downstairs to breakfast and enjoys lox, bagels, and whitefish." Dad, in the best stage acting of his life, looked at Phillip lovingly and, expecting a drumroll after this statement, had now added religion into the discussion.

Mom sat there totally frightened and silent while Dad was channeling a Johnny Carson monologue. Finally, Phil asked Mom, "How do you feel about all this?" Mom straightened up and said what I think was on the mind of every parent when they learned their child was gay: "I want Mark to be happy, I worry about him when he gets older, but most importantly I want him to find someone who he can love and spend the rest of his life with." She looked at my partner Phillip and smiled and placed her hand on his knee.

Donahue broke for a commercial, and when the sound was off he turned to my mother and said, "That was great, Mom." She was thrilled and Dad, still believing himself to be Henny Youngman, asked, "And what am I, chopped liver?"

After the taping Phil came over to tell us that it was a great show, and kissed Mom on the cheek. She smiled and blushed, and would never in her life miss another Phil Donahue show.

The staff handed us a piece of paper with the airdates and we departed.

Mom and Dad flew home, while Phillip and I headed to Provincetown on Cape Cod where I was the keynote speaker at the first New England Gay Conference. When I got home from the conference there was a bill in the mail from the Donahue people for eighty-six dollars for additional hotel expenses. Of course I couldn't afford it and wrote back promising to pay it sometime in the future. In the same letter I requested a copy of the taping. I'd never asked for tapes before, but this show was with my parents, and I thought it would be a great keepsake. They wrote back explaining that the company that handled those requests charged more than a hundred dollars per copy. They gave me their phone number and mailing address. Since I didn't have the money I didn't respond until a couple of years later.

Flash forward to 2013, at a meeting of Comcast's Joint Diversity Council, on which I serve as the national LGBT representative. The council was formed by company chairman and CEO Brian Roberts and Senior Executive Vice President David L. Cohen, with the mission to transform Comcast NBCUniversal into one of the most diversified companies in the Fortune 100. We were having a discussion about the history of television talk shows, when someone asked me about Phil Donahue and that February 1973 taping, saying that as far as he knew it was one of the first depictions of a gay family on TV. He said it was historic. I explained that he was almost correct, but that we were preceded by *An American Family* on PBS, which aired a year and a half earlier.

I'm still honored to have been a guest various times on Donahue's show. In the early days of TV talk, there was no other American media person or company who had done as much to make Americans aware of the gay and lesbian community. Ditto for the issues surrounding AIDS. Not only did Donahue broadcast shows on the subject before it became popular, it was, in some cases, dangerous. And he handled them always with respect and care. He got into the AIDS battle early, giving of his time when other celebrities hid the issues from their audiences and themselves.

At the 1993 March on Washington for Lesbian, Gay, and Bi Equal Rights and Liberation, I left the crowd to take a walk to the Washington Monument. As I strolled I passed thousands of people, most of them gay or lesbian. Over the loudspeaker I heard a familiar voice—it was Phil Donahue. On this early Sunday morning, long before the crowd reached capacity, he was once again giving his time to support our community in our fight for equality. He read a speech in which he told a story of discrimination, then paused and commanded America to get over it. Next, he shared a story of antigay violence. Again he said, "America, get over it." This went on and on. It must have taken hours of research to draft the speech. This man, who had brought so many Americans face-to-face with the gay and lesbian community, was rightly an opening act at our march. As I walked back to my group listening to Phil's voice, a chill ran down my back. I was so proud of him and his part in helping our movement progress.

While in the early 1970s the *Phil Donahue Show* was the leader in talk shows, I appeared on most of the others as well. The shows would fly me out to their studio, pay my travel expenses, and pick up the cost of meals and my hotel room. In each city, the night before the show, I'd invite a few members of the LGBT community to the hotel, order food and drinks, put it on the tab of the show, and mostly just listen to their stories. The talk shows were, in a sense, paying for me to witness LGBT America. Sometimes when I got a little downtime, the community would surprise me in some way. Yes, despite my upbeat disposition, I would occasionally get discouraged. In Detroit, for the *Joe Pyne Show*, some members of the community took me to the Cow Palace to see a traveling edition of *Peter Pan*. While I was in Chicago for the *Irv Kupcinet Show*, an incredible dinner party was given in my honor by Chuck Renslow, at his mansion that at one time had belonged to Al Capone. (It had a speakeasy in the basement.)

In between the talk shows I gave speeches, many of which have been long forgotten, or so I thought. In March 2014, the *Gazette*, which bills itself as the Eastern Iowa newspaper of record for over 125 years, published a report on the gay rights movement in Iowa. It chronicled the growth of the community and mentioned that in 1974 I became the first out gay person to speak publicly on the subject in Iowa. When I read the article, those memories washed back to shore.

It had started with Iowa State University sending me an invitation, one that included paying for my expenses and giving me a small honorarium. Honorarium? Progress for sure. At that point, the only thing stopping me from accepting an invitation was if I had dialysis duty. I always asked my parents if they could do without me for a few days before making a decision. They said that they'd be all right for this one.

When I told friends where I was going, their reactions were always the same. *Iowa, they'll kill you out there.* I'd like to believe my speech actually inspired a few in the audience. One guy there that night, Ken Bunch, would move to San Francisco and become one of the founders of the Sisters of Perpetual Indulgence, a beloved group of men dressing in outrageous nun drag while fighting the AIDS epidemic. His name became Sister Vicious Power Hungry Bitch. What a brilliant man.

On the homefront, Mom's kidney condition had deteriorated so much that she was now on the transplant list. Each family member was tested, and when only Uncle Stan was a match, my grandmother, who had been a free spirit her entire life, began to look shell-shocked. The emotional turmoil that she felt over the possibility that her daughter and her son could die on the operating table finally broke her spirit. Uncle Stan soon became her caregiver, and they moved into our house on Fayette Street. At the time it seemed very natural. There were three bedrooms. Mom and Dad had one, I had one, and Grandmom had one; Uncle Stan made good with the couch. Our family life became doctor appointments for Grandmom, dialysis for Mom, and demonstrations and zaps for me. I always told Mom and Grandmom as I left the house that they shouldn't worry; the worst that would happen is that I'd get arrested.

There were no complaints from them. At the time, they never told me about the numerous calls from relatives complaining about my activities. Most were about how I was embarrassing the family. Mom also never told me that she'd stopped going to the cousins club, one of the few outings she looked forward to, because some of her relatives had said derogatory things about my actions. Dad never said anything about the fights he got into until years later. Thanks to his time in the Army Air Force during which he competed as an amateur boxer, which had earned him the nickname Little Atlas, he always won. Years later, he boasted how proud he was of my actions and said, "We love you no matter what." He never lost an opportunity to let me know that I had made him proud. I cried every time.

Dad and Uncle Stan always held down the fort while my "career" without a salary continued. The press in Philly coined me "Supergay" and even the establishment wanted a piece of the action. The Junior Chamber of Commerce announced that I was one of their men of the year. The Jewish Community Relations Council voted me onto their board of directors, a gesture more symbolic than practical since my attendance was rare.

Meanwhile, Grandmom's condition grew steadily worse. My Auntie Mame, my muse, started to drift off into a world of her own. I liked to think that world was the one she loved, strolling on the boardwalk in Atlantic City, chatting with all her friends, and sashaying from one avenue to the next. She did listen to each word that we spoke to her, and always with a smile on her face. We never knew if she understood or not, and her speech slowly disappeared. Each night when I wasn't on the road, I'd go to the living room to sit with her and tell her about my day and future plans. She listened, reacted with that smile, and occasionally uttered a reassuring word. At times she'd perk up at the mention of some new success, but she wasn't that perpetual shining light anymore. I suppose those chats were more for me than her. I needed Grandmom and my family. They kept me grounded while I was becoming a public figure.

At home, my social world consisted of Phillip, my high school friend Randy Miller, and Randy's friends Jan Sergienko and Debbie Dunn. In the evenings we hung out and they'd help me come up with the next great idea. Except for Phillip, they were all non-gays, but today you'd call them LGBT allies. One initiative in particular comes to mind. We were still doing stunts in Philly every few weeks. Someone suggested that we paint a large sign with the words *Gay Power* and place it on the City Hall tower during rush hour. Soon we discovered what it would take to make a six-story "statement." We bought white sheets and began to do the lettering in Jan's parent's basement. Somehow we all agreed on this crazy project. It would be simple: white material, black lettering. It would be carried into the building in stages and Velcroed together.

We transported it to City Hall and found a friendly office where I stayed overnight. I awoke at seven a.m. and took the banner up to the tower but the doors were locked. I ventured to the top of the north side of the building and found an open window. I tied down the top of the banner and Velcroed the pieces together. Finally, I hung it out the window facing the traffic on Broad Street coming into the city center. It caused a huge traffic problem. The all-news radio stations began reporting on it every ten minutes. For some reason it took the powers-that-be about an hour to hoist the banner back inside. In the meantime I was across the street watching and kicking myself for not taking into consideration the wind, which at times made the words almost unreadable.

There was also Chicago's first gay pride celebration. The Reverend Troy Perry and I were to be the featured speakers in Lincoln Park. We agreed to arrive in Chicago days in advance to promote the event. Troy was fighting the religious establishment and I was off fighting the networks and elected officials, and both of us wondered when our community would begin to help us with building our vision. Troy not only struggled with mainstream religion, but also the antireligious sentiment in the LGBT community. My fight was with those who felt my actions put too much attention on the community and pigeonholed us all as radical.

The schism in the gay rights movement was hitting a fever pitch. Gay Liberation Front had disbanded in New York and the Gay Activist Alliance would see its last day soon thereafter, succeeded by the National Gay Task Force. The 1972 and 1973 Gay Pride Days at times seemed like war zones. In addition to the rivalries of the remainder of the GLF and GAA members, there was still infighting about whether the movement should be a diverse, inclusive civil rights movement or have a gay rights–only policy.

GAA had taken up roots in an old firehouse on Wooster Street in Soho in New York City. At that time, under the leadership of Morty Manford, it became the focal point of the movement. But a rift between Morty and Bruce Voeller resulted in the formation of the National Gay Task Force. The Task Force put several of the pre-Stonewallers on their board since by this point Voeller was in need of credibility. Barbara Gittings and Frank Kameny were brought in, but all that did was reopen the wounds of a past battle in 1970 over whether the community would march in New York to mark the first anniversary of Stonewall or continue the July 4 Philadelphia marches for equality. GLF members at the time unfortunately labeled Barbara and Frank, and all those associated with the Philadelphia marches, as the Uncle Toms of our movement. Most of the younger activists thought of them as dinosaurs. To further complicate matters, Bruce Voeller assumed the role as the first employee of a gay organization with a professional staff. This was the beginning of what we now call Gay Inc., the incorporation and branding of the gay rights movement. Previously, GAA had created what they hoped would be the symbol of our struggle, the Greek lambda icon, yellow on a blue background. But the Task Force took things a few steps too far on policy. No drag queens need apply; no care was given to street kids. Zaps or actions were discouraged; the primary activities were lobbying for issues within government, talking in moderate tones, and always wearing a suit when talking to the media. And then there was the constant stream of fundraising at upper-crust LGBT cocktail parties. To my mind they were complacent and afraid to really fight. They wanted to change laws, but not create community.

Bruce Voeller was as unpopular as a figurehead could get, not only among New York activists but nationally as well. My only relationship with the Task Force was to call and complain when they took credit for my work. Any time a story on the LGBT community would break, NGTF was always there to issue a statement and explain how they were involved.

Out on the West Coast, an investment banker named David Goodstein had purchased the only national LGBT publication, the *Advocate*, which was read by nearly all LGBT activists. It was how we learned what others were doing. We couldn't expect any reports from the mainstream media, and there was no Internet. But Goodstein agreed with Voeller's view on a more formal, professional, and organized gay rights struggle. He created a list of people who should be low priority in their news coverage. Along with longtime activists such as Morris Knight, I was on the list. It felt like censorship. Goldstein's strangest contribution to the movement was when he introduced "The *Advocate* Experience," where people paid to attend a Zen-like weekend getaway, with the emphasis on enlightenment and self-acceptance rather than public opinion and equal rights. At this point, the *Advocate*, a respected publication known for good journalism, slipped into the dark side of history.

Voeller eventually left what resulted in a decimated Task Force. A host of directors followed his departure, each of whom crashed and burned due to various scandals or were ousted for a lack of organizational and communication skills. Eventually the Task Force did find decent leadership and direction. Among those leaders were Virginia Apuzzo, Urvashi Vaid, and Matt Foreman. Under their stewardship, the Task Force became the respectable organization that it is today. And as the group was getting its act together, another organization came along, the Human Rights Campaign Fund. It later dropped the word *Fund* and become known as just HRC, but due to their early lavish fundraising events, it was coined by one activist "Human Rights Champagne Fund." As it stands, HRC is now the leading LGBT civil rights organization in the nation and their fundraising brings in over ten million dollars each year for LGBT causes.

In the mid-'70s, while the New York LGBT community was busy with their in-fighting, the Gay Raiders were beginning to blossom into new areas. What we had been doing with media, we now did with government. Seeing the need for concrete data that documented the treatment of LGBT people, we conducted surveys. Individuals donated stamps and stationery, and one of my new friends on the city council, Thomas Foglietta, who would become a congressman and then ambassador to Italy under President Clinton, allowed us to use his office and equipment to create the surveys.

One of the leading complaints from our community was police harassment and entrapment. We obtained a list of police chiefs in every major city and sent them letters asking how their department treated the gay community. We didn't expect much of a response and were surprised when over twenty responded. The answers were sterile, but at least we had opened their eyes to the issue. At the same time, we forwarded the responses to the local organizations should they want to follow up and create a relationship with their local police force.

We also did the first-ever survey of corporate America. We didn't have the funds to send surveys to the complete Fortune 500 list, but the top hundred would still have an impact. We asked each of them if they had a nondiscrimination policy in their human resources departments. It was again an eye-opening survey, for us and for them. Many wrote back that they had never even thought about it. A few said they'd look into it. In 1976, that was the state of corporate America on nondiscrimination.

And then my old friend from New York, Congresswoman Bella Abzug, along with then-congressman Ed Koch, asked me to help with something they had just introduced with little fanfare. The Equality Act (a precursor to the federal Employment Non-Discrimination Act) was first introduced by Abzug in May 1974. She and Koch (whom I always thought had a crush on me but never acted on it) felt that my luster at that time might help it along.

After countless meetings, it seemed to me that something was missing from the legislation: there were no African American Congress members as cosponsors. As the *Advocate* reported in August of that year, I worked to have Congressman Robert Nix, a founding member of the Congressional Black Caucus, become a cosponsor. He insisted that he reintroduce the legislation and later that year it became H.R. 166, with five sponsors.

Congrsswoman Abzug made one other request of me during that time: come up with a PR stunt to promote the legislation. That stunt became the lamest Gay Raiders zap of all time, a White House zap. Translation: we decided to have a public LGBT tour of the White House. In those days all you had to do was line up outside the White House in the morning. We publicized this, but since most of the LGBT community in DC was still deeply closeted, the tour consisted of me, a few members of the Gay Raiders, and a very large group of Secret Service agents. The only coverage it got was in the *Advocate*.

It is so impressive how much Human Rights Campaign has improved upon the effort to pass ENDA and how they've made their surveys so important—many Fortune 500 companies work diligently each year to obtain a 100 percent rating for their support of their LGBT employees. While our simple surveys consisted of one question, each year's Human Rights Campaign

Corporate Equality Index has a booklet of questions that each company's human resources department must fill out. It touches on the full range of LGBT issues that individuals and corporations face. Many of the Fortune 500 corporations now covet a top ranking in the index and advertise and promote the fact.

In the middle of all of this, I wrote a letter requesting a meeting with the governor of Pennsylvania. It seemed simple, but at that time, in 1974, no governor in the nation had ever met publicly with anyone from the gay and lesbian community. So when Governor Milton Shapp agreed, it caught me by surprise. His office called to arrange for a meeting the next day. In all honesty, it never occurred to me that he'd actually agree to such a meeting. Preparation was virtually nonexistent and as was often the case for me, the meeting was off the cuff. We met in Norristown, Pennsylvania, while he was on a statewide tour. When Harry Langhorne and I walked into the room, the governor stood up, walked over to us with a big smile on his face, and gave me a hearty handshake. His smile grew as he said, "I've seen you on TV." When I didn't get it, he added, "Cronkite seemed to be surprised to meet you, but I'm not." It was the first time that I'd ever felt comfortable with an elected official so quickly.

Rather than ask what he could do for us, he asked what he could do to help our cause. This caught us completely off guard. And, as always, I went for the brass ring: "Governor, gay men and lesbians are discriminated against in almost every part of state government."

This was all I got out before he said, "How can we change that?"

I replied with the brass ring again: "Create a commission to explore these problems and find solutions." At that point there had never been an official governmental body to look into

LGBT issues. He knew it, I knew it, and we just looked at each other for a while, knowing that what was requested was, in fact, unprecedented.

Governor Shapp finally said, "Let me consider the options and get back to you." He then did something else unheard of: he asked his press secretary to allow the media in to our meeting, which we had believed was to be off the record. This was another surprise to Harry and me.

The press was out in force. When the door to the room opened, they rushed in. Questions were yelled at the governor, too many to answer, but he gave the usual political statement, "We had a good meeting," then added, "It's a start." To further assure us, he actually posed for pictures with us. At that time most elected officials were running from gay activists; some wouldn't even touch a gay person—but not Governor Milton Shapp. The next day, pictures of the two of us shaking hands were splashed across the state's newspapers. He relished the idea of helping; after all, he was the man who came up with the idea of the Peace Corps (not Sargent Shriver, as most people believe).

Our friendship grew, and it was not unusual for him to call the house in the evening to talk about the LGBT community. He wanted to know all the ways in which we were discriminated against. We started to discuss the organization of the commission. During one of these calls, he said, "It's going to take all the departments of the state." If Milton Shapp was from a different state, such as New York or California, he would be hailed as a national hero of our community rather than a footnote. Shapp, the first Jewish governor of Pennsylvania, also became the first governor in the nation to issue a statewide executive order forbidding discrimination against gay people in all agencies and departments, and the first governmental chief executive in the world to create a commission to look into the concerns of the gay and lesbian community. When he was up for reelection, his Republican opponent, Drew Lewis, was forced to write *Philadelphia Gay News* a letter stating that he opposed discrimination in housing employment and public accommodation, and my favorite part of that letter was where he added, *I do not feel that your preference should result in criminal liability.* If elected, Lewis would continue to support civil rights for gays and lesbians. This marked the first gubernatorial election in America where both Republican and Democrat candidates supported LGBT rights. The credit is due to Shapp, and it also underscored the power we as a community had garnered by 1975.

In April of that year, Shapp established the Pennsylvania Council for Sexual Minorities. He ordered each department to appoint a top official to be a member or liaison. This was real. Yet there was also one disappointment for me, and one that I'd have to become comfortable with if I wanted to continue to plow new ground. I might have provided the seed, but I was not allowed to grow my own child. As the governor told me, "Mark, you're too much of a firebrand, and if I allowed you to chair the commission it would get nowhere, and we both want it to make change, you understand."

I was given two subcommittees: prisons and insurance. Tony Silvestre would lead the commission. The governor appointed Barry Kohn to be his liaison. It seemed to me that both Silvestre and Kohn believed, as had the Task Force, that I projected the wrong image. That old feeling of isolation that I experienced in grammar school returned. Gee, if only I'd worn a suit.

Shapp continued to engage me in new ways. While the commission was toiling, he put me to work with the state police and the legislature. One day he called and asked me to meet him in the governor's residence later that afternoon. "Governor, I'm in Philadelphia, is it so important that I come to Harrisburg?" He insisted, and after a two-hour drive, I was pulling up to the gate and the guard said, "Mr. Segal, the governor is waiting for you."

Entering the governor's ornate residence, I found him standing there, smiling with his arms crossed against his chest. He said, "There seems to be one thing that is lacking in your lobbying efforts, and it's about time someone tells you." With that we went into the state dining room where there was a coatrack with about ten jackets on it. "If you're going to lobby state senators and representatives, you need to look the part. You don't have to wear a complete suit, but a blue jacket will do the trick. Here, try these on." The rack contained blue blazers in various sizes. "Find the one that fits you, and I'll see you in Philadelphia next week." He had me drive all the way to Harrisburg just to give me a jacket!

In quick succession, Shapp issued an executive order banning discrimination in state hiring and services, created the Council for Sexual Minorities (whose title, according to the governor, had to contain the word *minority* since that was something the public would respond to), and, in June of 1975, became first governor in the nation to have his state officially proclaim Gay Pride Month.

Shortly after the governor issued his executive order, I was lying down in my bedroom on Fayette Street one morning when the phone rang at six a.m. I ignored it and just turned over in bed. Then, a knock on the door. Mom said: "Mark, there's a guy on the phone who say's he's Lieutenant Governor Ernie Kline and he wants to talk to you."

Picking up the extension in my room, I greeted, "Governor, what can I do for you?"

He explained that Governor Shapp had had a knock-down

screaming match with the head of the Pennsylvania state troopers over his executive order banning discrimination against sexual minorities in state hiring. It seems that when Colonel James Barger heard that the executive order included his department, he marched directly to the governor's office and told Shapp that there was no way would he have "those people" on his force.

My reaction was, "So what can I do to help?"

"The governor wants you to go to the state police barracks at Belmont today at nine a.m. and sign up to be a state trooper." As my mind was trying to grasp this idea, he went on, "Just show up, fill out the paperwork, and we'll do the rest."

All I could get out before he hung up was, "Ernie . . ."

So on May 14, 1975, I jumped out of bed and began hatching a plan of action, one taking place in an unfamiliar landscape. I knew the police, that was for sure, but from a completely different type of experience. I wondered what one wears to sign up to be a state trooper. Then it dawned on me: How far was this going to go? Would the governor actually make me go to some sort of state trooper boot camp? By this time, in the two years after I had been summoned home to help care for my mom, my parents had adjusted to almost anything. So as I left the house, I called out, "Well, at least today you won't have to worry about me being arrested by the police, seems I'm signing up to become one of them." Mom gave me a strange look and I added, "You know, Mom, I'm marching off to war." She smiled; it was our private joke about that day in grammar school and "Onward, Christian Soldiers."

As I drove into the Belmont police barracks parking lot, a swarm of media surrounded my car. Clearly, the governor's office had put out a press release. There was a new reporter for KYW-TV named Jessica Savitch, who in just two years would become an anchor on the *NBC Nightly News* and in short order lose control of her life, then actually lose her life in an automobile accident. But in 1975, she was still a cub reporter. When I got out of the car, she shoved a mic in front of me and said, "Mr. Segal, you're a homosexual."

Like that was something I didn't know. Before she could say anything else I replied, "Isn't that obvious?" After all, I was wearing a button that read, *How dare you presume I'm straight.* Then I added, "I see you got the press release."

She continued, asking why I was applying to become a state trooper. The rest of the media gathered around and I said the first thing that came to mind: "I like men in uniform." Everyone laughed, and then I got down to the serious business at hand. "This is about employment discrimination. If I'm able to do the job, then I should be given the same opportunity as anyone else." Sounded perfectly logical to me, and to the press; they got their three-minute story for the evening news. But no one mentioned that the guy signing up for the state troopers was five-seven, dressed in torn blue jeans, a T-shirt with a peace sign on it, and hair down to his shoulders. This was political theater, and the only way to make it work was with a little humor.

One reporter who saw through the theatrics and went right to the facts when covering one of my political actions was Andrea Mitchell, then with KYW-TV and one whose battles with Mayor Frank Rizzo are now legendary. Our relationship was cordial, but once the camera was on she was as professional and well-researched as any reporter I've ever known.

The activity with the state troopers was written about and broadcast throughout the state. Here's an example of how the media of the day handled this:

Philadelphia AP—Mark Segal, an admitted homosexual, applied Wednesday to join the Pennsylvania State Police, but admitted later his application was a test of state police policy. Segal said, and state police confirmed, that he applied at the state police barracks in the Belmont section of Philadelphia.

But my favorite headline came from the *Times Leader:* "Shapp Aide Tells Berger to Reconsider Homos Ban."

After one long day of fighting, I asked Shapp why he was taking this on, and he told me, "Mark, I'm in the closet as well." When I looked at him strangely, he laughed and followed up with, "My real name is Shapiro, I had to change it to Shapp to enter politics. So I understand discrimination."

Almost thirty years later I received a call from a young girl who explained, "My father suggested that I contact you regarding a report on gay rights I'm doing for a school term paper." My questions were the usual: What school? What aspects of LGBT history are you interested in? She replied, "I'm not calling you about your activism, I'm calling you since I understand that my grandfather was involved with the gay rights movement and my father told me you worked with him." Her father was Richard Shapp, and she was Milton Shapp's granddaughter. She had no idea about her grandfather's important work in this area, and unfortunately most Americans still don't. And believe me, he's one of the most important figures in the early gay rights movement. He was a pioneer in his own way.

Those official Pennsylvania gay pride proclamations started by Shapp kept coming through various administrations, including Republican governor Richard Thornburgh, who was later appointed US attorney general by President Ronald Reagan. When elected governor, Thornburgh wanted to show inclusion in his administration. He chose an African American Republican doctor who had been elected to the Philadelphia city council to be his secretary of the commonwealth. Her name was Dr.

Ethel Allen, and she was diversity-inclusion all rolled up into one neat package. She was also a personal friend, and a closeted lesbian.

Closeted public officials often look for ways to be a part of the fight for equality. Ethel had been in numerous struggles; as a woman, as an African American seeking a medical degree, and as a black Republican in a Democratic town. She was a fighter.

Soon after Thornburgh chose Ethel, she gave me a call and asked if I'd write the governor's gay pride proclamation. Something felt odd. I asked her, "Does the governor know you're asking me this?"

She responded, "Not to worry," and got off the phone.

A month later she called to ask how it was going. My reply was simple: "It's not going, since if the governor isn't going to issue it, why should I waste the time?" She guaranteed me he would, and then she set up a lunch date for us to write it.

We sat in an empty restaurant called Bramwell's one afternoon, looking over the previous gay pride proclamations and making changes and additions. When we finally completed our task, I grabbed her hand. "I think I know what you're going to do, and you know he might fire you over this."

She smiled and said, "Over this small little thing?"

June rolled around and, lo and behold, one morning I read in the newspaper that Governor Richard Thornburgh had become the first Republican governor ever to proclaim Gay Pride Month. That point had slipped both our minds. It created more of a dustup than we expected. A good deal of the media congratulated the governor on making a brave gesture and an opening to the LGBT community, but they didn't know the real story.

Each week, Ethel had a regularly scheduled meeting with the governor where she'd inform him of the various documents that needed his signature. The last item on the docket was usually proclamations. She read off a list of what they were, she put the pile in front of him, he'd sign, and she'd take them back to her office to issue.

It seems at one of those meetings where she was reading off the list, she didn't mention the Gay Pride Month proclamation that he was about to sign. Now, with the positive media editorials, he didn't know what to do. As with all smart politicians, you wait for the clamor to die down before making a move, and that is exactly what he did. A couple of months later, Ethel was unceremoniously fired. The reason given: she abused her expense account by making too many long-distance calls.

Soon after, she contacted me and suggested that we have a celebratory lunch at Bramwell's. We met and chatted about other things before the subject came up. She told me there was no reason for me to say a word. She was proud of what she had done. It was her contribution to the struggle, and in her eyes it was worth the cost. She never regretted it, and I believe it was one of her proudest moments. While Thornburgh went on to be part of Reagan's presidential cabinet, Ethel took a downward medical spiral. It has always been my belief that she knew her time was limited and she intended to make the most of it. She was a brave and dignified woman.

And one last item: at that lunch she presented me with the signed proclamation from Governor Thornburgh that hangs on my office wall to this day.

It was a busy time. Beyond the media zaps, negotiations with the television networks, the groundbreaking surveys of police chiefs, and workplace nondiscrimination efforts, we issued a survey of all fifty state governors, which actually resulted in replies from half of them, including New Jersey's Brendan T. Byrne, Tennessee's Ray Blanton, and one from Massachusetts by Michael S. Dukakis stating, "If this [nondiscrimination] bill is passed by the General Court, I expect to sign it." Alongside the countless speaking engagements and interviews, and my duties at home, at the end of 1975 I managed to do a press tour of eastern Ohio and western Pennsylvania at the behest of Jim Austin.

Jim, a longtime newspaperman who had the knowledge to make a success of one of America's first local LGBT publications, the *Pittsburgh Gay News*, was now branching out. He had decided to create the *Ohio East Gay News*. To launch his first issue, he thought a speaking tour with the nation's most outrageous gay activist would generate good publicity. We did speaking dates in Cleveland, Youngstown, and Kent State University, and our last stop would be Pittsburgh.

Jim made up posters for the tour, one of which still hangs on my office wall. There's a picture of me in my youthful handsomeness with the line, *Meet Mark Segal, Gay Activist Extraordinaire*. The tour was a hit. A lot of people showed up when I spoke, and there was good press coverage, but it was Jim's show and we always turned the message to the new *Ohio East Gay News*.

On our way back to Pittsburgh, Jim asked why Philadelphia didn't have a gay newspaper. I explained that we had a weekly mimeograph publication, the *Gayzette*. His reply was no, you need a newspaper on newsprint with stories on every issue affecting our community, a professional publication. Then, out of nowhere, he said, "Why don't *you* do it?"

I responded by sharing an account of a recent lobbying experience. I told him that while I never had the pleasure of meeting Princess Grace of Monaco, her brother Jack and I were acquaintances. Jack, a rower and member of the US Olympic Committee, was also a Philadelphia city councilman who at rare ambitious times had higher political dreams. I say rare since Jack was a fun-filled guy who worked to live, not lived to work in a political campaign.

We became acquainted while I was lobbying for a gay-rights bill. On our first meeting he invited me into his inner office to ask some questions. None of them concerned anything to do with the law, rather he asked about what it was like to be gay and about gay relationships. After several visits with Jack we were on a first-name basis and I felt comfortable enough to ask him to be a cosponsor of the gay-rights bill. He replied, "Mark, I'd like to assist, but Mother wouldn't understand."

Our relationship remained that of councilman and lobbyist until an item appeared in the *Philadelphia Daily News*, in a column by a mutual friend of ours. Larry Fields's personality (a.k.a. gossip) column kept tabs on the who's who of Philadelphia society and visiting celebrities. Larry was also a friend to Mayor Frank Rizzo. It was in Larry's column that the Rizzo camp would send up trial balloons or political warnings. Rizzo, nearing the end of his first term in office, didn't want any problem in his reelection bid. There was disgruntlement among Philadelphia Democrats over the manner in which Rizzo had governed both the city and the party political machine; many thought that he was acting more policeman-like than mayoral.

In an unusual mood, Jack had let it be known that he might be interested in challenging Rizzo in the Democratic primary for mayor. It was in this atmosphere that I entered City Hall one morning to do my regular check-in with city council members. At each corner of City Hall there are circular staircases. On various occasions, when feeling that I hadn't gotten my exercise or just wanting to marvel at the magnificent building, I'd take the staircase to Jack's office.

On this day, as I made my way up, I noticed Jack sitting

on the stairs holding his head in his hands. I called up to him, "How's it going?"

He looked distressed and, picking up the *Philadelphia Daily News*, said, "Have you seen this yet?" He told me to check out Larry Fields's column. Then he began to cry.

There we were, the gay activist and Princess Grace's brother, sitting on a staircase in the middle of City Hall as the latter started to sob. I turned to the column and read the tidbit, which began by stating that Jack was thinking about challenging Frank Rizzo for mayor. It then stated that if he did so, several members of Rizzo inner circle would rent a billboard with a picture of Harlow, a well-known transsexual in the city, with the caption, *How would you like her as your next first lady?*

As I read the threat, Jack moaned, "I only went out with her on one date." (Harlow, an incredible beauty, insists to this day that it was more than once.) He continued, "Can you imagine what this will do to my mother?" Jack's mother, though sickly, still controlled his life at this point. As he continued to sob and mumble, I stood him up, put my arm around his waist, and walked him back to his office. He got control of himself and thanked me, saying, "I don't have anyone else to talk to about this." How sad I felt for him.

That evening Jack called me at home, thanking me again and asking me not to talk to anyone about his "breakdown." He said that he was feeling better, and if there was anything he could do for me, I should just ask. To get a laugh out of him I said that he could arrange a date for me with his nephew, Prince Albert. He chuckled, and thanked me once more. I told him that I was always available to talk. Days later it was reported that Jack would not be running against Frank Rizzo. The Rizzo team's dirty work did what it was supposed to.

When I ran into Jack from that point on, I'd always say quietly, "You still owe me that date." He knew that just like every-one else, I really wanted to meet his sister, Princess Grace of Monaco, but I was aware that this was unlikely. One day while sitting at my desk the phone rang and it was Jack on the line. "Mark," he said, "I have someone here in my office I want you to meet. Do you think you can come over immediately?"

My office was only a ten-minute walk from City Hall. When I arrived it was apparent that something was up because there were police everywhere. Since City Hall also served as a court-house I thought there was trouble with one of the courts or an inmate. As I got to Jack's office, the crowd was overwhelming. I made my way to the door and was stopped. After telling the police officer that I was expected, I was allowed to enter. I was then ushered into Jack's inner office. Several people who I didn't recognize were there, but Jack saw me and said, "Mark, I want to introduce you to my nephew."

There sat Prince Albert of Monaco. He rose and said in a soft voice, "My uncle has told me how helpful you've been to him."

I nodded, speechless, and after a very short while I made my way to the door. Jack noticed me leaving and said with a smile, "I guess I'm off the hook now for that date," then added, "He doesn't bat for your team."

After relating this story to Jim Austin, he looked at me and asked, "What does Princess Grace have to do with you publish-ing a newspaper?" My response was that I was an activist, what did I know about publishing or business? He remarked, "Mark, someday you'll need to earn a living—this is that way, and it will allow you to remain an activist, just in another form."

We shook hands and became partners on the spot, and my life was about to change yet again. Meet publisher Mark Segal.

Chapter 6

Talking Sex with the
Wall Street Journal

P*hiladelphia Gay News* was among the first local news-papers for the LGBT community. Like the others, we were building a network where one had never existed before. Until being catapulted into my position as publisher, my knowledge of journalism was limited to school yearbooks, the *Gay Youth Journal*, and a few freelance articles I'd written for *Gay Sunshine* and other small publications. Actually publishing a forty-page newspaper each month was a daunting task.

Jim would do the lion's share of the work in Pittsburgh. Jim now had three newspapers, and this made him the owner of the first-ever chain of publications for the LGBT community. He was smart and knew the networking I had done as an activist would pay off.

Like all that I have done in my life, my newspapering was learned from on-the-job experience and a thirst to give our community the best. I had gotten to know numerous main-stream journalists in my travels and I utilized many of them to help guide us in those early days. Among them were Pulitzer Prize–winning writers such as Richard Aregood, Michael Pak-enham, and even Walter Cronkite, who had quietly befriended me after we ran into each other in Miami in 1976 at a debate before the Florida primary he was moderating among Democrat candidates for president, and then later in the year in Philadelphia where he was moderating a CBS-TV bicentennial salute to the 1776 American Revolution.

When he'd spotted me in the wings in Miami, he walked over with a smile and asked, "Mark, what brings you here?" I was really surprised that he recognized me. I explained that I was helping one of the candidates, Pennsylvania Governor Milton Shapp, who had a strong record on gay rights. Walter wrote a note and asked if he could use that in his introduction since all he had about Shapp related to a threatened national independent truckers strike. Governor Shapp had stepped into the negotiations and won praise from the truckers for settling the dispute without a national strike. That night Walter's introduction of the man was, "Governor Shapp of Pennsylvania hopes to bring a coalition of truck drivers and homosexuals together to win the nomination," spoken with that Cronkite air of assurance.

By late 1975, we were laying out the first edition of the paper, which was to be issued in January 1976. Never did I expect the battles that would follow over journalism. Our vending boxes would be bombed, and we would clean them up, repaint them, and put them back. People would run over them with their cars, and we would, again, clean them up, repaint them, and put them back out. People threw bricks into our windows and sprayed graffiti all over our building. The death threats were something we got used to. Me being put on the American Nazi Party's hit list in their magazine was a little more unique.

Another person put on the hit list was the publisher of the *Advocate*; both of us were "Jewish fag publishers." *Philadelphia Gay News* covered myriad gay bashings and murders, crimes that most of the population didn't seem to care about. Many times we were the sole voice yelling out in the darkness of a silent press. We covered the issues of transgender people from day one, while many in LGBT media tried to ignore that part of our community. We were one of the first to publish Alison Bechdel's wonderful and funny cartoon strip *Dykes to Watch Out For.* And she was always thankful that she got paid. (Alison's career blossomed along the way, and she was a recipient of the MacArthur Genius Grant in 2014; her life story was made into a Broadway musical *Fun Home.*) In those early days of LGBT media, many freelancers were never paid. *PGN* got a reputation for not just paying our freelancers but paying them on time.

The news could be emotionally nerve-wracking. One week's story continues to haunt me: the murder of Anthony Milano. His death was covered by our then-editor Tommi Avicolli Mecca. Milano's throat was cut dozens of times, and he died by drowning in his own blood. Then there were other murders that only the *Philadelphia Gay News* seemed to care about. In reporting Nizah Morris's story we hounded the police department and district attorney, and requested assistance from the US attorney general. We even took the city to court to release records. The potential for physical intimidation and harm that Tim Cwiek, the reporter on that story, put himself through was akin to any top-notch crime reporter for any major newspaper.

After twelve years of reporting on a single case—that of transwoman Nizah Morris, who was given a late-night courtesy ride home by the police and later found dead—in June 2014 *Philadelphia Gay News* staff writer Tim Cwiek, editor Jen Colletta, and I found ourselves at the Society of Professional Journalist's awards dinner at the National Press Club in Washington, DC. Our table partners were staffers for the *Wall Street Journal,* who were, like Tim, receiving the award in investigative journalism. As we were preparing to accept the highest journalistic honor that any LGBT media had ever received, we found ourselves in conversation with our tablemates about three things: the murder of a transwoman, the business of pornography, and gay for pay. We explained what we knew about the trans community's relationship with the police and why there might have been physical intimidation. The *Wall Street Journal* people looked like they had entered an alternate universe. We all chatted until it was time for our award to be announced. Everyone in the room heard about the twelve-year struggle *PGN* had waged to answer questions surrounding the death of Nizah Morris. And just like any professional publication, we continue to follow up on the story.

When we started in the mid-1970s, we often covered police raids on gay bars and their wholesale blackmailing of gay men. *Philadelphia Gay News* took on organizations such as the American Red Cross, Blue Cross and Blue Shield, and even the United Way.

I once asked Tommi Avicolli Mecca, an early *PGN* staffer and later editor, what his most memorable story was, and he replied, "The police district that was keeping a list of people with AIDS so that it wouldn't respond to calls from those addresses"—the police chief had to denounce that after the dailies picked it up from us—"and the investigation of the murders of several black transgender women that the police weren't even bothering to investigate."

Al Patrick recalls investigating the AIDS Ride fundraisers that took place in Philadelphia, Los Angeles, and San Francisco, among other cities, and unveiling how lucrative they were for the organizers and how little they did for AIDS organizations who received only a pittance from them. After that report, the group threatened to sue us from their Los Angeles offices and we wrote back explaining we'd be happy to meet them in court in our state. They never took us up on this. Eventually the *New*

York Times did a series about them and in a matter of time they were out of business.

Our community was not always pleased with us. We pushed every envelope; from that very first issue we were defining ourselves as a real paper with hard news. In those first two years we published many features that no other LGBT media would touch. We hit a major nerve nationally with the first-ever feature on lesbian nuns by Victoria Brownworth, which made Victoria the national expert on the subject. We reported on the poor and homeless in our community, the countless "thrown away" gay and lesbian youth; we went to Rikers Island prison in New York City to visit their new experiment with a gay men's wing; we wrote about the perils of Susan Saxe, a lesbian who was accused of robbing a bank; and we led a major investigation into aversion therapy.

Aversion therapy was used in an attempt to change a gay man or lesbian's sexual orientation through the use of drugs or electroconvulsive treatment. The latter was done mostly with electrodes strapped to the genitals. Psychiatrists and other health professionals practiced it nationally, since up until 1973 homosexuality was still considered a mental illness. It was also widely used in prisons—the most notable being Atascadero State Hospital in California, on which writer and activist David Mixner reported extensively.

In Philadelphia, aversion therapy was being conducted at Eastern Pennsylvania Psychiatric Institute, which was part of Temple University and got its funding from the state of Pennsylvania. The paper investigated the institute and was able to have the practice ended, one of our first major victories.

In previous years, doctors had one other treatment to use if the "illness" persisted: lobotomy. And yes, there was a method known as the ice-pick lobotomy popularized by Dr. Walter J.

Freeman. It is estimated that Dr. Freeman submitted over a thousand gay men and lesbians to this torture. When you factor in other doctors who employed the practice as well as the prison systems that used it, this figure increases to the tens of thousands. LGBT media has hardly touched on this dark time in our history.

In 1977, Tim Cwiek conducted one of the first interviews in LGBT media with a presidential assistant inside the West Wing of the White House. Tim wrote a sidebar called "Mr. Cwiek Goes to Washington" where he detailed his experience waiting in the West Wing lobby with Senator Sam Nunn of Georgia, who was there with Miss America to be photographed with the president. Miss America, being polite, asked Tim what he was doing at the White House. Tim told her that he would be interviewing the president's assistant about gay rights. Miss America looked nervously to Senator Nunn, bringing a speedy death to that conversation.

I can't help but get emotional when I think about the beginning of our newspaper. We were in a building with no electricity, no plumbing, and it leaked so badly that we needed a plastic tarp when it rained. Our bathrooms were cans in the basement. At times, the only way we could pay our bills was to use the quarters from our few vending boxes. Don Pignolet, our distribution manager who had many roles at the paper, recalls taking those quarters to the hardware store to buy supplies to shore up the plastic tarp with two-by-fours.

If those issues weren't enough of a headache, our "neighbors" came in one night and removed the small amount of electric wiring we were able to install. To their chagrin and astonishment, we went out and got a generator and were back up and running in just a few hours. When someone trashed a vending box, Don would have another out in twenty-four hours. We continued repairing the boxes until the people gave up. We would not be defeated. I'm proud of this paper and its staff for believing we could make it.

Dr. Walter Lear was the main story of our first issue. With that report he became the highest-ranking public official in the country to come out. He was Pennsylvania's first deputy health commissioner and he came out at a time when some state health boards wouldn't give licenses to openly gay doctors. Any mainstream newspaper of the day would have loved to run that story, but we got it first.

To keep the ball rolling, in our second issue we went even bigger and featured a groundbreaking interview with the governor of Pennsylvania. Others began to notice, especially the dailies that couldn't get an interview with the governor no matter how many times their reporters called. We made it a point that if you were running for office, you'd speak to the LGBT community through its media or be held accountable. But we also went further: it was not only speaking to the LGBT community that mattered but keeping the promises of equality.

In 1975, on that trip to Pittsburgh that had sealed the deal to create *Philadelphia Gay News*, I can honestly say I really didn't understand what I was signing up for. The last forty years as seen through our pages proves that it is our own media that best chronicles our community. You can find reporting on all the debates within our community and recall the struggles that we've long forgotten.

LGBT publications had to battle the mainstream press to be recognized. Moreover, we had to get our community to appreciate that it was not our job to be a mouthpiece for them, but rather to be an independent voice that allowed public discussion in and out of the community. We do share our positions in editorials so the community knows where we stand, but we allow people to voice their differences with us in our letters to the editor and even guest op-ed pieces. That's a key strength of *Philadelphia Gay News*: our willingness to invite people to write in our pages when they disagree. I have received plenty of flack for allowing LGBT Republicans and others whose views do not reflect our own to have space in the paper. But their perspective should be heard, since any good story presents various points of view in order to be balanced and complete.

Our news must contain what all professional stories should have, the simple *who, what, where, when, why,* and *how*. When there's a scandal, run to it, not from it. It might sound strange but if you cover a story objectively, even one that the community doesn't want you to cover, you'll earn respect. And like all communities, someone always thinks they are above the law, or gets a little greedy. In those cases we need to be the first on the scene to report our own misdeeds.

In the early days, one of our advertising representatives was running an escort business on the side. When I discovered this I explained that he had a choice to make. The paper would not be affiliated with a prostitution service. He chose to keep his escort business and start a competing paper, taking one of my editors with him, but it never gained any traction. The sales rep was a pretty indecent guy; he pimped his lover as part of his escort service. To me this became a comedy that could serve a purpose. Why not have competitors who were inept to bolster our own standing. Needless to say, I found ways to help keep them in business.

The earliest American LGBT publication I know of was from 1937. It was a slick magazine that looked like *Life*, but only had articles and pictures about men. It had no masthead or any names in it, or even an address. It was more of a fashion magazine. Then, in 1947, a lesbian magazine appeared called *Vice Versa*, completely written and typed for publication by Lisa Ben. In the 1950s, LGBT organizations such as One Inc., Daughters of Bilitis, and Mattachine were publishing magazines or newsletters of their own, but it wasn't until 1967 that the first professional newspaper for our community appeared. The *Advocate* was launched in response to a police raid on the Black Cat, a gay bar in Los Angeles, and is the only national pre-Stonewall news publication that is still in print today. It is an invaluable resource and reference in researching the community's history.

Local LGBT publications began to flourish in the midseventies. Boston's *Gay Community News* (GCN), the *Washington Blade*, the *Bay Area Reporter* in San Francisco, *Pittsburgh Gay News*, and *Philadelphia Gay News* were soon joined by a host of others in almost every major city. In June 1976 we held our first LGBT media conference, organized by GCN, to discuss our mutual concerns and to find ways to work together. Since few of us had the funds to travel to Boston and pay for hotels, GCN stepped in to arrange housing for us. The second meeting was held in Philadelphia. During this period I was elected president of the first LGBT media organization, the Gay Press Association, which was renamed the National Gay Press Association. We soon changed the name again to the National Gay and Lesbian Press Association.

We were officially incorporated in May of 1981. At our convention in Los Angeles in 1984 we received our first city resolution, and there's one clause that tells volumes about building LGBT media:

Whereas, the Gay Press Association has instituted the International Gay Wire service, an intercontinental computer network which provides instant transmission of information around the world and provides greater access to news and information to its subscribers, be it resolved . . . that a suitable copy of this resolution be presented to the Gay Press Association, member resolution No. 155, dated this 21st day of May, 1984.

Before I received that resolution onstage at the Sheraton Universal in Burbank, I had lunch with a man I had searched for over many years, my cousin Norman. Norman had read about my coming to LA in *Frontiers* magazine, and called my office. He was living in Long Beach, California, and in order to meet me for lunch I had to send him a check since he had no spare funds. We met in the Sheraton's dining room. I was eager to see him, so I arrived early. When he showed up, he looked like a haggard old man of seventy, but he was only fifty-three at that time. Wearing a white shirt with some print on it and brown jeans that had seen better days, he was escorted to my table and we just stared at each other. I stood up and hugged him and it seemed like he didn't want to stop.

At first he was timid, but after ordering lunch he began to tell me the story of his life. As a youth his dad beat him every time he thought Norman was not acting manly enough. When he saw that a sixteen-year-old sissy was developing, he beat him one last time and told him to get out of the house for good. Penniless, Norman took whatever job he could find and was abused and used in every way imaginable. This led to booze and drugs. He even claimed that in a drunken rage while squatting in an old abandoned building he'd tossed a longtime lover out the third-story window and might have killed him, but he didn't stick around to find out. He finally made his way to California and was now living on public assistance. He was the only person I've ever met who had no joy in life. He had kept in touch with his sister, my aunt, but she couldn't deal with his needs and issues.

As we finished lunch, I invited him to the auditorium where in true Hollywood fashion I was to be sworn in by the actress Lynn Redgrave as president of the National Gay Press Association. Why Lynn Redgrave? To this day I have no idea. Norman said he wasn't dressed well enough to attend, but I insisted. After Lynn Redgrave swore me in, I said a few words about our industry, then, looking at Norman in the back, I added, "I have a special guest here with me today, a member of my family who at the age of sixteen had to leave his home because he was gay. Like other gay youth he learned to survive in a cruel world. Please welcome my cousin Norman."

The audience started to applaud, and then rose to their feet. Norman didn't know how to react. It was, most likely, the first time in his life that a group of LGBT people had given him sympathy for what he had been through. He stood nervously and took a bow, and just started to cry. When the audience sat down Norman rose, blew me a kiss from the back of the auditorium, and left.

He called a few times after that, always in need of funds. Then one day the calls stopped, and there has been no trace of him since.

At the 1984 convention, we were looking for ways to get news and information to our readers faster. This was at a time when there was no Internet, and the wire services, Associated Press and United Press International, didn't carry many LGBT stories. Even if they had, most of us could not afford the monthly fee for their services. Out of necessity we created the first wire news service for the LGBT community; we simply agreed to exchange news stories between us. The reality was that given the limited functionality of the computers of the day, it really didn't work so well.

Like other publishing organizations, we also shared strategies on building circulation and advertising. Our news coalition began to create a list of freelance writers and stringers. Early members included Phil Nash of Denver's *Out Front*, Joe DiSabato, founder of Rivendell Marketing, Morgan Pinney, Pat Burke of *Update* in San Diego, Sally Tyre of *PGN*, Chuck Renslow of Chicago's *GayLife*, Bob Swinden of *Cruise Atlanta*, Richard Rogers of *This Week in Texas*, Mike Rutherford of *Out* magazine, Don Michaels of the *Washington Blade*, Bob Ross of San Francisco's *Bay Area Reporter*, and our vice president Henry McClure from Texas, among others. Like most media and journalism organizations, it was overwhelmingly white and male.

Our first resolution was to request that the National Gay Task Force stop attempting to interfere with the operations of gay media by its "request to editors." A stronger condemnation of the codirectors of NGTF was tabled, but this resolution made it clear to activist organizations that we were independent and that any attempt to control our news coverage would be dealt with, and transparently.

The most serious member of the group in those early days was Don Michaels, publisher of the *Washington Blade*. Don always stressed a good business plan and was often heard lending the advice, "Pay your taxes." Thinking back, it's amazing how important that statement was and still is. Many a publication went out of business because they didn't pay their taxes. Don was echoed by Robert Moore of the *Dallas Voice*, who hosted the next convention, where we shared a hotel with a Bible group and the National Rifle Association. (Our treat on one very hot, humid Texas evening was Robert taking us Eastern city boys to a bar to learn how to line dance.)

Don's early advice was welcomed at the *Philadelphia Gay News*. Understanding the playing field and the absolute necessity of learning good business skills to keep the doors of the paper open were paramount. This began my quest to join every professional journalism organization I could. They knew how to make newspapers work and we needed that information. But like the many LGBT lawyers and doctors who tried to join their industry's associations, *Philadelphia Gay News* was similarly rebuffed for years.

New publications continued to sprout from LGBT organizations, and were operated by volunteers. I was determined that *Philadelphia Gay News* would no longer rely on volunteers; everyone was paid something. In addition to being fair, this was also a form of control. We bought used vending boxes from the daily newspapers and charged fifty cents an issue, which we later raised to seventy-five cents. As I've said, many of those quarters were taken to restaurants for meals, as well as to the lumber store to buy wood to create a ceiling in our office. Some nights I would even buy my dinner with them. We also learned to pay a decent commission to advertising representatives, our bread and butter as we learned the canons of journalism.

After nine months, Jim decided he'd had enough. Running three newspapers was more work than he'd expected and he had been in the business his entire life. Plus, I was moving way too fast for him. He somehow believed that I'd make it all work so we made an agreement, and with nine months of experience under my belt I became the sole publisher of a newspaper chain that included *Philadelphia Gay News*, *Pittsburgh Gay News*, *Ohio East Gay News*, and eventually *Atlanta Gay News*.

My relationship with Phillip had been over for some time now. My friends set me up on blind dates since most of them felt I was not doing anything to improve my own home life; in other words, they thought I needed a partner. One of those men had what I thought was a great sense of humor. We went out once, and while it was fun, I didn't see it as a lasting relationship. He kept calling until I finally went on a second date with him. I still wasn't convinced so he kept calling and calling, which led to a third date. Finally, I asked him what he saw in me and he replied, "Your potential to make money and thereby make me happy." We both laughed, and that was the start of a twenty-year relationship.

One afternoon, in complete disgust over the Catholic Church's history of fighting against our issues, I wrote a column called "Shut Up, Pope," which was prompted by Pope Benedict's speaking out against condoms in Africa where the AIDS epidemic was out of control. For that piece alone, I won several awards. Writing what you're passionate about helps generate discussion. You can't be afraid of debate; just make sure to debate with respect.

There's a question that pops up in almost every interview I give. It goes something like this: "What is the state of the LGBT press?" Or, "Is the LGBT press having the same issues that mainstream media is dealing with?" And some even ask if LGBT media is dying. From my vantage, sitting on the boards of several mainstream media organizations, it became apparent along the way that many news outlets were spending barrels of money on their new web ventures without an understanding of where the Internet was headed. Thus far, most traditional media haven't seen a payday and, worse, have needed to cut back on their print editions to pay for their web expenses. It's not a good move to lose seasoned journalists to pay for your web expansion. Your journalists are bringing you the product that you sell, and the good ones are the reason people buy it. You don't just sell information; you sell accurate and well-told information, which, for the most part, only seasoned journalists can give you.

Local LGBT publications serve themselves and their communities by sticking with the stories of their individual communities, and owning those stories. For us, national marriage-equality stories take a backseat to local news that we own, meaning you won't find it anywhere else. Newspapers have to be alive with opinions and information unique to the community they serve, both geographic and cultural. They cannot just be the same thing you find elsewhere else. Local LGBT publications have to be the first place your community looks for details.

The Internet has something that print doesn't: an instantaneous forum to publish and gather opinion. It satisfies those who need instant gratification and can be extremely inexpensive to run. That last advantage is problematic for the print medium, since it allows for more and more websites and blogs to come online and create competition for those already serving the community. It is also a vehicle for misinformation, and thus needs to be watched carefully.

New media is something that needs to be embraced. In 1997 my friend Andy Cramer was in search of people who would assist in his dream of a gay online site. It was Gay.com and I was one of its first nine investors/founders.

I still believe that print is light years ahead of the web. In almost every major city, there's a local LGBT newspaper with numerous full-time staffers and they are excelling at fusing print and the web. There are few, if any, local blogs or websites with full-time employees. Nationally, it's a different story. *Out* magazine and the *Advocate* have both traditional and new media outlets. They are the top websites as far as hits and clicks go, but their print editions are hurting. *Queerty* and *Towleroad* have also become popular sites and have full-time staff. Aside from those, you might have a few out there with one or two staffers. Here's the big problem for websites and blogs: it takes very little capital to start one, but all the new sites are competing for the same audience and advertising dollars.

Publications like ours have had to count on our local advertising for a long time. Relatively recently we've seen national ads in local LGBT publications because many companies want to be on the right side of history. As President Barack Obama has stated, LGBT rights are the civil rights of this generation. In some sense, the ads from Ford, GM, McDonald's, Taco Bell, and other mainstream corporations make a statement about how far we have come. Or is it how far those corporations have come?

At the 2013 annual National Lesbian and Gay Journalists Association (NLGJA) convention in Boston, it amazed me to hear most print journalists there bemoaning the condition of LGBT media. I was honored to be there to get inducted into the NLGJA Hall of Fame. In my speech, I was originally planning to simply thank the NLGJA and get off the stage, but this feeling of impending doom for LGBT media led me, at the last minute, to change my address.

To offer an air of optimism, I explained that *Philadelphia Gay News*, which is now the nation's most awarded LGBT publication, owns its own building and equipment. All of our bills and taxes are paid to date and we employ a full-time staff of thirteen with full benefits. That is success in print media. Then the most important part—how did we become so strong and how do we stay that way? It's a simple formula, at least to me. One must have a strong business department that embraces the need to hire award-winning journalists. Period. It is imperative to put out not only an LGBT newspaper, but a high-quality mainstream newspaper. The key is hard opinion pieces, unbiased news coverage, and investigative reporting. Here I recalled the Nizah Morris case, which at that time prompted a new report by the Philadelphia Police Advisory Commission and caused rule changes at the Philadelphia Police Department. No other paper that I know of would put the resources into such a story for so long, but it paid dividends in the end.

In the early days of AIDS we began to hear about insurance companies dropping men they discovered to be gay or otherwise refusing to insure gay men. We had a reporter call every major insurance company nationwide. This was at a time when there was no Internet and long-distance calls were expensive. The bill for those calls alone was nine hundred dollars. But it was a story that we owned. Few other publications were producing that kind of in-depth material.

Hard news and features keep you relevant. We were out front on the Boy Scouts issue, reporting on the city of Philadelphia's decade-long battle with its local chapter. We also covered the dangers of pumping parties, attended by poor trans people to get the hormones they can't afford from traditional medical resources. These innovative and relevant stories pushed boundaries and appeared nowhere else . . .

At the *PGN*, we expected controversy, but it managed to find us even when we weren't looking. We conducted a public service campaign that stemmed from a series of features on drug addiction in the LGBT community. We spoke to Nurit Shein, CEO of the Mazzoni Center, the local LGBT heath organization in Philadelphia, which in 2014 had over a hundred employees. The campaign sought to highlight the issue of addiction—how it destroys lives and how to seek help. Many in the LGBT community do not feel comfortable in mainstream drug treatment programs, since they are often judged on their sexual orientation rather than their drug use. We never expected a deluge of letters and calls asking, "Why would *Philadelphia Gay News* show our community in such a bad way?"

Nurit and the *PGN* staff felt the campaign was worth the outrage and continued forth; I suspect that the anger and debate about the campaign might have reached more people than the campaign itself. I explained to the audience at the NLGJA awards ceremony that our paper has partnerships with Philly. com (the *Philadelphia Inquirer*) and the *Philadelphia Business Journal*, the first such partnerships in the nation. We also work with the Philadelphia Multicultural Media Network, which has helped more than twenty newspapers, and allowed us to work with a wide range of publications, making Philly a vibrant, diversified newspaper city. There was much more that I could have added, but my time was limited. My desire was to bring new ideas and optimism, and I believe I succeeded.

The reality is that *Philadelphia Gay News* has been on a winning streak for the last decade; in 2008 something very special happened, which made this really sink in. The paper was informed by the Suburban Newspapers of America that journalistically we were one of the top ten weekly newspapers in the nation. Not one of the top ten LGBT weeklies, but top ten of *all* weeklies. Our then-editor Sarah Blazucki basked in the spotlight, as she should have. Sarah, now working for the Peace Corps in Washington, DC, came to her position at *Philadelphia Gay News* after starting as a reporter.

Our staff has gone on to garner more individual awards than could possibly be listed here, but the overwhelming majority of them are from mainstream journalism organizations. As mentioned, our strength is built on our reporting and our appreciation of our community's needs. You can see this same dynamic in the other successful LGBT publications across the nation.

The *Washington Blade*, due to its proximity to the capital, breaks more national news than any other LGBT publication, and their local coverage of the marriage-equality movement should be studied in journalism schools. Chicago's *Windy City Times* and its publisher Tracy Baim pulled out of their files a questionnaire that a state senator by the name of Barack Obama had signed, stating that he supported marriage equality; they did this while he was president and publicly still evolving on the subject. That is the power of local newspapers. The *Bay Area Reporter* in San Francisco, along with the now-defunct *New York Native*, showed the rest of us how to cover AIDS, and do so professionally, even with the widespread anger surrounding the issue. *Bay Windows* in Boston played an important role in what would result in the first state with marriage equality. In Michigan, *Pride Source* staged what could be called the mother of all wedding expos, made a huge profit, and ended up with an e-mail list that would be the envy of any blog, website, or print publication. Their publishers Susan Horowitz and Jan Stevenson are pillars of our LGBT legacy.

LGBT publishing is awash with new publishers and new ideas. The *Dallas Voice* and *Frontiers* in Los Angeles are pioneering the integration of print and web in what will become the new LGBT media, each with a different viewpoint and style. While they do this, they still foster hard news reporting by writers like Karen Ocamb. The *South Florida Gay News* keeps reinventing itself as all media must do in a time of change, and in Portland, Oregon, Melanie Davis, a second-generation publisher with a long history of involvement with Latino media, has created *Proud Queer* magazine. Along with Chris Cash of Atlanta's *Georgia Voice* and Lynne Brown of the *Washington Blade*, women constitute a major presence in today's LGBT media.

* * *

Like any industry, LGBT journalism has suffered low points. Our brothers and sisters who worked for a chain of LGBT newspapers owned by a company called Windows Media showed up at their offices one Monday and discovered that their publications had closed. At the time, Windows Media was the largest chain of publications for the LGBT community, and included the *Washington Blade*, Atlanta's *Southern Voice*, *David Magazine*, *411 Magazine*, and the *South Florida Blade*. In prior months, the same company also closed down *Genre* magazine and the online-only *Houston Voice*. To say this was the biggest failure in LGBT-media history is an understatement. But what does it say about LGBT media in general? The short answer: nothing.

While the media industry is going through changes, there are some basic publishing lessons that can be learned from this. In some ways, these developments make LGBT media even stronger. Those who were behind Windows Media had little idea how to market to this community and little understanding of the struggle for equality that some of us were covering on a daily basis. From the outside it appeared that journalism took a backseat to advertising. It also seemed like substantive articles played second fiddle to fashion and professional features or just plain fluff pieces. At one point, the *Washington Blade* had an escort featured as a columnist on the front page.

As a local paper your first line of advertisers should be the community itself, which should support its publication of record. Next are the gay-friendly businesses in gay neighborhoods and the non-gay businesses frequented by the LGBT community. Once those bases are covered, this should also cover your bottom line. Any national advertising is just icing. It seemed that Windows Media turned this strategy upside down.

Windows Media's failure affected the employees of their publications and the cities they served, but not local publications elsewhere in the nation. New publications would rise in each of those markets since the communities were strong and loyal. In some of the markets the Windows employees themselves set up the new publications. This all shows growth in LGBT media. The best example is the *Washington Blade*. Lynne Brown and Kevin Naff took it from the trash can that Windows had left it in, and have brought it back even better than it was before. Chris Cash has likewise revived a publication in Atlanta, the *Georgia Voice*.

Media, whether it be newspapers, TV, radio, movies, magazines, or the Internet, continuously evolves. One example pertains to young people. Due to the success of our community's efforts, LGBT youth are coming out at a younger age. Many organizations have popped up to deal with their needs but few publications have given them a voice. Jen Coletta at our paper decided to try amplifying their voices by featuring a quarterly supplement written and edited by LGBT youth. They decide on the content themselves and do almost everything to get their stories ready for publication other than the final edit and layout, which is left to the professionals in our offices. This has served various purposes. In addition to allowing their voices to be heard, it provides an opportunity to work in the publishing business. Worst-case scenario: this experience becomes past employment on their resumes.

The aging gay and lesbian community is a topic that we address as well, via a supplement for seniors. As our community ages and we begin to deal with the first out generation of seniors, there are unique issues of ageism that can be urgent.

PGN also spearheaded an alliance with other multicultural publications in our region to seek advertising that would normally go to mainstream print media. Along with several members of the African American regional media, Asian publications, the *Jewish Exponent*, and *El Día*, the leading Spanish-language publication, we've created a united force. Our value to advertisers is strong in an ever-changing and diverse landscape as together our combined circulation is near that of mainstream print media. Forty years ago, none of these publications would have wanted to be associated with a gay newspaper. Now we're one of the leaders of the coalition.

On of my fondest memories from the early days was learning how to do my first newspaper promotion. A former pro football player by the name of Dave Kopay had recently come out and had published his autobiography, *The David Kopay Story: An Extraordinary Self-Revelation*, cowritten with Perry Deane Young. He was doing a book tour and had arranged with his publisher that *Philadelphia Gay News* would host a cocktail party.

It was the first such event we'd put together so we wanted it to be a success. This meant a packed house and publicity for the paper and Kopay's book. We arranged for a venue called The Steps to let us use their space during an afternoon when it was not usually open. In exchange we gave them some free advertising. We invited LGBT leaders, business and government people, some folks from the pro sports teams in Philly (quietly), the press, of course, and our own friends and families.

The Steps had an upstairs bar with a balcony. With the entire party on the ground floor, I stepped out onto the balcony when the time was right to introduce Kopay. I welcomed all the elected officials in the audience by name, and read the introduction that the publisher had prepared for me. Then I concluded, "Ladies and gentleman, please welcome Dave Kopay!"

He took the microphone and spoke so softly that no one could hear him. He looked nervous. Later, I found out that this was one of the first times he had to address this type of crowd and it was the largest audience of his tour. Unable to hear him, the people began to mingle and we were losing control of the room. At that moment, my four-foot-seven grandmother decided to act. Standing in the middle of the audience, she put her fist in the air and shouted, "Right on, Dave!" And she repeated it, "Right on, Dave!" and then again. She kept going until everyone was shouting along with her. Grandmom, my Auntie Mame, once again saved the day.

It was an exciting, heady period. Things were humming along. We were helping invent a microprofession we termed *advocacy journalism* at a time when little was known about this. Exhausted but elated, every night I'd return home to Mom and Grandmom. I'd spend as many evenings at home as possible and I still cherished every second sitting on the couch with my family.

Chapter 7

Tits and Ass

In early 1978, Mom wasn't getting out much due to dialysis. The drugs she was taking had her staying close to home most of the time; the hospital had given her a beeper in case a donor kidney became available. And she couldn't shake the cold of the winter. Unable to get warm no matter how hot the house was or how many sweaters or blankets she had, she never complained and still attempted to cook dinner each night. Mom loved cooking for my brother and me and she certainly loved our appreciation of her time at the stove. But to be honest, she wasn't a good cook. Her beef was always well done and very dry, her tomato sauce, of which we always requested seconds, was so heavy that antacids were required quickly after the meal. (She never understood why we headed for the bathroom directly after having her spaghetti sauce.) Her meatballs, however, were a bouncy delight. They were more like matzo balls then meatballs. But ever since we were little boys, we were always told by Dad that Mom took pride in her cooking and that we should never say anything that might upset her. So we ate, and we loved it, knowing that this made her happy. What's a little indigestion among family?

The newspaper was beginning to make money at that time. To celebrate and to try to get Mom's spirits up, I decided to take my parents to a restaurant and a show. The restaurant's name

I don't recall, but the show was *A Chorus Line*. I had recently interviewed the show's author, James Kirkwood Jr., who had offered me tickets anytime I wanted, so we went to the theater and Mom was delighted just to be out and about.

During the show I couldn't keep my eyes off her. It was so important that she enjoy herself. Any misgivings I might have had vanished with her first smile, during the second number. After that, she laughed and smiled throughout the evening. Dad and I could feel it and that was magic enough for us. Despite my love of musicals and eagerness to see the show, that night I was focused only on her.

As we left the theater I asked Mom what song she liked best. She looked at me with a sheepish grin on her face, and in the tiniest of whispers she said, "Tits and Ass." She put her hand over her mouth in embarrassment. Dad almost fell over in laughter and he and I just started to howl. Even Mom joined in. For her to say "Tits and Ass" was simply earth-shattering. But as the laughter was dying down, the hospital beeper went off. Then she said it again: "Tits and Ass." This time none of us laughed.

We called her doctor and were told she had to come in right away. We hurried home, she put a few things together, and off to the hospital we went, along with Grandmom and Uncle Stan. We were told that since it was so late, the kidney transplant operation was set for the next afternoon. Mom stayed the night and we all returned the following morning. For the first time in my life I saw my mom nervous. This was the mom who went to battle for me over "Onward, Christian Soldiers," the mom who bought me a shiny red train set when we had no money, the mom who went on the *Phil Donahue Show* and walked in gay pride parades. I wasn't as strong as she was. All I could do was be present and tell her it would all work out. I know I was trying to believe that myself.

This was a dread that I had never felt before. My mother was about to go under the knife for an operation that the doctors explained was very serious, very risky, but necessary. Further complicating things was that at this time in medical history, rejection of transplanted organs was a 50/50 proposition.

Mom tried to look brave. She kept any fears in the back of her mind and remained her gentle self, trying to reassure us, as she was readied for the operating room that afternoon. We hugged her and watched as a nurse pushed her through the double doors and down a long, dark hallway leading to the operating room. Then we were all ushered into the waiting area. We sat there as the quiet hours ticked by slowly, only intermittently interrupted by a nurse or doctor who would come out with prepared statements like, "It's going as planned."

Somewhere during that long night Grandmom became silent. When any of us would ask her something she'd just nod. No one thought anything of it at the time, we were all just worrying about my mother on the operating table. Very late in the evening, or perhaps early the next day, the doctor came out and told us the operation had gone "as well as expected." When pressed, he simply stated: "Now we'll see if her body accepts or rejects the kidney." He sounded more like he was building a car engine than transplanting a kidney. It left me with a sinking feeling. He suggested that we go home since she was in isolation. There was not a word spoken on the entire ride back.

I awoke the following morning to a gloomy winter day and immediately felt something wasn't right. When I got downstairs my father called me over and said, "We think Grandmom is sick." The pressure had gotten to her, and she still wasn't talking. Uncle Stan arranged to take Grandmom to her doctor while my father and I went to the hospital. Mom remained on a ventilator and had numerous transfusions going at the same time. She was very woozy, but we wanted her to know she made it through the operation and we were there with her. She looked as if she desperately wanted to talk with us, and it frustrated her that the tube down her throat prevented her from doing so. The hospital didn't allow much time since they were afraid of germs being brought in from outsiders. So we went home to get a report on our other sick family member.

Grandmom's doctor could find nothing wrong with her and suggested that it was merely nerves and depression due to Mom's hospitalization. When things settled down with my mother, most likely Grandmom's "depression" would pass. He didn't even give her any medication. Just a pat on the back, accompanied by unhelpful reassurances.

As the days wore on and as Mom's condition improved, we were able to visit her more often and for longer hours. Every time she saw me she'd ask how the paper was doing. I appointed myself comedian-in-chief and tried as often as possible to get her to laugh. All I had to say was, "Tits and Ass." She'd put her hand to her mouth so we couldn't see that she was smiling in embarrassment.

Even though my partner and friends Randy and Jan were giving me support by getting me to the hospital, staying with me, or just talking, I continued to drift and feel alone. I'd spend the nights chatting with Grandmom. I'd talk and she'd just smile, but there was always hope that something I said would get her to speak again. I even told her about "Tits and Ass," at which she smiled a little wider, but still made no sound. The two most important women in my life were in trouble and there was nothing I could do.

Dad was a complete wreck, but he wasn't on my radar at all, nor anyone else's. Poor Dad. His whole life was my mother and nobody recognized what this was doing to him. Growing up in our house there was one indisputable fact that you knew: my parents adored each other. In a sense it's a true love story. They saved each other. Mom was from an upper-middle-class family and she had been a sickly child who was not, as we discovered later, expected to live into adulthood. Grandmom took her out of school in the tenth grade so that she could help with the family's grocery store. But this proved to be counterproductive; since she was already not expected to amount to much, being taken out of school only deepened her feelings of failure. When she survived and married she was advised against having children.

Dad grew up in a home where his father had abandoned his mother, which was rare in a Jewish family of those days. My other grandmother couldn't afford to feed her kids so Dad was put into a Jewish home for children, sort of like an orphanage. He stayed there until the Second World War, when he enlisted in the Army and became a tail gunner over the Pacific. When he came home from the war, his dreams of going to college slammed head-on into reality. He needed to help feed his mother and siblings. So he put his own interests aside, only occasionally having a night to himself. During one of those Saturday nights, at a dance, he met Mom. According to both of them, it was love at first sight. Dad made Mom feel like she had a future and could have that family she so wanted, and Dad married up and into a loving, stable family. We might have been poor in my early days, but emotionally we were very rich. My parents set my ideal of a successful marriage. Neither of them began to truly live until they met each other; Mom was Dad's life and vice versa.

Their wedding picture tells it all. Dad looks dapper and Mom is a beautiful bride in a long, flowing gown. The smiles on their faces are incredible. They carried that unconditional love to their children; seeing it between them impacted me in ways I didn't even recognize until many decades later. As it stood, if ever that unconditional love was put to the test, it was by me. Even as a child, my independence was evident. At nine years old I hopped a train to New York to see my first Broadway show and called my mother from Manhattan to express how thrilled I was with myself, unaware that I'd given her the fright of her life. When I did it again at age thirteen, she was no longer surprised. This time she asked what show I saw, and I replied, "*UTBU* with Tony Randall." From her voice I could tell she was happy for me, and somehow I instinctively knew that my happiness more than anything was what she wanted from life. If her son wanted adventure, she'd be happy when he had adventure.

Other kids ran away from home; I went on trips. For me it felt like I had broken away from the projects for the day. Times Square in all its awe was no match for my excitement. Passersby on the streets were in such a rush they hardly paid attention to me, a nine-year-old kid strolling by himself. In that big city, this little boy could be just like anybody else, not the poor Jewish kid from the projects. I can still recall going to the stage door and asking to meet Tony Randall. He actually came to the door in a white bathrobe and asked how I picked his show, and I replied, "It was the only one which had a name I knew." He smiled and patted me on the head. I felt special; I'd met a movie star. If ever I thought I was different, this moment solidified it for me. I was different from my schoolmates and relatives, not because I met a movie star, but because I was there, taking a trip on my own. It was the moment I knew that one day I'd create my own destiny. I had no idea what that would be, but on that day I began thinking about my future.

My parents of course knew that I was a slightly different breed of child. One night, my father decided to punish me for something bad I'd done, and told me to go upstairs and miss my favorite TV show, something about a big-top circus. I hesitated and Dad gave me a wallop on the ass. I screamed and yelled as he again suggested I head upstairs. I kept the crying act up as I climbed the steps in dramatic pain. Dad wasn't going to get the best of seven-year-old me. At the top of the stairs and just out of sight I let out another yell for good measure. Then, as if in a trance, I found myself in my parents' room and saw the makeup on my mother's dresser. Soon I was like a chemist pouring one liquid into another until I found the perfect blend and color. I took off my trousers and my underwear and started to apply the liquid to the underwear. It was a nice deep red, and resembled blood. I quietly went to the stairs and laid them out with the fake blood showing. Then I started to howl. My father came running to scold me, but upon seeing the underwear he thought he had actually hurt me and rushed to my bedside. I just looked at him, and slowly started to smile. At first he didn't know what to say, then finally called out, "Shirley, you won't believe what Mark did." And he was laughing. We were a very forgiving family.

Once, Mom was working to make ends meet in a local department store. She was the manager of the pet department which gave us an excuse for having every kind of pet, from goldfish to piranha, from dog and cat to snake. (Ours got lost in the closet one day and wound up in the coat pocket of the housing project manager. We never figured out if this is why our rent was raised.) We had an alligator named Moishe that Grandmom brought back on a leash from Miami, the fruits of her annual winter pilgrimage. She took to walking the alligator until it died of fright from the bark of our German shepherd.

One day when my brother was working on some chemistry experiments, he let our parrot out of its cage to fly around the room. It had been imprisoned too long, he said. My brother was boiling his specimen and the bird decided to land on his shoulder, but somehow miscalculated and flew directly over the

Bunsen burner. His wings caught fire. My mother, who was preparing to go out that evening with my father to a cousins club function, was lavishly dressed, awaiting my father's return from work, when she heard a yell from my brother, something about fire. It seems the parrot with its burning wings landed on the curtains; they caught fire, which then spread to the bed. My mother, seeing the problem the minute she entered the room as only a mother can, shouted, "Everything stay exactly where it is!" I was scared and I know that my brother was scared, maybe even the bird was scared, but that fire didn't give a damn. Mom, thinking fast, opened the window and threw the curtains and bedspread out. Then, once all was quiet, she noticed herself in the mirror. Her dress was full of ash, her hair was fried, her makeup smeared. She was not going to the cousins club that night. Seeing the look on her face, somehow I wished she had tossed *us* out that window. Her only response, with a half-smile on her face, was, "At least I'll get to spend the night with my favorite people in the world." That was Mom. She didn't even scold us, not one word about the fire.

My brother and I never truly bonded. We never had what might be called a brotherly relationship. To me it seemed he resented me from the time my parents brought me home from the hospital. We seldom talked. Once, in anger at something he had done that I've since long forgotten, I stormed over to my parents and said, "I'll never forgive you for giving me him as a brother." Even though he was three years older than me, I always felt more mature. I was the one taking care of things, especially our parents. But I do recall, at the hospital following my mother's kidney operation, him trying to comfort our father.

While she was still in isolation, Mom's numbers began to go south. And then we were told that septicemia had entered her bloodstream. The doctors used lines like, "We're trying to do everything we can." And finally one night while we all sat in the waiting room taking our turns to visit with Mom, one of the younger doctors whom I had become friendly with called me over and told me the truth: "It doesn't look good." It was left to me to tell Dad. I suggested that he and everyone else go home and I'd stay the night.

There was no one but me in the waiting room this time. My partner and my friends Jen and Randy all wanted to stay with me but I asked them not to. For whatever reason, I had to be there alone, and when I think of it now I believe that I didn't want anyone to see me so vulnerable. I spent that night in the tiny waiting room pacing back and forth. Every so often the doctor would come out and say nothing, just stand there. And what could he say? He was just trying to comfort me; it was one of his first cases, and he took it personally. When he'd leave I'd curl myself into a ball on the floor and cry with a sick feeling in the pit of my stomach. I felt as though I was the loneliest person in the world. In an uncharacteristic move, I had a personal chat with God. It was a one-sided conversation.

At about six a.m. the doctor came out and said, "You might want to talk to your mother." By the sound of his voice I knew he meant a final conversation. As I went into her room, all I saw were her arms flailing around in pain. It was the most frightening sight I've ever witnessed. The doctors were holding her down, trying to stop her from hurting herself. There was no conversation possible. It was a scene out of hell.

Going back to that tiny waiting room, I sat on the floor and wondered why there was nothing I could do to solve this. Then the doctor suggested that I call my father. At that point I turned into a machine, no longer human, no longer feeling, just doing whatever had to be done, whatever was asked of me. Dad arrived just in time. Fifteen minutes later Mom passed away, and when she did, Dad screamed and cried in pain and kept saying, "Let me die, please take me." Then he fainted on the spot. They needed a wheelchair for him.

A nurse gave him a Valium. He was so out of it that he just popped it into his mouth without question. Another nurse came over to check his blood pressure and gave him another Valium, and then the doctor who was attending my mom saw him and gave him another. We wheeled Dad to the car and he slept until the following day, which was a blessing. It was February 27, 1978. I was twenty-seven years old.

The next day, with Dad out of it and me still in machine mode, I made the funeral arrangements. My brother just agreed to whatever plans we worked out or were suggested by the undertaker. Word had gotten out that my mom had died and the *Daily News* wanted to run an obituary. It was from that obituary that I learned about what my parents had been through with some of my relatives. In the obituary I'm quoted as saying, "My mom was a gay activist." On the day of the funeral, my Uncle Ralph asked me if I had really said that, and I said of course. He said, "Then maybe it's good she's gone." Can you ever forgive someone for saying something like that? I couldn't.

There is only one part of the funeral itself that I clearly recall. It was the part where they ask the family to review the deceased. All I can remember is Grandmom looking at Mom. She was smiling and I wondered if she understood what was happening. We were ushered into a side room as the lid of the coffin was closed. My mind and body remained on autopilot, doing whatever needed to be done.

My father remained a wreck for some time, so I began to make household decisions to keep things moving as best as possible. My mother and father's best friends were Dot and Gouch who lived up the street. Most nights, Mom and Dad would go up to their house and either play cards or just sit around and talk. Now, every night they came down to sit with my Dad, to sit with their Marty. They were his best medicine. And they were funny. Dot spoke like a truck driver, and I could see why the couples were friends. Like my parents, Dot and Gouch adored each other. It might have taken months, but they nursed Dad back to living.

As for me, it might seem strange but my feelings were mostly guilt. Was there more that could have been done? Why did I not have more knowledge on the subject and should I have asked the doctors more questions? There was no WebMD then, and at that time patients relied, for the most part, on whatever the doctor said. It would take an epidemic less than five years later to explain to me the value of patient involvement and self-advocacy for one's own treatment.

My tears only came when I was alone, and they were slight and silent. I wanted to have a big cry, to break down completely, but somehow it did not happen. To me, this was private. For weeks I was in a zombie state, going through the motions and moving forward but without feelings. A friend finally thought it might be good to get me out of the city and took me to Key West. One night while walking on the beach alone and looking up at the stars, I sunk to the sand and cried. I don't remember how long I cried but I do remember thinking, *Let me get it all out now*. I can tell you that even after more than thirty years, you can never get it all out. What you can hope for is that the pain transitions into the fondness of memories and the good that a person brought into your life. My mother's gift to me, the gift of love and support, was immeasurable.

The pages of *Philadelphia Gay News* did not see my byline again for several months, but the editorial responsibilities were in the good hands of Jack Veasey. Jack was a talented writer with a sharp wit. My favorite line from him was when he was doing a review of a cabaret singer whose voice he just could not tolerate. In describing this Jack wrote, "His voice was so flat that you could land a 747 on it without spilling one cocktail."

In April I finally wrote an editorial. It was titled "Up with Parents":

The old adage that says you don't appreciate something until it's gone is never more true than it is with gays and their relationships with their parents. In most ethnic and minority communities, children who are feeling depressed or somewhat different from other segments of society could always look to their parents for needed support in dealing with their problems. Unfortunately, gays do not, for the most part, go to their parents for support. In fact, many shudder at the thought of outing themselves and asking for help seems insurmountable.

Parents can help ease the suffering of guilt, anxiety, and pressure that many of us go through, but most of all, they can normalize a life torn between different worlds. In a time when we feel so unloved, the attentive love of parents can bring us home to reality and ease the hurts that we all come across on the path of life.

We are not all able to express to our parents the realities of our lives; some might not understand, others might misunderstand. In some cases we are not strong enough to burden them with something that may take them the rest of our lives to digest.

This is a very personal editorial because its meaning brings home the memory of my mother, who recently passed away. She not only knew and accepted me as I am, but became an important part of my work. I have no doubt that were it not for my parents, I could not have achieved what I have thus far.

I remember the first time I tried to tell my mother that I was gay. I called her on the phone, dropped the line very shakily, and listened for her reply. She asked, "What are you going to do when you're old, who do you have to keep you company?" I answered, "I would have my friends and family, and you." I was wrong, but the short period I did have my mother proved to be the most productive and rewarding time in my life. She not only accepted and supported my work but she was proud of that work, so much so that she wanted to be a part of it.

My mother's enthusiasm kept me going when times were difficult, and at times she seemed to be more liberated than I. When her cousin was planning a wedding, my mother was outraged when an invitation was not extended to my lover and balked at attending until my father persuaded her otherwise. She's spoken at gay pride rallies even though illness should have kept her indoors, and when speaking on the Phil Donahue Show, she said in reference to my lover Phillip, "He is also my son." She'd planned to reorganize a local "Parents of Gays" group to aid parents in understanding and accepting their gay children, but illness kept her from completing that goal.

I know that the warmth, love, and encouragement that I received from my mother have resulted in numerous successes, and the existence of this newspaper is one direct result.

I still have my father, who I know will continue to be supportive and loving as he has always been. I am particularly grateful for that when I realize that even only one supportive open parent is more than many gays will ever have.

I'd like to encourage readers, who haven't already, to seriously consider sharing your gayness with your parents. You may be underestimating the power of their love. Closeness with the moral support from parents can be an invaluable source of strength to cope with the day-to-day oppression we all have to face.

Chapter 8

Post-Traumatic Stress Syndrome

There's more to a problem than just finding a solution. There's the creativity used to find that solution. Like most boys of my age in 1969, which happened to be during the height of the Vietnam War, the single biggest personal concern was being drafted into the US military and ending up in that hell. Like all eighteen-year-olds, I was required to register for the draft. Then I awaited the dreaded call to go in, to be questioned, and to be examined, hoping that my birth date was low on the list and I'd escape the draft. Many of us looked for ways out. It would have been simple just to say I was gay and I'd be immediately denied entry and receive what they called a 4-F. The problem would be that a 4-F remained on your record permanently and could affect future employment. So most gay men never used that option. The closet was safer.

I had read somewhere that anything you sent to your draft board was required by law to be kept on file, in a permanent capsule of sorts. Given that, it seemed to me that they would try to figure out what was of interest to an individual, and therefore know whether or not they were a suitable candidate for the draft. Each Sunday, I religiously bought my *New York Times*, and every Monday, after faithfully reading it, I'd package it up and send it to my draft board. I wonder if there is a file somewhere out there with my name on it with over a year and a half worth of the Sunday *New York Times* taking up valuable governmental office space.

The point being that if they called me in, the reviewer would have had to sign a paper saying that he or she had read my complete file. Most likely, unless they had hours and hours to spend sifting through newspapers, they would not have. I'm not sure if that was the actual reason, but I never did get a call from the draft board.

If there ever was a time for creativity in the gay community, it was when we were fighting for our lives in a different deadly war. This war started with one word: AIDS. To put it simply, AIDS in the US affected and defined the LGBT community more than any other issue in our history. Everything from coming out, politics, organizing, to how we dealt with each other changed due to AIDS. To this very day, its impact on the LGBT community has not been fully and honestly dealt with. For many, the anger still seethes of being witness to a government that callously ignored our very existence. For others, the residual effects are pervasive grief, crippling fear, personal, emotional, or physical trauma, and the experience of what is commonly known as survivor's guilt. Even in these days of drug cocktails and preventative care, there are always new controversies that arise around the AIDS crisis. When it first started, every single aspect of the disease was a raging battle. In many ways, it still is.

We seem to still be afraid of saying the obvious: AIDS was a virulent war that an entire generation of gay men got drafted into, whether we wanted to serve or not. It's not enough to say that it was on par with serving in Vietnam, Iraq, or Afghanistan. Vietnam cost 58,000 American lives; AIDS, so far, has cost more than ten times as many. Does the US government owe restitution for ignoring the safety of millions of gay Americans? They provided it to people with hemophilia, who contracted HIV from tainted blood products. They gave it to Japanese Americans who were imprisoned during World War II. We weren't imprisoned; we were just left to die. After all, it was merely the gay disease—the gay cancer, as they first labeled it. What harm could it possibly do to them as non-gays?

Something should become very clear, no matter who you are. Whether a member of the LGBT community, a government bureaucrat, a health professional, or just someone attempting to understand our community, we should still be afraid of AIDS. It seems that most people don't even want to know the statistics of the heavy toll, nor do we want to deal with the trauma of those left behind. We pretend that it's over. It's not.

A couple of years ago at the Walter & Elise Haas Fund's annual LGBT media conference, organized by Bilerico Project's leadership, Bil Browning and Matt Foreman (formerly of the National Gay and Lesbian Task Force), one of the attendees, Mark S. King, asked if the LGBT media had dropped the ball on the coverage of HIV/AIDS. This spurred an incredible e-mail dialogue where many of the journalists pointed out areas where LGBT media might be lacking. As one of the longest-serving members of the LGBT media, my answer to that question was and still is yes, there are areas where we are deficient. I'd suggest that the question might be asked in a different way, but the answer, no matter how it is framed, is still yes.

From 1955 through 1975, the US was involved in a war in Vietnam. During that time 58,220 American service members were killed. If we add the Gulf War, the second "Desert Storm," and our subsequent involvement in Iraq, where 7,000 service members were killed, we find that America lost approximately 65,000 lives to these wars.

In 1982, as reported by the Centers for Disease Control, AIDS became an official disease in the US. Since then, over

600,000 people have died of AIDS here. So you may ask, what's the connection? Survivors. Many of those who went to any one of the aforementioned wars, or endured other US military involvements, have suffered what is called post-traumatic stress syndrome (PTSS). Post-traumatic stress syndrome came from the stress of being in a war and witnessing fellow soldiers get badly injured and die. Would those who witnessed their friends die from AIDS also suffer post-traumatic stress syndrome? I think so. That said, there are many external differences between the two groups of people. While the surviving soldiers of war were considered heroes (with the exception of Vietnam vets who were often mistreated), AIDS patients were treated as trash. Those who died were sometimes refused embalming, funerals, and burial. Some were actually put in the trash heap outside of hospitals. Those of us who fought for dignity in death were forced to take on the government, the health care system, and, in some cases, our very own community. It was a war and it was hell for the victims and survivors. Anybody who lived in that period has their own stories of survival, and they are as terrifying as any of the wars mentioned above. Have we in the LGBT community tried to ignore what we went through? The answer is yes. How often do you hear someone of my generation talking about it?

One treatment for post-traumatic stress syndrome is coming to terms with it by repeated discussion. We in our community shy away from this discussion, and the health care resources that could have helped us deal with it were never given to us. Today, when we try to talk about HIV/AIDS with our youth, they are often uninterested and don't want to hear about a time when sex was dangerous. After all, youth is a time for sexual experimentation, and with the advances of HIV medications and treatments, it can seem like a moot discussion. Conversations around the topic are sometimes labeled old and we are told that we shouldn't deny the young their freedom.

We lost scores of friends. Our people were refused treatment. We had to beg to get our friends buried with any level of dignity. Families of those who died from AIDS were forced to feel ashamed, and many times the funerals were held in secret and the death certificates were fraudulent. Causes of death were listed as cancer, heart failure, pneumonia, or anything else but AIDS. Those of us who survived and were up close and personal with the disease now have what is traditionally called survivor's guilt.

There is not a gay man alive today who went through that time period and, at one time or another, did not think he was going to be infected. Just a bruise would make you believe you had AIDS and were going to die. While taking a shower on a trip to Israel, I noticed two bruises, one on each arm. For three sleepless nights and days I was consumed with fear until I got back home. The reality was that the bruises were from the way I was carrying my hand luggage, yet the anxiety from worrying about my health status was real.

Did people actually want us to die? Was that a solution to societal issues with gay people? During the height of the plague we had just begun to find sexual freedom. Once we knew that the disease was transmitted through sex and through sharing needles, some believed that the government would use AIDS as a way to recriminalize sodomy or any form of gay sex. Joe DiSabato, who represented many of the newspapers in the LGBT community to national advertisers, went to the largest maker of condoms and asked them to advertise in LGBT media. They refused, saying that the content in our publications was too sexual. More sexual than condoms? They didn't want the world to think of their condoms on gay dicks. Perhaps they thought straight dicks wouldn't buy them. We were too dirty, we were trash, and our lives were not to be saved, at least not by condoms. To be fair, they'd sell them to us for a cheap price, but publicly they wanted no connection to gay men.

AIDS to Americans was a gay disease, and to many uneducated people it was a disease carried by *all* gay men. Gay equaled AIDS, AIDS equaled gay. In California, there was a discussion about a referendum on whether to set up containment camps. Proposition 64, a California referendum that would have required mandatory reporting of AIDS to the Department of Health Services, actually made it to the ballot (and was ahead in the polls at one point). Torie Osborn, Bruce Decker, and David Mixner ran the campaign to defeat it. People like Reverend Pat Robertson and Jerry Falwell took to their pulpit and declared that this disease was a punishment from God. It still haunts me that on a television talk show that I did on AIDS, the union stagehands refused to attach the microphone to me. They left it aside and explained how to do it myself. They did not want to touch a gay man.

According to the government, whose primary job is the security of its citizens, we weren't people. During the early years of the Reagan administration, the government spent more funds on protecting livestock, fish, and poultry than they spent on AIDS. Even the surgeon general at the time, C. Everett Koop, later expressed sadness that during his first four years he was not allowed to touch the subject. Finally, when he issued the first detailed report on the study of AIDS, his attempts at spreading the word were seen by some as an effort to victimize gay men and brand us as outcasts.

Sean Strub's book *Body Counts: A Memoir of Politics, Sex, AIDS, and Survival* has a good description of the community's actions during this time. His perspective as a survivor is invaluable to anyone studying the subject. At a speaking engagement with him in 2014, he impressed me with his incredible scope of knowledge, and unlike other survivors he tries to be diplomatic and create needed discussion. Another top-notch depiction of that era can be found in Larry Kramer's play *The Normal Heart*, which shows the utter conflict within the community over this issue. In addition to being one of the founders of Gay Men's Health Crisis (GMHC), he also established the AIDS Coalition to Unleash Power (ACT UP) in 1987. In my view this was his finest achievement. ACT UP went back to the roots of Gay Liberation Front, and even zaps. It used street-theater tactics to get the public's attention, and succeeded far beyond anyone's expectations. ACT UP was Political Theater 101, and Larry is certainly theatrical.

According to David France, the award-winning filmmaker of *How to Survive a Plague*, the New York City government spent a paltry $24,500 on AIDS by 1984, even after the city had created the Office of Gay and Lesbian Health Concerns. A *New York Times* article of August 27, 1989 reported: "Mayor [Koch] says he is meeting the challenge. 'We do more on AIDS than any other city or state in America . . .'"

There are two main speculations about the Koch administration's lack of attention to the AIDS crisis. The first is that he was a closeted gay man and the second is that some communities affected by AIDS rallied hard for it not to be publicized, specifically the black community, where homophobia in some segments of the church was rampant. In the case of the latter, I believe the LGBT community did not work closely enough with the black community, which could have provided greater lobbying and thereby galvanized more support from the city. The effort to combat this public health catastrophe required public, private, and government intervention.

While in New York the funding for AIDS was limited, in other cities the funding grew and information flowed. This is all somewhat amazing when you realize that in the private sector, New York was actually a leader. GMHC was at the forefront of showing the nation how to serve the needs of patients with AIDS, and certainly how to fundraise. American Foundation for AIDS Research (amfAR), the first major organization to fund AIDS research, was also based in New York.

But compare New York's public officials with those in a city like Philadelphia and the differences are striking. Around the same time in the eighties, Philadelphia's first African American mayor, W. Wilson Goode, announced that he was not only creating the AIDS Action Coordinating Office, but he was also doubling the AIDS budget. The city did not have the same resistance from the African American population, possibly because the mayor provided better leadership and faced the issue as a human crisis.

The media in Philadelphia also came out in support of a stronger response to the epidemic. Unlike New York, where such enlightened publications as the *New York Times* downplayed AIDS until much later, Philadelphia stood with the community. While mainstream media might have been light on coverage, it was during this time that LGBT media all across the country stepped up to the plate and found their collective voice. It was to the LGBT media that the community looked to find information about new research and proper organizing. Out of necessity, some of the LGBT publications published only AIDS news and information. Needle exchanges, safer sex practices, condom distribution, and buyers clubs were broadly written about.

On June 26, 1987, Mayor Goode, along with media heads, public health officials, and AIDS activists, held a morning press conference to declare AIDS Awareness Day in Philadelphia. If you lived anywhere near the city it was literally impossible to ignore the messages. The primary purpose of the conference was to give people the information they needed and allow them the opportunity to apply that information to their own lives.

For AIDS Awareness Day, the two daily newspapers, the *Inquirer* and the *Daily News*, along with the *Philadelphia Tribune*, America's oldest African American community newspaper, and *Philadelphia Gay News*, all ran the complete multipage supplement of the surgeon general's report on AIDS. If you read a newspaper in the city, you saw the supplement in print. The community also partnered with local television stations. All three network affiliates and some independents started out every newscast of the day with the story, and they also made it a featured subject on their talk shows. Even Oprah's schedule was changed in Philly that day. We lined up experts from the various AIDS organizations to be guests on radio shows throughout the day. The copy for ads was provided by a committee of the AIDS organizations headed by Jane Shull, cochair of the day. What I am most proud of is that all of this was done without a single dollar changing hands. Not one TV station, radio station, or newspaper asked for a dime. The print publications all donated the space and wrote news copy. The *Inquirer* printed an additional twenty thousand copies of the official AIDS report, which AIDS organizations in the city handed out on the streets.

Thanks to the efforts of the various HIV/AIDS organizations and the political clout of the LGBT community, we were able to keep the issue front and center in Philly up to the 1991 mayoral election. During that election cycle, an HIV/AIDS forum was held in which all the candidates had to present their views on treatment and city services.

One of the candidates running in the Democratic primary was my old friend, former District Attorney Ed Rendell. He and his campaign manager, David L. Cohen, decided that they needed to brush up on the issues before the forum. They came to my office to meet with various AIDS experts. What surprised me most was their ability to quickly memorize the treatments, drugs, and afflictions of HIV.

It was the first time that I got to experience up close the brilliance of David L. Cohen. He was someone who could not only strategize and organize, but he also showed genuine empathy for the people he was dealing with. He and I struck up a friendship almost immediately. David later went on to do great things at Comcast NBCUniversal, specifically around diversity inclusion, and became one of America's top corporate leaders.

When Ed became mayor and David took on the role of chief of staff, David mentioned that Ed was not on good terms with one of the state's leading Democrats, State Senator Vincent Fumo. David knew that I had a decent relationship with Vince and suggested that since I had asked the mayor to come sit at my table for the first ActionAIDS Dining Out for Life fundraising event, I should invite Vince too, in the hopes that they might develop a working relationship.

Vince was chairman of the Senate Appropriations Committee, which of course dealt with the budget of the state, and from that position over the years he literally brought billions of dollars back to Philadelphia. But beyond balancing the budget, I thought the mayor was going to need state dollars to be successful in helping to combat the AIDS epidemic and of course for other programs in Philadelphia in general.

With my somewhat shameless hosting style, I got them both to agree to sit together, explaining that it was the event's head table and all the press would be there. Vince came with his wife and Ed came with one of his assistants who over the years had seemed to take on the role of jester, giving an audience to Ed's adolescent humor. At dinner, all was going well; Ed and Vince seemed to be getting along. When Ed spilled a dessert covered with powdered sugar on his black suit pants, he jokingly leaned over to his assistant and asked him if he wanted some of it. I heard Vince's voice in my ear: "I didn't know he batted for your team." At that point I had to explain to the senator that the mayor was heterosexual but felt liberated enough to make such jokes. The dinner, powdered sugar and all, was a tremendous success, and Ed, Vince, and David developed a solid relationship, allowing for continued funding and support for HIV/AIDS among other issues. The three of them became a force for great change in a growing city, and are proof of how networking and collaboration, even in the face of a crisis, can benefit all parties.

Despite the progress we were making, both medically and politically, all gay men were still suspected by some of being "carriers." If you visited a person with AIDS in the hospital, you had to prepare for something out of a science-fiction novel. The yellow and red tape was everywhere, along with ominous warning signs. You were asked to wear hospital gowns and face masks. Sometimes, hospitals emptied an entire floor for one patient, and nobody would attend to them. Some patients were lucky enough to have friends visit them; some were not. I still hesitate to ask friends about people I've lost contact with from that time, afraid I'll hear the dreaded line, "Oh, they died." Or just get a telling nod of the head.

But from the trauma, the LGBT community learned an invaluable lesson. With little assistance from the government or medical community, friends and loved ones continued to die. When we saw our friends commit suicide rather than go through the daily horrors of being sick and stigmatized, this community learned how to react, fight back, and organize. ACT UP and those who preceded them are the real heroes. In Dallas, the hero wasn't the glamorized heterosexual cowboy in *Dallas Buyers Club*, but Robert Moore, cofounder and former publisher of the *Dallas Voice*, who put a spotlight on the issue. Other heroes were the real-life doctors who put their practices on the line. Those few elected officials who found dollars in their tight budgets to house, feed, and care for people who were tossed aside by society—they are heroes. And yes, clubs allowing members' collective buying power were heroes too, but not the Matthew McConaughey movie versions.

During the height of the epidemic, I was watching TV at home one night and a show on PBS got my attention. It was called, simply, *Plague*. It explored various plagues throughout history. For me, the one takeaway from the show was that most plagues last about twenty-five years. So I began to hope that by 2005 or 2006 we'd be at the end of AIDS.

Soon after watching that show, the AIDS drama hit home in a very personal way. There had to have been some clue to the change in my partner of twenty years, that guy who always joked that he wanted me for my potential to make money, but I hadn't noticed. One night at dinner he said with a tentative smile, "There's something I have to tell you." It wasn't long before he began to cry and told me he "has it." I knew exactly what "it" was. Stunned, sitting there frozen, the seconds seemed like an eternity until it finally sank in. We embraced, and I whispered in his ear, "We'll get through this." Even with this painful disclosure hovering in my mind, I knew we were going to somehow make it through.

That night, the answers to the questions I asked were not reassuring; he said that I was the seventh person he had told. *What?* He explained he hadn't known how I'd react. That was hurtful. After twenty years, he didn't know me!

While I was attempting to stay calm for his sake, inside I was torn apart. Was our twenty-year relationship just a show? I was furious and began to believe that I had somehow let him down. Had I also failed the community? I don't believe I've ever had so much anger inside but I couldn't allow it to explode. There was no sleep for me that lonely night.

This was also the night before I was scheduled to host Mayor John Street on his first venture into a skeptical LGBT community. Though Street hadn't been our ally while serving on the city council, he was making a public statement of his switch to now supporting LGBT rights by having a full-scale tour of the William Way LGBT Community Center, with press in tow. I knew that by leading this tour, I'd be ridiculed by some in the community, but I also knew that Street, as mayor, could make a difference. It was important that I be focused that night. I had twenty-four hours to get my head straight, but the hurt remained palpable. My partner had told six other people of his condition before me, and chose the night before a major press event to share the news.

The tour was somehow going really well, and after taking in several rooms and having a demonstration of the computer-learning center, we came to the ballroom. At that point, acting out of pure impulse, I asked the executive director of the community center to continue the tour without me, saying that I'd catch up later. I pulled the hand of someone who I knew could help, and the two of us stayed behind while the press junket moved on. In an empty ballroom I looked at Jane Shull and blurted out, "He has AIDS, what should I do?"

Jane, president of Philadelphia Fight and cochair of AIDS Awareness Day, was a strong woman, politically smart, and one of the most knowledgeable people on the subject. She shot me a nice smile and said: "Let's finish this up, and we'll get to it."

As the tour continued, questions wound around in my head. Questions I hadn't asked or thought to ask. How did it happen? What was his viral load? How do we tell his parents and my nephew Jeffrey, who was living with us? Should we tell him at all? What should I prepare myself for? What care procedures will I need to learn? The questions never stopped, but somehow no one noticed. I went on talking to people, discussing the evening and how the mayor could help us as a community. I was on autopilot, which was my fallback position when overwhelmed.

After the tour was over Jane took me aside and said, "Have you cried yet?" This sounded so strange, but Jane knew what she was talking about; she had been through this many times before. In a flash I realized that I hadn't, and then the watershed began.

As the city's foremost expert on the subject, Jane knew that there were a number of issues to deal with, both medical and psychological, regarding our relationship. Her next question was one that hadn't even occurred to me: "Do you want to continue the relationship?" How could I not continue the relationship? Me, I'd deal with it like I did with everything else that had been tossed my way.

In short order, my partner and I became clients of Philadelphia Fight. At our first visit, the counselor asked me, "Have you been tested yet?"

That hadn't dawned on me either. I scheduled a test with Karam Mounzer, one of the doctors who dedicated his life to help fight AIDS. Getting tested wasn't a new experience for me, but this was different, as the closest person to me now had the disease. The test was negative.

When it became public knowledge that my partner was HIV positive, things went from bad to worse. While most friends were supportive, a number urged me to leave him, saying things like, "Do you realize he's put your life in jeopardy?" It also spurred on friends to tell me what they knew about him, most of which I had earlier refused to believe, chalking it up to idle gossip. It soon became apparent that he had a secret life I had no knowledge of.

He needed more than what Philadelphia Fight could offer; as the months went on his drinking became worse, and friends told me to wake up and confront my denials. Instead, I did what many people do—blame myself—all the while not realizing what was happening around me. He would openly hurl insults my way, giving venom to a previously humorous line of his—"I always told you the only reason I married you was for your potential to make money." He now told me that it was the *only* reason he had stayed with me. He bragged about his recent infidelities and reminded me of past ones that I had forgiven or tried to forget. He began to confess all facets of his life, a life alien to me, and to viciously ridicule my person. A friend told me I was in an abusive relationship. It broke me, and then rage set in when I discovered that little has been studied about abuse among same-sex couples. Anger, depression, and self-doubt took over my life.

How my nephew Jeffrey made it through this time I'll never understand. As I write this, I'm full of sorrow for putting him through it and realize how much he loves me to have stuck by my side all these years. Some of my friends were not so loyal. To them, I now apologize. I apologize to all my friends whom I didn't believe.

The end came the day I picked him up from yet another stint at rehab. I believe it was his seventh time. We got home and before dinner he already had a glass of wine in his hand. Denial had ended. Calmly I spoke the words, "It's either the wine or me."

He threw the wine at me and was out the door. Later that night, Jane Shull called to tell me that he was at one of her fundraisers, drinking and happily telling people that we were through. She asked if it was true. The answer was yes. It would be great if I could say that life went on, but for me, after a nearly twenty-year relationship, it felt like life was over.

I was about to see bottom, thinking that I'd failed myself and the community too. I could no longer claim that we'd have a normal, long-lasting relationship like some of our straight counterparts, like my mom and dad. In hindsight, I know that every relationship, no matter what kind, is different. But I felt that I had something to prove, from my early days of activism; seeing my parents' and their friends' happy marriages . . . until the end, so happy.

Friends tried to help pull me out, but I built a brick wall around myself. Instead of going to the office, I'd spend days holed up in my house on the Jersey Shore, which I had bought a few years prior. Jim Austin had been correct: I could earn a living as a publisher. It became real to me in 1994, eighteen years after the first issue. We had steadily picked up advertisers and circulation climbed. I had wanted to rent a house at the Jersey Shore for the summer and didn't know if I could afford it, even with others sharing the cost, so I called my accountant and asked if I could do it. I essentially pleaded with him that I needed some time off. He laughed and explained that for the money it would take for a summer rental I could make a down payment on a house and it would serve me well each year with taxes. He also suggested that I give myself a raise, and for the first time in my life I actually felt middle class. Walking into the house for the first time, I felt great pride. Things were beginning to get a little easier, to the point that I was able to purchase a house—rather, a shell of a house—in what was becoming a gentrified neighborhood. Indeed, *I* gentrified it, as the first non–African American on the block. It had one of these bathtubs with the four legs, but one of the legs was missing so when you took a shower it sometimes felt like you were surfing. It actually fell through the ceiling at one point, and we then used it in the kitchen. And when the dining room ceiling plaster started dropping one day, we covered it with egg cartons. The house was falling apart, but it was mine.

But now, after the breakup, I used that house as a place where I could drink in excess and take various prescription drugs for sleeping or depression. I wouldn't even answer the door when my friends Larry Furman and Dennis Cook, who had a house at the Shore a few blocks from mine, came by to check on me. Soon it didn't matter which pill it was or how many. I'd come undone.

It was Pattie Tihey, our editor, and Rick Lombardo, my assistant, who kept *PGN* afloat during that time, as I was useless to the publication. Convinced that my ex-partner's problems were my fault, I had taken an emotional beating and internalized his scathing remarks.

I stayed in that fog for over a year, until one day Pattie stormed into my office and said she'd had enough. "This has gone on too long. You have responsibilities. This publication which you founded supports fourteen people and their families." She then added, in understanding some of what I was feeling, "That is success!"

Get up and get on with it was the message I received.

Patti urged me to get help; she even suggested several psychologists. As always, she was prepared, and her words about supporting fourteen people became my new guiding light.

Seeing a psychologist set me at ease. "Tell me about your last twenty-five years."

Thinking for a minute, I said blankly, "Death, suicides, AIDS, the breakup."

She looked at me for a few moments, remarked at my lack of emotion, and then asked whether anything positive had happened. There was nothing in my mind. Empty. Then she had me tell the full story, sparing no detail.

My last twenty-five years had included my mother's death from kidney disease, Grandmom's Alzheimer's and ultimate death, Uncle Stanley's gambling and death, the suicides of my friends Jan Sergienko (after a gang rape), my friend Carol (after sexual abuse from her husband), my friend Michael (after becoming fed up with medical treatments and watching his own deterioration from AIDS), and my former sales manager and close friend Sally Tyer (who after a bad business deal shot herself in the head). Then there were the AIDS deaths, chief among them my friend Bill Way, and the numerous funerals that were left for me to plan. Then there was my failure as a partner. All relayed in a stream-of-consciousness monotone.

She had one more question: "Did you ever cry?"

I took a long pause before I replied, "We had a demonstration at the city council where we disrupted the session and I took over the president's desk, tossing the papers in the air. The police were called in and it became rough. Several of our members were hurt. The TV reporters rushed me and there were tears coming down my cheeks. In an emotional state, I said on camera that our people are being hurt. Later, a few friends told me sternly that I should never cry during an interview, that it was unmanly."

She didn't judge me, instead asking me to keep relating my life story. Soon I was in tears, hysterical uncontrollable tears; surprisingly, so was she.

Afterward, she stated the obvious: "You need to get in

touch with your emotions and stop covering them up." She also encouraged me to meet with a pharmacologist.

That was the first time I'd ever heard of such a profession. Those two hours with the psychologist were perhaps the best investment in myself I'd ever made. Without her, along with the other key people mentioned above, I'm sure my life would not have had any more chapters. Jane and Dr. Mounzer got me the help I needed, and Pattie and Rick kept the newspaper moving, even hiding the fact that I wasn't at the wheel.

This story isn't unique; it was common to many gay couples when one partner was diagnosed with HIV. Like others, it took me years to accept the situation and move forward, and that is another lesson that those of us affected by HIV/AIDS had to learn. PTSS is real.

By that time in the mid-nineties, the pharmaceutical industry was competing to see who could come up with the best regimen of pills, or "cocktails," to manage the disease. HIV was on the road to being treatable—just like that PBS show had promised—but it couldn't be cured. Those cocktails did indeed work and they have been improved upon. Now there are pills advertised to prevent a person from acquiring HIV. But there's no telling what effect these new pills will have on younger people, if they'll simply forget the lessons we learned and deem themselves invincible. Will we see the return of Fire Island circuit parties—no air of caution and no end to the high? With medical advances in prevention, will those who already have the disease be alienated and forgotten? Even after we've gotten through the worst of it, the work of educating people is not over. Not by a long shot.

Above, the official White House picture of President Obama's first state visit to Philadelphia in 2010, for which I was one of the hosts. Below, the president and I engaging at the event.

My grandmother Fannie Weinstein, the suffragette.

Wedding photo of my parents, Martin and Shelley Segal.

Mom and Dad on honeymoon in Atlantic City, New Jersey.

Eight-year-old me at 2333 South Bambrey Terrace.

The receipt from my first arrest in 1970.

Mark Segal, taxi driver.

The picture that appeared in the *Philadelphia Inquirer* the morning after I held a party in Arlen Specter's office in October 1973.

My first meeting with Governor Milton Shapp in 1974.

Disrupting Nixon's reelection fundraiser on November 1, 1972.

Above, handcuffing myself to the camera during a live taping of the *Mike Douglas Show*. Below, addressing Douglas and his guests Helen Hayes and Tony Bennett.

The Walter zap (December 11, 1973).

Publicity shot from one of my appearances on the *Phil Donohue Show*.

President Clinton and I in a photograph taken by Governor Ed Rendell.

Befriending Republicans along the way. George W. Bush's Homeland Security Secretary Tom Ridge and my old friend City Councilman Thacher Longstreth.

Patti LaBelle, my diva, dedicates a song to me at the mayor's official LGBT inaugural gala on January 3, 2004.

Patti LaBelle with her new backup singers, Governor Ed Rendell and Mayor John Street, wearing blue feather boas as I look on.

Looking from above the stage at the Philadelphia Art Museum on July 4, 2005, and realizing for the first time that we had over a half million people on the Parkway.

Sir Elton John and I at the official July 4, 2005 ceremony at Independence Hall.

Congressman Barney Frank, Elton, and Mayor John Street.

At the Independence Hall ceremony in 2005, I became the first out LGBT person to speak publicly at this annual event.

Robert Key of the Elton John AIDS Foundation and I make our entrance into the Freedom Ball at Philadelphia's Museum of Art. The Philadelphia Boys Choir sings on either side of us as we descend.

Dedication of a Pennsylvania state historical plaque at Independence Hall, honoring the pioneering LGBT public pickets of 1965–69. (L to R) Lilli Vincenz, William B. Kelley, Randy Wicker, Ada Bello, Barbara Gittings, me, Frank Kameny, and Kay Lahusen in the chair.

Original participants from the first gay pride march in 1970, which was then called Christopher Street Gay Liberation Day. Members of my New York Gay Liberation Front family reunited for this photo on Pride Day 2013 in front of the Stonewall.

Four Chairs in Search of a Table
from left to right
John Chiafalo, GY Chair 1973-4
Mark Horn, GY Chair 1971-73
Tom Approbato, current GLYNY Again Board Chair
Mark Segal, Founding Daddy, GY Chair 1969-71

Gay Youth reunion. Top: John Chiafalo, Mark Horn, Tom Approbato, and me.
Bottom: Michael Knowles, Mark Horn, Jeff Hochhauser, and me.

Messing around at a fundraiser at my home: Congressman Barney Frank dancing with Congressman Bob Brady.

Soon-to-be Mayor Jim Kenney with Jason and me after he paid for our wedding license (yes, he really did).

At home talking policy with California Lieutenant Governor Gavin Newsom.

Our wedding on July 5, 2014. (L to R) Jason's sisters Jennifer, Ryan, and Lill, Jason's parents Clyde and Rosalina, Jason, myself, Judge Dan Anders, my cousin Ilene, and my nephew Jeffrey.

Jason meets President Obama and the First Lady for the first time.

Gay History Month, front page of the *Philadelphia Daily News*, October 13, 2011.

Chapter 9
Clout

In 1993, *Philadelphia* magazine named me the resident with "Most Clout" in their annual Best of Philly issue, crowning me above union leaders, corporate heads, and elected officials. By this time I had been in the public eye for nearly twenty-five years. It wasn't a quick rise, and the clout they attributed to me was garnered out of necessity. Any social justice or civil rights movement needs not only to understand the politics swirling around, but also to have insider clout. Change does not happen without working the system.

One can develop clout from a number of factors, like building coalitions with other communities, organizations, and leaders. Other important facets are the ability to raise funds and deliver votes, and being able to stop a candidate dead in their tracks. And the simple fact is that to get a large program on the boards or to get any sort of legislation passed, you need to be in tune with elected officials, both those who support your issues and those who don't. Knowing how to navigate the latter may indeed be even more important. One last item is getting the attention of media. Today, that means having an understanding of the power of both traditional and social media.

Two organizations that prove this point and deserve recognition for a job well done are Lambda Legal Defense and Education Fund and Freedom to Marry. They get it. They know how to spend funds wisely and use media to their full advantage. Evan Wolfson, founder of Freedom to Marry and formerly of Lambda Legal Defense and Education Fund, is a community treasure: he is bright and articulate, and understands how to create a message that the public can consume. He has been creative with his approach, and no one can doubt that it has worked. Like many activists, he was ahead of his time and kept to his vision, no matter the opposition in the community—and that has a place in my heart.

The LGBT national all-star team also includes the Human Rights Campaign, which exemplifies the slogan that money and media are the mother's milk of politics. It takes funds to elect candidates and launch campaigns that change public perception.

Each time I hear a complaint about the lobbying efforts of Human Rights Campaign, it makes me want to hurl. While one might disagree on the issues, HRC is excellent at raising funds and using those funds to lobby, which is simply playing the game, and playing it correctly. You have to be in the game to win it.

Another member of the all-star team is the Victory Fund. Cofounded by Vic Basile in 1991 to support and groom politicians for LGBT equality, and later infused by the incredible energy of Brian Bond, the Victory Fund raises money and teaches people the fundamentals of campaigns. Their efforts have led to scores of victories around the nation. Both Vic and Brian became important members of the Obama administration and have helped shape the path of LGBT issues, providing a blueprint for future administrations to follow. Human Rights Campaign and Victory Fund can take a bow for the work they have done with Barack Obama to make him the most inclusive president in our country's history.

Along with money and organization, an additional path to clout for our community is to have a mainstream media watchdog, which has largely fallen to the Gay & Lesbian Alliance Against Defamation. GLAAD has had a few bad years but they're getting back on their feet. The low point for them (and Human Rights Campaign to a lesser extent), and our community in general, was the Chick-fil-A disaster. That campaign will also be a blueprint for gay activists—of what not to do.

The quick story: It was discovered that the Chick-fil-A Foundation was giving money to anti–marriage equality organizations. Some LGBT groups and bloggers went off the rails. The Human Rights Campaign and GLAAD, however, were caught off guard; the LGBT community and the marriage equality bloggers were angry, but they were given no direction from our leaders. They grew frustrated, and many began to ask where HRC and GLAAD stood on the issue and what countermeasures should be taken. With no apparent plan, the organizations simply issued press releases about the facts, without offering any leadership of what to do next.

The LGBT community ultimately had to find its own answer, which entailed a national kiss-in at Chick-fil-A restaurants all across the country. Unfortunately, this resulted in perhaps one of the best business days for Chick-fil-A. Our equality was reduced to kissing, we looked weak and silly, and opponents staged a Chick-fil-A appreciation day, which drove more profits to the chain.

People forgot a fundamental aspect of our struggle from the early days of the movement, which was not to allow the opposition to simply reduce our community to sex. Compare the Chick-fil-A story with a similar struggle that occurred much earlier in our climb out of oppression, the Anita Bryant fight against gay rights in Florida. There, the local community had control and leadership. Anita Bryant was a devout Christian and a popular singer of the day who in 1977 went on a crusade against "homosexuality," attracting national notoriety and support. She used as her slogan "Save Our Children." That played into the stereotype that gays were child molesters and predators.

Dade County, Florida, where she lived, had passed non-discrimination legislation, and she used the platform of repealing that legislation to assault the LGBT community. She was endorsed and supported by Jerry Falwell and his Moral Majority, who threw in millions of dollars. In 1977 we had little national organization, so the locals led the way. Lacking major funds to combat Bryant, they first fought her and her supporters with logical, tempered answers. And then they dropped the hammer on her. Bryant made most of her money as the spokesperson for Florida Orange Juice, so activist Bob Kunst called a press conference to announce a boycott on orange juice from Florida. Today you'd say the campaign went viral, with people around the nation hearing the call.

In Florida, Bryant did ultimately win the ballot initiative, but by 1979 she was fired as the spokesperson for Florida Orange Juice. A win and a loss for her, but that win ultimately faded. She never regained the support and stature she once had. Anita Bryant, in the eyes of history, looks similar to George Wallace, standing in the doorway to uphold segregation—or in her case, discrimination.

If I had my way, I'd have taken all the money that went into the battle against Chick-fil-A and given it to Democratic National Committee treasurer Andy Tobias, the master of all political LGBT fundraising for the Democratic Party and its candidates, through the LGBT Leadership Council. Andy understands LGBT oppression well. He's best known for his financial writing, but early in his career he also published a book in 1973 about growing up and coming to terms with himself. Using a pseudonym, the book was titled *The Best Little Boy in the World*. It's my favorite book of a boy coming of age. He also showed me how to turn my involvement in the political system into clout to gain equality.

My first foray into congressional funds, also known as *earmarks*, came in 1993. The LGBT Community Center at that time did not have a permanent location. Their slogan was "A Community Center without Walls." Fundraising was volatile, the board of directors mostly transitory, and the vision simply lacking. Tony Green, chief of staff to my old city council friend Congressman Thomas Foglietta, met with me for lunch to see what he and the congressman could do for our community. Formerly married to a woman, Tony was now openly gay. I told him about the center's predicament and he was receptive to earmarking funds. With funding, we'd be able to get a permanent location. He sent me the paperwork and we began the process. Along the way, he mentioned that "LGBT" could not appear anywhere in the paperwork, since that would alert the Republicans, who would vote it down. Our solution was to describe the building as "a place for the community most impacted by AIDS." That $300,000 earmark, the largest funding the organization has ever received, made it possible for what is now the William Way LGBT Community Center to purchase its building at 1315 Spruce Street.

Thanks to my early work with media and our efforts to pass a city nondiscrimination bill, I knew most of the city officials well. We asked for their support and also got valuable contact information to build my Rolodex. At my urging, Governor Shapp created the Governor's Council for Sexual Minorities, which further cemented my relationships with state leaders. Invitations to my house parties became coveted, especially by city officials and those hoping to break into politics. Where else could you see a Jewish governor singing Christmas carols with the Gay Men's Chorus? Along with regional bank presidents, union heads, a Socialist, and a drag queen all mingling with one another.

In the midst of all of this, District Attorney Ed Rendell, who was thinking about running for mayor, suggested that I form a political action committee (PAC). Almost as quickly as the ink was drying on our PAC filing, there was a fight in the city council regarding a gay pride resolution. It was a perfect reason to launch the Pride of Philadelphia Election Committee. Within weeks a cocktail party was held with leaders of the community, and Ed gave a speech about the importance of raising money in a campaign and the clout that the community could gain. There was also a hint that Ed might run for office again and could use a supportive PAC behind him.

That first fundraiser was memorable, to say the least. Pride of Philadelphia Election Committee at that time saw itself as a local version of the national Human Rights Campaign, and set as its first goal to gain passage of the pride resolution the following June in the city council. But in order to do that, we needed funds. Enter Barney Frank.

Barney Frank was the new gay hero to many of us, an openly gay man in Congress representing both his district and the greater LGBT community. Using the gifts of wit, intelligence, knowledge of history, and his famous Massachusetts drawl, Barney commands attention when he speaks. In 1989, when I first met him, you could say "Barney Frank" was synonymous with "pride." A PAC board member who was involved with one of Philadelphia's namesake organizations, the Franklin Institute, arranged for us to use space in the institute for our kickoff fundraiser. The plan called for cocktails in the observatory, then down to the planetarium for speeches and a private show. We had the venue, but we still needed a headliner. Congressman Tom Foglietta wrote a letter to Barney in July of 1989 asking him if he'd assist an old friend in starting a local gay and lesbian PAC. Tom's letter was accompanied by another letter from me telling Barney about my work.

Barney soon called and told me that he had followed my escapades over the years and would be glad to help. I then called Congressman Bill Gray and Mayor Goode to ask them to serve as honorary hosts. Both accepted.

Next came the arrangements of caterers, printers, mailing lists, advertising, and ticket sales. The date for the event was set as September 15, and by the fourth week in August ticket sales far exceeded our expectations. Then, with less than two weeks to go, Barney was figuratively caught with his pants down. The scandal involved a callboy who was living with him and the rumors that the guy was running a service out of Barney's house. Barney told the nation that he knew about his roommate's background, but was trying to help him change his life.

As with all Washington scandals, it dragged on and on, and the roommate even started to do talk shows and tell about his sexual antics with Barney, true or not. As the scandal broke I tried to talk with Barney about the September 15 fundraiser. He did not respond personally, but several staff members kept telling me that they didn't know his plans. Some of my political friends offered to pinch hit, but none had the same level of name recognition. Others suggested that I drop Barney, but I felt that was a bad signal to send out with our first major fundraiser, not to mention downright disloyal. To me the issue was clear. Loyalty mattered, along with the notion that all are innocent until proven guilty. What's more, Barney was still a national treasure; the public was just coming to terms with the fact that he was human, like the rest of us.

At the same time, board members were calling me every day to ask about Barney and the fundraiser. We continued to run advertisements, but Barney had walled himself in, and nobody was getting any answers. Finally, I wrote to him and explained that the test of a friend's loyalty is when you are down, and in this instance we still wanted him since he was a hero, and heroes are heroes, even after falling from their pedestals. A week before the event, I returned home from a meeting to discover a message on my answering machine: "Ah, hello, Mark, this is Barney Frank, sorry that I've kept you in the dark this long. It's not fair and I'm sorry. I promised you I'd be at your function, and I'll keep that promise. Call my office tomorrow to make the arrangements."

This, it turned out, was the easy part. His staff was concerned about media. The press was now camped outside both his office and home. They followed him everywhere, and he was not commenting to them on the scandal. It was a typical DC feeding frenzy. Someone suggested that our gala premier of a new PAC should be staged without press. Then Barney's staff told us it would be a mandatory condition for his participation. I had to find a way to get this man, embroiled in the nation's number one sex scandal, into the city to attend a cocktail party, give a speech in a public place, and leave, all without the media catching on.

I faced the situation like it was a Gay Raiders zap. We stopped the sale of tickets. Only friends of board members could buy tickets. Security was set up at every entrance of the Franklin Institute. Drivers were informed that no reporters were to come near Barney no matter what. And no press releases were allowed. Meanwhile, a strange thing occurred: since most politicians run for the hills, away from their scandal-ridden colleagues, I was surprised to find that both Congressman Tom Foglietta and Ed Rendell called to offer support, and while neither had planned to attend, they both now felt compelled to in order to support Barney and the cause.

September 15, 1989 was a damp, drizzly, and windswept day. It matched my spirits. Members of my board were telling me that Barney would cancel at the last minute. After all, he had not made a public appearance since the scandal began other than a few attempts at talking with the press. It was decided that I'd be the one to pick him up and welcome him to the city. With my friend Bill Davol, who I thought would have a calming effect on Barney, we set off in the rainy night.

Barney arrived at the train station alone with one bag. I introduced myself and we shook hands, then made a quick exit before he was noticed. Bill was close by in the car. En route to the institute, I expressed my gratitude to Barney for coming, considering the toll that other matters might be taking on him at this juncture. He was mostly quiet, keeping his head bowed. Finally, worried about his state of mind, I said, "I recently wrote you about heroes and the way they sometimes slip. To me a hero is someone who fights for a cause no matter what might fall around them. The heroism is the cause, not their private life. To me you are still a hero." Barney lowered his head some more and began crying. We said little else for the rest of the ride, but I was worried. At the reception, the first thing I discovered was that we had succeeded in keeping the mainstream press unaware of the event. Since we sent out no press releases or advisories, the only way for reporters to know was to read the gay press. Imagine the firestorm that would have greeted us if they read the gay press regularly. For the first time in my life, I was thrilled that they didn't.

At the venue, some members of the board took Barney around the room and introduced him to the attendees. Several local politicians arrived to assist and lend support. It became apparent almost immediately that Barney was mentally not with us. We quickly arranged for a friend in attendance, a psychologist, to usher Barney from person to person, but he told us that he wanted to mingle on his own. Then he sort of ambled around the room, just nodding his head in acknowledgment whenever someone tried to talk with him. At one point he came up to me as I was going over the rest of the schedule with the board, and asked in a low voice, "Where's the bathroom?" I suggested that we'd have someone show him, but he declined and asked us to point the way.

We watched as he slowly made his way to the bathroom. Once the door had closed behind him, we looked at each other in total fear. We honestly believed that he was going to do some harm to himself. As we waited, I found myself thinking of how I would respond to reporters' questions about the dead congressman in the bathroom. Eventually, we all agreed to send someone inside. I asked Jeff Moran and his partner Richard Bond if they would make sure the congressman was okay. As they reluctantly approached, the door opened and Barney came sailing out. My sigh of relief could be heard all the way in Washington.

Congressman Tom Foglietta showed up, and we moved to the planetarium where the program was to begin. After everyone was seated I took to the podium and thanked the attendees for their support. The first speaker was Ed Rendell, followed by Tom who would introduce his colleague Barney. Tom spoke stronger and more eloquently then I'd ever heard him before. He reaffirmed his support of Barney and said he looked forward to working on a progressive agenda with him for many years to come. He then concluded, "Friends, let me introduce a fine gentlemen and a great congressman, my good friend Barney Frank!" The assembled rose to their feet en masse, and I could see the tears in Barney's eyes. Like magic he woke up from what seemed like a walking sleep, and was full of energy. As he spoke he became stronger, and with each comical story he slowly became the Barney the nation had grown to love and appreciate.

After the speech, we had to get him to the airport to make his flight to Boston, and I hugged and thanked him, offering to help in any way I could. The next time I saw Barney was in the spring of 1994 when he and Congressman Gerry Studds came to my home for another fundraiser, this time for Tom Foglietta. My fondest memory, though, came many years later at a different event at my home. He and Congressman Bob Brady were both there, and Bob talked about how close he and Barney had gotten in Washington. Barney was so comfortable and upbeat that he slow danced with Bob, the same blue-collar guy from the tough neighborhood, the sergeant at arms who had the job of carrying me out of the city council thirty-five years earlier.

That first fundraiser at the Franklin Institute was merely an appetizer for the Pride of Philadelphia Election Committee. Over the next couple of years, the committee continually brought political surprises. One development in particular cemented the strength of the LGBT community; it was a perfect storm that I could exploit, and that storm was Fran Rafferty.

Rafferty was a city councilman with strong religious beliefs. He was a blue-collar Irish Catholic who had imaginative ideas about God and AIDS. He had a temper, which once resulted in a brawl with another councilman on the floor of the city council. When a gay rights issue came up in the council, he'd yell slurs like, "Fairies!" Beyond his antigay views, his other behaviors were, shall we say, not representative of the pride Philadelphians took in their city.

Most people thought of Rafferty as the most homophobic

elected official in the city. It all came to a head when we introduced a resolution recognizing Gay Pride Month. He suggested
that it be called AIDS Pride Month. This led to a series of mis-
haps and ended with a televised debate on a KYW-TV talk show
hosted by Jerry Penacoli, who went on to Hollywood to report
for the entertainment show *Extra*. My plan for the debate was
simply to be as quiet as possible (for once in my life) and let him
talk as much as he wanted. Just allow him to flaunt his hate and
ignorance on the subject, let him be the bully he was. Of course,
I'd encourage him along whenever I could.

Just before we went on the air and were having makeup applied, I looked over to him and saw what appeared to be malice
in his eyes. I smiled and said, "Franny, you look so good in all
that makeup."

At every commercial break, my mind found another line
that just kept him roiling. During one commercial he actually
suggested he might punch me. It was difficult to hold tight, but
people viewing saw a bully in action. All we had to do was let
it sink in. We were about to do something that had never been
done in American politics: try to defeat a candidate in a citywide race simply for being a homophobe.

It was 1991 when we announced our campaign against Rafferty's reelection. The political elite of Philly thought the idea
ridiculous. To be truthful, so did I. After all, he was endorsed
by the Democratic City Committee and running in a city controlled by an entrenched Democratic machine. He had also
been the top vote-getter in the previous election. In our own
style we were attempting to take him from number one to number six, since the top five vote-getters would be elected. People
thought we could lower him to two or three, but certainly not
cause him to lose office.

The campaign organization was formed with two goals in

mind. The first was to help Ed Rendell become mayor and the second was to defeat Fran Rafferty. Ed was almost a sure bet to win, but defeating Rafferty didn't seem realistic—until we realized that we could use Ed's campaign to work the ward leaders. We would need to find an acceptable candidate to replace Rafferty who the public could embrace and we needed to make the community and the city believe this was all possible. Television was what I knew, so we decided to produce a commercial. We had little money and a commercial campaign would wipe out most of our funds. This, we realized, would be a smoke-and-mirrors campaign. But it was worth a try. No pain, no gain.

Richard Bond, a public relations executive on our board, had a friend who sold airtime on KYW-TV. Together, we began to research hot-button issues and put together a storyboard. In the end, the commercial would be a thirty-second spot. It was filmed secretly at NFL Films studios in Cherry Hill, New Jersey, at a deep discount. Yes, NFL Films must be thanked for helping produce the first-ever citywide LGBT political campaign television commercial in the nation. We sent Peter Lien out to photograph Rafferty with the instructions to get as many shots as possible with him looking mean. Mission accomplished. From my days at a radio station called Talk 900, we got Bill Davol to agree to do the voiceover. The spot was a collage of Rafferty photos; in each one he appeared progressively meaner. With the voiceover, we used his quotes and his votes to lay out the issues.

"You may have thought it was funny when Fran Rafferty insulted lesbians and gays. But was it funny when he had to apologize to Philadelphia for saying he would salute the Statue of Liberty by getting drunk? Or when he voted against more money for our children's education? Or when he made the city council a laughingstock by having not one but two fistfights there? The sad thing is, Fran Rafferty could be elected again to the city council. If you're serious

about Philadelphia, don't waste $65,000 a year . . . Say no to Fran Rafferty."

I believe the commercial cost us under a thousand dollars to produce. We then tried to place it. There, we ran into a surprise: most of the stations were afraid to sell us time. No one had ever run an ad against a sitting city council candidate without being a candidate themselves.

We called a press conference and announced that only two TV stations would sell us time for the commercial. This was outrageous. We thanked the two stations, KYW and WPHL, and told the assembled press, which included the stations that wouldn't sell us time, that the commercial would begin running the following morning on the news shows. That night the six p.m. and eleven p.m. news on most stations led with the press conference, with the commercial as part of the story. We ended up getting the commercial on TV free of charge and it ran more times on the news than the airtime we'd actually purchased.

But the true magic of that moment was that we were the first LGBT group to ever fight a standing councilman with a TV campaign. We made bumper stickers with the *Say No to Rafferty* logo next to a snarling Rafferty. We handed them out and they began to appear all over the city. People like activist Mike Marsico and members of ACT UP kept coming back for more stickers for their army of friends and colleagues. People saw them and recalled the commercial, and it appeared as if we had a citywide campaign going.

This led to the most powerful member of the Pennsylvania Senate calling and asking to have lunch with me. Enter Vince Fumo, not only a state senator, but also a ward leader, who was trying to help get his friend Jim Kenney elected to the council. Vince felt that if our campaign took votes from Rafferty, it would help Kenney win. The idea was to take Rafferty off the list of endorsed five and replace him with Kenney, and to do it ward by ward. Finally we had found our candidate! Once agreed, Vince began to call ward leaders and I'd take them to lunch at The Palm.

Ed Rendell was at the top of the ticket, and thus far I had not asked him to do anything for us in this election. But now things were moving fast. So fast that Rafferty began to believe he needed to get a stronger campaign together. I was so focused on our own campaign I didn't have time to pay attention to Rafferty's response. It seemed, like other city council candidates, Rafferty expected that the City Committee and Rendell would carry him on their ticket. I don't think he ever expected any ward leaders to request that his name be removed.

I took ward leaders to lunch almost every day, which became one of the largest expenses of our campaign, since there were sixty-nine of them. I became such a regular that my picture now graces the wall of The Palm. We printed new bumper stickers and announced new commercials that didn't exist. There was not a week without some announcement. A month before the election, ward leaders were now publicly announcing that Rafferty was off their ticket.

We now went shopping for an election-night hotel ballroom. We secured the ballroom next to that of the Ed Rendell campaign in the Warwick Hotel. That night saw an early win for Ed. He, his wife Midge, and his son Jesse came over to our ballroom as soon as he declared victory. Our night was just beginning, and to the surprise of everyone our little smoke-and-mirrors campaign had been widely embraced. The city council election was still close, too close to call. We already knew at that hour that Rafferty was no longer at the top, but had we toppled him? We wouldn't know until the following day.

Ed and Midge gave me hugs as they prepared to leave, and I

witnessed a beautiful family moment in politics: the two of them bent down to their little son Jesse to explain that, with his dad becoming mayor, life would now change, but the two of them would always be there for him.

The following morning, I was awakened by the phone ringing. It was Senator Fumo, who greeted me with an incredible laugh: "Congratulations!" He went on to say a lot more, but all I heard was that one word. When I finally roused and regained some ability to understand the situation, Vince made me realize the importance of what we had done, but also some of the finer points of the game of politics. "Mark, you won, but Fran has a family to feed. We have to give him something. How about if we put him on a commission?" This was a level of politics I had no knowledge of, and all I could say to the man who had first reached out to help was, "If that's what you feel is correct."

In hindsight, I realize Vince was explaining to me that we had just knocked off a giant, and in victory we should offer an olive branch. After all, the giant could rise again, if not placated. The fact that Vince even asked me was a sign that he respected the campaign we had launched, and understood that this made the LGBT vote a powerhouse. In the subsequent election, we continued to make a pro-gay difference in local politics, leading the president of the city council, John Street, who at that time was considered a homophobe, to spend $400,000 to protect his own seat.

As Ed began building his mayoral team, he appointed members of our board to his administration. Some elected officials suggested to me that Ed should offer me a position of deputy mayor. This went to my head, and I let it be known to media friends that out of respect, I *should* be asked. Word got around to Ed's campaign manager, David L. Cohen, who called and made the offer, but also told me that I wouldn't be happy, since taking that position meant that I was no longer independent. I'd be part of the administration and would have to voice their positions. David was right, and I quickly declined the offer.

The first week as mayor, Ed called me to his office. He was leaning back in his chair with his feet up on the desk.

"What commission or board do you want?"

"How about the airport board?"

Ed was surprised, and suggested several boards and commissions that offered compensation, and I responded, "The airport board."

He looked at me sternly. "Why? It doesn't pay anything."

My answer: "Mr. Mayor, I want to be Philadelphia's first official flying fairy."

Ed still likes to tell that story.

James Carville, one of the nation's most renowned political consultants, showed me his tremendous charms during our first conversation. Jim is often credited for the Clinton White House victory, and the man knows how to win debates. He is a lover of the political deal and I got a taste of that early in his career. Robert Casey Sr., the father of future US Senator Bob Casey Jr., was running for Pennsylvania governor in 1978, and Carville was his manager, willing to do whatever it took so that this would not be Casey's fourth failure in getting to the governor's mansion. It was during this campaign that Carville uttered his famous description of Pennsylvania. He said in his Louisiana drawl, "On one side of the state you have Pittsburgh, on the other Philadelphia, and in the middle is Alabama." Some have since remarked that his description is an insult to Alabama.

The polls were running pretty even and Casey needed one more thing to go his way to pull off a victory. The old Democratic coalition was drawing together to support him, but the gay community was suspicious of Casey and his devotion to the church. He had not met with gay leaders or made his position on gay rights known. What's more, my newspaper was not offered an opportunity to interview Casey and find out what he stood for and how he would apply that to the gay community.

It was in this atmosphere that I picked up my phone one day and was greeted by: "Mark, what the hell do I have to do to get you to support Bob? This is Jim Carville." Taken aback, I said hello and asked why he was the one calling. He explained that since Bill Bateoff, a campaign fundraiser and acquaintance of mine, had been unable to make a deal and get me on board, he thought he'd give me a talking-to.

I replied that it was very clear what was required for my support. Unlike others, there was no need of patronage, state funding of any particular organization, or bond issues to any law firms I was associated with. All I needed was for Casey to support the state's gay rights legislation when introduced in the legislature, and to recreate the Pennsylvania Council for Sexual Minorities that Governor Shapp had started and which had died under Shapp's successor.

"That's all?" Jim uttered.

I immediately said, "And one more item: an interview in my newspaper, so he can give his remarks on these issues."

"Done deal," Jim responded.

After the interview was published, Jim called to thank me for handling Bob in a polite and professional manner. At that point I asked what I should do when Bob doesn't keep his promises. After telling me that should not be a concern, since Bob always keeps his word, Jim said, "You have Bill [Bateoff] talk to Bob, and if he can't take care of it, you call me and I'll set him straight."

Governor Robert Casey broke every promise, and I'm still waiting for Mr. Carville's return call.

It was around this time that I got a call from an up-and-coming union leader by the name of John Dougherty from the International Brotherhood of Electrical Workers. We set up a meeting and he asked what he could do to help the LGBT community. Never one to shy away from the big ask, I explained that we had just purchased a building to be used as our community center and it needed some electrical work. Being a generous guy, John replied, "Not a problem, consider it done." He sent over a few apprentices to take a look and unfortunately, the building needed a completely new electrical system, which would require more then a few apprentices. To his credit, John never told me what the price tag on that job would have been. Certainly a price tag the center could not have paid.

Later I'd discover that John was doing this in part as a way of showing his daughter his support of the LGBT community since she had recently come out to him. We've gone on to engage in many battles together, sometimes even opposed to one another, but we remain friends and enjoy a special bond.

Councilman Jim Kenney, our replacement for Fran Rafferty, showed gratitude from the beginning. Soon after being sworn in, he arranged a meeting with Council President John Street and me. Basically, we were quickly shown the door. Leaving the office, Jim laughed and said, "Well, that went well."

We thought that Street, who had been opposed to domestic partnership legislation for religious reasons, might see the writing on the wall. Not a chance. Thus began the fight for domestic partnership and another national first when we connected tax savings to LGBT relationships. Yes, we did beat Vermont to become the first government to recognize that domestic partners mean taxation as well.

By Ed's second term he had created a peaceful, working relationship with Council President Street, who was still opposed to domestic partners legislation. Ed was somewhat boxed in, since Street controlled the council with an iron fist. Without the council, Ed wouldn't have a city budget. Knowing this and having to straddle us and Street, he publicly said that if passed by the council, he'd sign domestic partnership into law (though I believe he expected Street would never allow it to pass).

Street was all about power. He understood how power could be a force for good, and he believed his community hadn't gotten the benefits it deserved. We were like-minded in that respect. Enter my partners in this effort. From our PAC's board, Andy Chirls, who would later become the first openly gay chancellor of the Philadelphia Bar Association, and Andrew Park, executive director of the Center for Lesbian and Gay Civil Rights, both stepped up. As with the Rafferty campaign, we knew we had to define our characters. This meant that we had to paint Street as the homophobe who was blocking the door of equality.

Andy Chirls's job was to stay close to Street's coalition members who we knew would be uncomfortable with being labeled homophobic. That was the behind-the-scenes campaign. In front of the camera, Andrew Park commissioned surveys, brought out people who had lost their homes due to unfair tax laws, and showed people in hospitals unable to see their partners on their deathbed, all with the tag line: *John Street Did This*.

Street felt the heat.

He called a special evening session of the city council. It was rumored that he actually intended to force a vote on the legislation while he still had some control. What he didn't know then was that one of his strongest supporters on the council, Republican Thacher Longstreth, was wavering. This was a vote I really hadn't counted on even though he was someone with whom I had developed a friendship. Thacher, his girlfriend Melanie (who he lived with, and who was employed by the council), and I would sometimes have dinner together. Hearing the life story of one of Philadelphia's most blue-blooded and beloved characters was a joy, and as word got around about our friendship, it bemused the city. The conservative, Republican, blue-blooded socialite being friends with the out, loud, and in-your-face gay activist.

So on that fateful night, Street needed Thacher there, but he didn't show. Street went as far as asking the police to find Thacher, requesting his presence in the council chambers. He didn't give up until almost midnight. Which of course irritated the other council members. Later, when I asked Melanie where they were, she said delightedly, "I took him to the circus so John couldn't find us."

The first call to break Street's coalition was from a councilman whom I expected would feel the guiltiest, Michael Nutter, himself a future mayor and president of the US Conference of Mayors. Nutter asked if we would allow him to reintroduce the legislation that Jim Kenney and Councilman Frank DiCicco had previously submitted. Kenney and DiCicco were gracious and stepped in as cosponsors. The votes were now moving in our direction. It became a race, and for the first time Street knew he was in trouble. His designs on power were in jeopardy.

Andrew Park and his team of lawyers had written companion bills to create a domestic partners registry and give tax benefits similar to those offered to heterosexual married couples. As we came closer to a vote, only Street, the Catholic Church, and evangelicals publicly opposed the bill.

On the morning of the vote, I was shuffling from one council office to another. It was clear how close this vote would be. Street would sometimes be coming out of a councilmember's office just as I was going in. Our union friends had packed the galleries and it was said that a certain councilman was told that if his vote was needed, he would give it to us. I must admit that I didn't believe what I heard, until I entered the council and saw two muscled giants having a chat with that councilman.

Thacher was playing it cool, telling both Street and me that he'd make a final decision when he actually voted. Street had to face the fact that he might actually lose a vote in the council he controlled. As council president, he hadn't yet lost one vote. So at the very last minute, he proposed his own domestic partners legislation. Of course it was a sham.

Andrew Park recently shared with me his memory of the vote on the John Street decoy bill, just before the vote on the real domestic partners bill: "I was standing next to you on the railing of the city council behind all the desks. You were on your cell phone with Vince Fumo. You handed the phone to Janie Blackwell who was going to vote in favor of Street's bill. I don't know what Vince said to her, but it changed her vote. I think he offered her a campaign contribution. She was the deciding factor."

By the end of the day we had passed real domestic partnership legislation with a surprise vote from Thacher Longstreth.

Street, to his credit, quickly began to reach out to me. It might be relevant that he was about to run for mayor. I gave him an education on the subject of domestic partners and we soon became friends. I wouldn't be endorsing him for mayor, since he was still painted as a homophobe, but he and I knew that this didn't mean we couldn't start a dialogue.

In time Street began to question his own position on the matter, and this led to us having long discussions. As mayor, he actually did more for the gay community than Ed Rendell. He fought all the way to the state supreme court to protect Philly's domestic partners law, the one he originally fought against. And he won. He also launched a war on discrimination against gay people in the Boy Scouts and he both funded LGBT organizations and hired LGBT staffers.

The highlight for me was when he personally performed the domestic partners ceremony for his gay staffer Micah Mahjoubian and his partner Ryan Bunch. In a front row seat in an ornate City Hall room, I watched as Mayor John Street talked about marriage and how it should be afforded to all. This was the end result of legislation that he had opposed five years earlier and a testament to the power of education. To conclude the ceremony, Street brought out a broom. He told a story about slaves who were forbidden to marry without the permission of their owner. "They'd call the ceremony 'jumping the broom.' Since it is outlawed for LGBT to marry in our country, like it was for slaves, it is appropriate for you, Micah and Ryan, to jump the broom." When he laid it down before them, there was not a dry eye in the room.

When people ask me about Street, my reply is that we're friends and that he's really funny and often surprising. After winning reelection as mayor, he invited me to lunch one day. I thought we'd meet at the Capital Grille or maybe The Palm. But he had another idea: we'd dine in his office. When I got there, a table had been set up in a little back chamber where Ed used to keep a soda machine. It had white linen on it with china, crystals, and even lit candles. A server was at the ready. It was elegant, and I do not know if I've ever felt more out of place or uncomfortable. Yet he did it for two reasons: first, to show thanks and appreciation for our unlikely friendship, and second, to prove a point.

During Street's inauguration, I had attempted to stop him from limiting the power of the new city council president, Anna Verna. In a strange twist of circumstance, Verna had a delightful and upbeat assistant named Pat Rafferty who I became friendly with, and it turned out her husband was Fran Rafferty. Street had known the power of that city council presidency and didn't want it to get in his way. My attempt at blocking this power grab had failed.

Street said over lunch, "Mark, without a soldier who is willing to fight, you can't win. Anna will never fight."

I told him he was correct, then said, "We're now even."

My coalition had beaten him on domestic partnership legislation and now he had won the battle for city council supremacy. We both had a good laugh to accompany our lunch.

In 2011, the Philadelphia city council passed the most far-reaching LGBT legislation in the nation. It was a well-needed update of an old piece of legislation. Sponsored by our friend and Rafferty replacement, Councilman Jim Kenney, the legislation now included trans issues; it even gave tax credits to corporations that offered trans benefits.

On August 28, 2008, my partner Jason and I, along with our friend Nia Meeks, were sitting in Invesco Field listening to will.i.am and waiting for Senator Barack Obama to make his speech accepting the Democratic nomination for president when my cell phone rang. I tried to answer, but due to security measures in the stadium it was hard to keep a signal. It took several callbacks for me to get the message. Just before accepting the nomination, the Obama people got a tip that the Republican nominee, Senator John McCain, was about to announce his VP choice in order to mute the publicity Obama would receive from his acceptance speech. One of the prospective candidates was former Pennsylvania governor and secretary of Homeland Security, Tom Ridge. If that happened, the Democrats wanted me to be prepared to speak on the subject.

Political pundits and columnists were falling all over themselves trying to guess who McCain would pick and when. Several weeks earlier I'd made a few guesses and offered a detailed analysis on two leading candidates in my weekly column. At the top on my list was Ridge, who as governor was a zero on LGBT rights. Just before becoming governor, I had met with him in Washington. He was serving out his final days as a congressman. In that meeting, he made it clear to me that he was not a friend to the LGBT community. My question to him at the time was simple—was it political or personal? His answer was both. I thanked him: "Congressman, you've saved me a lot of time."

That night, McCain didn't pick Ridge. It wasn't until the next day that we heard his decision. In hindsight, Ridge might have been a better choice than Sarah Palin. I'm not sure how the Obama team would have used me, but it's a testament to how well structured, organized, and disciplined the Obama campaign was in 2008. They had contingency plans for any issue. Ridge, to his credit, went on to support marriage equality in a brief before the US Supreme Court, and of course Barack Obama was elected president.

Chapter 10
Adventures with a Publisher

We drove up to the gate at Fort Indiantown Gap, Pennsylvania, and noticed that it was well guarded. It was one of the detention centers where the administration of President Jimmy Carter housed Cuban immigrants from the 1980 Mariel boatlift, and they were keeping it a secret. Actually, the center was holding prisoners and captives of various types.

I was in the driver's seat. J.R. Guthrie, our reporter, sat shotgun, with photographer Harry Eberlin in the backseat with an interpreter we'd hired for the day. We were all nervous as we pulled up to a guard.

"Reason for requesting entrance," he said, stone-faced.

Looking him straight in the eye I replied, "I'm Father Segal, sent by Metropolitan Community Church to talk with the refugees." He stared at me skeptically, so I added with equal parts seriousness and calm, "It's my missionary work. We should be on your list of clergy." I tugged at the clerical collar around my neck and cleared my throat. We were granted entrance.

Father Segal and *Philadelphia Gay News* became the first media to get inside one of America's military detention centers in the wake of that 1980 Mariel boatlift. The secret that President Carter had not wanted made public was something we in the LGBT community were well aware of. A great number of gay Cubans—considered "undesirable" by Fidel Castro—were put on those boats to Florida in an attempt to rid the island of homosexuals. Castro thought he'd play a joke on the US, since it was our policy to accept all Cuban refugees.

By June the rumor was spreading in the LGBT community. The State Department ran a quiet campaign to find foster homes for the gays through the Metropolitan Community Church and other church groups. Our military and State Department were not used to dealing with gay men, from Cuba or anywhere else. I smelled a story. J.R. and Harry agreed to come, which surprised me, and I happily put on a black jacket and shirt to look like a priest.

Once we'd gotten inside, instead of checking in, we headed straight to where our source said the gay Cubans would be held. We found two full barracks of gay men, well kept and wearing a hodgepodge of clothing. Our interpreter explained to them that we were from a gay newspaper in Philadelphia, and we began handing out copies of the paper. Few spoke English, and those who did spoke poorly at best, but we got permission to interview and photograph them. I kept watch at the door as J.R. and the interpreter asked questions to as many of them as possible. They talked of their lives back in Cuba; of how the police often raided their homes, imprisoned them, and attacked them with guard dogs. Even when showing us the scars from various abuses and atrocities, they radiated joy at being in the US even if they were in a detention center. Those who'd finished interviewing with us went to another barracks to tell a second group about us. Soon there was almost a party atmosphere as these guys paraded and danced before us with their stories.

The carnival soon drew attention and we suddenly found ourselves surrounded by soldiers. One of the higher-ranking men walked in and asked what we were doing there. By that time J.R. and Harry had hidden the recorder and camera.

"Sir," I said, "I'm just doing my missionary work for Metropolitan Community Church and I'm sorry if we have caused a ruckus. It seems we're giving them too much hope." I extended my hand.

"Father Segal, it's a pleasure to meet you." He shook my hand. "I think you've done enough for today."

The soldiers showed us back to our car and we drove off the base. Going through that gate was a relief. We were quiet for a few miles, and then we all broke into laughter. Awaiting us when we got back was a message from the general in charge of Fort Indiantown Gap, who had finally discovered our true identities and intentions. When we returned his call, the general demanded the recording and pictures we took. Apparently we were in deep trouble.

Thoughts of Watergate kept dancing in my mind, but I wasn't about to give in so easily. "General," I said, "I'm a publisher, and as far as I'm concerned we have a great story. You gave us entrance, we left when you requested. I see no reason not to publish. It's our First Amendment right."

He offered a few choice words, more loudly and a tad more threatening, before hanging up with a flair. We published the story on the cover of our August 8, 1980 edition, under the headline, "Meet the Gay Cubans."

Nine years later I spent a week in Cuba, traveling there without any prior contacts or government approvals. I did not want propaganda from either side; all I wanted was to report on the actual state of the gay community there.

I had learned from friends who'd visited the country that there was an ice-cream stand in the center of Havana where gay people went to meet up. After walking around for an hour, trying, albeit poorly, to cruise some of the guys, one of them came up to me and started speaking in Spanish. Seeing my confusion, he brought a friend over who spoke English. The two of them wound up being my tour guides for the week. I didn't tell them I was a reporter, not at first, since I didn't want to scare them. After a few days I told them the truth, and realized I should have done so from the beginning. They opened their lives to me, just as the men in the barracks had.

On my final night, they took me to a private party on the roof of a four-story walk-up in downtown Havana. We paid a dollar to enter, which I quickly realized guaranteed us all the bathtub rum we could drink. I learned that these parties happened at the same hour several times a week. It was an incredible sea of diversity, both men and women, and like most Cubans they were fairly poor. A few hours into the party, there was a commotion and people began to scream; some bolted for the exits. I made my way down to the ground floor with my friends, and as we left, I saw policemen pull up and begin to storm the building. After the raid, I watched from a distance as those who didn't flee the party were carried out and carted away. We returned to my hotel, where I decided to treat my guardians to a good meal.

Fidel Castro later publicly apologized for his government's discrimination against the LGBT community and treatment of people with HIV/AIDS. His brother Raul is a supporter of LGBT rights, and his niece Mariela has become an international voice on behalf of the cause.

In the eighties, I tried my hand as a radio talk show host on a small AM station in Philadelphia. WDVT (Delaware Valley Talk) is what is known as a daylighter, which simply meant that according to Federal Communications Commission rules, the station could only operate during daylight hours. The limited hours, plus competing against the other talk radio stations in the city, meant that the station had to do something revolutionary to garner an audience. Hence, *GayTalk*—the premier commercial gay and two-way talk radio show with your host, Mark Segal.

GayTalk launched on November 1, 1986. Stu Bykofsky, writing in the *Philadelphia Daily News*, described the show as "sort of a cross between Ralph Nader and Ethel Merman . . . *GayTalk* will twit heterosexuals, but not bash them." My first guest ever was Mayor W. Wilson Goode, who pleased me to no end when he said, "I didn't know what kind of show this was when I agreed to come." This is the same mayor who just four months later, during a heated reelection bid, appeared in front of a packed crowd at the annual *Philadelphia Gay News* Lambda Awards ceremony. In the Grand Ballroom of the Warwick Hotel, Philadelphia's first African American mayor stepped onto the stage to great applause. Wanting the gay audience to appreciate his commitment, he said with excitement, "I'm glad to be here, I've come three times." The audience roared. He meant he had attended the award ceremony three previous times.

Every Saturday afternoon for two hours, *GayTalk* held court. My format was to interview guests for the first hour and host a community roundtable for the second. Our guest list was surprisingly varied considering the subject matter and the station's small size. We had visits from politicians, TV personalities, and community leaders. On one particular Saturday we decided to discuss the pope. The Vatican had issued a statement on homosexuality written by one Cardinal Ratzinger, later to become Pope Benedict XVI. The statement declared that homosexuality was intrinsically evil. To which Stanley Ward, managing editor of *Philadelphia Gay News*, opined: "The pope is just a pimp for those abusive priests." Being a special-interest show, on a small station in the middle of Saturday afternoon, you might imagine (and you'd be right) that we didn't receive many calls. Our lines were always open and anyone could get through to us and on the air at almost any time. Once Stanley made that statement, however, the phone lines lit up like the proverbial Hanukkah bush.

Monday morning I heard from the station. While they did not agree with the statements on my show, they felt that speakers had the right to express their views, but in the future I should make it clear that those views were that of the individual, not the station. Several days later the station received a letter from the Anti-Defamation League of B'nai B'rith, supporting the church and asking for an apology on my show.

After I had fully digested the crux of their letter, I wrote back expressing my surprise at their support for an organization that not only has a historical record of oppression against the LGBT community but also the Jewish community. Then I cited the material on sexual abuse of children by priests. In 1986, most were unaware of this rampant abuse; the issue hadn't yet made it to the mass media. After receiving my reply, B'nai B'rith made no more requests for an apology.

A friend by the name of Wade Alexander began to gather clippings on issues that he thought would make good conversation for my show. I soon noticed that in every packet of clippings there were a number of articles on the papacy, so many that I figured there must be an eleventh commandment just for journalists: *Thou shalt not kill a story about His Holiness.* Considering the large audience response to our first foray, we soon had a regular feature—the weekly Pope Report.

We constantly corrected the misinformation sent out by the church, like comparing homosexuality to pedophilia, or the attempts to hide various issues that were, at that time, very prob-

lematic within their organization. Week after week, we covered
the issue of abusive priests, and we made sure that any attempts
by the church to denigrate the LGBT community were answered with facts.

As much fun as this was, it was bound to end sooner or later.
After two years of being on the air, the station, always on the
brink, succumbed to a buyout offer from a company that owned
religious tape stations. These were radio stations that played religious shows on tape from various fundamentalists who paid
the company for air time, then would plead with their listeners
to send in a prayer offering to keep them on the air.

My friends Bill Davol and Phyllis Furst were running the day-to-day
operations and coordination with on-air personalities. When I'd
started at Talk 900 I was green to radio. Bill and Phyllis had
taken me under their wings and helped me make my show more
professional. They loved my energy and applauded the freshness
that the show brought to the station. So for my last show they
went all out.

My guest was a conservative TV talk show star named Mor-
ton Downey Jr., who paved the way for people like Bill O'Reilly
and Glenn Beck. I relished the chance to interview a poster
child for the right wing. I'd debated many people with his views
before and knew what buttons to press. Downey strolled into
the studio with a confident air. He was there to promote a new
book. My agenda was to get him to tell his followers that he
would not accept violence against gays. If possible, I wanted to
set him straight on the issue of AIDS; his remarks about the issue were inflaming the nation. An example, which he repeated
on my show, was that AIDS wouldn't be a problem if gays would
just learn that God gave us the anus with only one purpose in
mind.

As soon as we went on the air the telephone board lit up. Most of the early calls were from Downey's fans, then an abortion question or two, and then I asked him about AIDS. He started out by using the same gay-baiting language, and tried to tug at heartstrings by talking about his brother who had AIDS. He said he loved him, but often told him that if he had a different lifestyle, he would not be in that position now. He was chain-smoking at the time and I asked him if he'd say the same thing to someone dying of emphysema. He continued on, insisting that he'd do anything for his brother, and you could almost hear tears in his voice. Then we went to a commercial. During the break, I tried to tell him about a new drug that was being tested that might be of help to his brother. He just asked to use the phone and didn't seem to hear me. When he returned I tried to tell him again, but this time he interrupted me and changed the subject.

The next topic we tackled was violence. It took me some time but I finally got him to say that violence of any type was wrong. Then another break. He told me that while he wasn't as extreme as he appeared on the air, his act was going strong and if he could stand it for another two years he'd make a couple of million and then blow. He was cancelled in two years, right on target.

The lesson learned was that professional right-wing broadcasters like Downey and Rush Limbaugh, and even the shock jocks like Howard Stern, are more entertainment than enlightenment. They have every advantage by controlling the audio button, that magic ability to just cut someone off. They also have their regular callers and supporters, and they control the commercial break. Those things, no matter how good a speaker you are or how professional, mean that you cannot win a debate on their show unless it is agreed beforehand.

As for Downey, he filed for bankruptcy and would later suc-cumb to lung cancer. These people must be admired for the pro-fessional show-biz personalities that they have become. When Howard Stern's show first aired in Philly, his producers did their homework and tried to get local personalities on the air. At one point I was attacked for several days. This was a time to put my ego behind and realize that Stern controlled his own airtime. I didn't take the bait, and I didn't become another of his chewed-up guests. Within a few days I was never mentioned again on his show. But one fun episode: In August of 1994 my editor learned that Stern had a twenty-something gay intern for the summer. He assigned our intern, also a twenty-something, to interview Stern's charge, who arrived with his own public relations repre-sentative. That showed the level of control that must be exer-cised when you're crafting a media personality.

The one unfortunate fact with television media is that many Americans buy in to the unreality of what they see. Many let the shtick influence how they treat people. Ask any Rush Limbaugh listener about gay issues, and it's likely they will simply spurt out his views rather than try to form their own. This misinformation is something that the LGBT community combats every day, and is why it's so important for us to make human connections, talk about the facts, and, whenever the opportunity arises, speak the truth on any relevant or so-called controversial topic. We must protect ourselves as a community, and that includes being able to spread the real word, which is to say, the truth.

Years later, while sitting at my desk one morning and looking over mountains of paperwork and wondering where to begin, the phone rang and it was the ACLU. They asked if I would be willing to go to jail in order to protect the First Amendment. When I told them I'd gone to jail for less, they perked up and explained COPA.

The Child Online Protection Act was passed by Congress and signed into law by President Bill Clinton in 1998. It was an attempt by Congress to restrict access by minors to online material deemed harmful to them, an attempt to control Internet pornography. They were using pedophiles as a justification for the legislation. Any government official or agency that was offended by something placed on the web could somehow argue that it was harmful to minors and then prosecute.

The ACLU representative wanted to know if PGN would be interested in being a plaintiff in the case and help sue the US government. She explained that this had inherent danger, like being found guilty and carted off to prison for example. For me, it was an easy decision. *Salon* and *PGN* were among the plaintiffs. As expected, the case made it all the way to the Supreme Court. The plaintiffs were invited to be present while our attorney argued her points and then took questions from the justices. The night before, all the plaintiffs were in DC for a planning meeting, or rather we were told what was expected of us, which was very little. As plaintiffs this was the end of the trail for us. We were instructed to sit respectfully in the court and listen.

The following morning, just going into the elegant Supreme Court building was intimidating. Truthfully, there was very little to be worried about since by this point we had won all three lower court rulings on the First Amendment rights. Indeed, the US Supreme Court eventually ruled that legislation, which was signed into law by President Clinton, unconstitutional.

On another occasion I had an encounter of a different kind with President Bill Clinton. He was in town to deliver a speech to the party faithful at the Warwick Hotel. Several months before I was unable to accept an invitation to the White House due to a trip to China. I asked Ed Rendell, who had then become chairman of the Democratic National Committee, if he'd arrange a photo of me with the president. Once again Ed and I began to act like children. He said, "You bring the camera and I'll take the picture." This was before cell phone cameras. Somehow I got through security with the camera in my coat breast pocket and made it to the front where there was a red velvet rope separating us from the podium. Standing next to me was the city's district attorney, Lynne Abraham, with a Secret Service agent directly in front.

President Clinton's party entered the room to thunderous applause. They took their places onstage; Ed stood directly behind the president. As Clinton finished his remarks, Ed put his hands to his face like he was taking a picture and mouthed, *Do you have the camera?* I nodded. People began to stare at us. The president's speech ended to more thunderous applause. Enter the Marx Brothers, Ed and Mark. The president tried to leave by the left side of the stage but Ed steered him to the right where I was waiting. Clinton climbed down the stairs and Ed, who was directly behind the president, shouted, "Toss me the camera!" Without thinking I reached in my pocket, pulled out the camera, and tossed it over Clinton's head. Ed caught it, then told the president he wanted to get a few pictures, and we began to pose with him. It is amazing that I didn't get shot. The president started laughing and the crowd was stunned.

In my weekly column of November 10, 1994, titled "Presidential Charmer," I told the story. I sent a copy to the White House with the following note on my three-by-five stationary pad with the *Philadelphia Gay News* logo.

Mr. President,
    If you'd sign and send this back to me it will be the highlight of my life . . . Okay, ONLY ONE of the highlights.

Thanks,
Mark

A few weeks later a brown envelope from the White House arrived at my office. Inside was a large piece of white cardboard and in the middle was that three-by-five stationary. Scrawled over my writing were the words, *To Mark, Warm Appreciation, Bill Clinton*. The picture that Ed took is now on my office wall; it shows Clinton and me with the surprised crowd looking on with open mouths.

Most Communist countries have had trouble dealing with LGBT issues. In 1991, soon after the fall of the Berlin Wall, Patsy Lynch, then a photographer for the Associated Press, was covering what is now known as "Soviet Stonewall," a phrase coined by journalist Rex Wockner. It was the first LGBT conference tour in Russia. The organizers chose a wide range of speakers from around the world to showcase gay activism. Bob Ross of San Francisco's *Bay Area Reporter* and I were representing LGBT media. The tour had two stops, St. Petersburg and Moscow. Thanks to President Mikhail Gorbachev, there was new freedom in the air that spring and people wondered how far they could take things. Our conference was a test. The International Gay and Lesbian Human Rights Commission (IGLHRC) had gotten us invited to Russia on a ruse from a medical institution. We didn't know what to expect.

During a break in the proceedings in St. Petersburg, after taking a photo of me on the throne of Peter the Great, Patsy wanted to go shopping. We found ourselves on Nevsky Prospect, one of the main streets in the city. Walking along we noticed that most shop windows and shelves were bare. The streets on the other hand were filled with peddlers hawking their goods on carpets and cloth. These wares were mostly knickknacks, tattered old clothes, family mementos, and Soviet memorabilia. Everywhere you walked, if they knew you were from the West, people would just take things out of their pockets to sell you. A pack of cigarettes would get you a car ride to any destination in the city. People were poor, and the country was on the edge of political and financial collapse.

Patsy had only one shopping item in mind: a watch from the Soviet navy. While tensions in Russia had eased up a little, there still was some restrictive protocol, and military items were not to be sold. A man came up to Patsy at some point and showed her a Lenin pin and a Stalin pin, but she just brushed him off. She started to move on but then turned around and asked him if he had a watch, and lo and behold, her dream item appeared. She haggled for a moment and as the watch and currency changed hands, a black car screeched to a stop in front of us, just like in the movies. Two men in black trench coats grabbed the guy, threw him in the backseat, and made a quick exit.

I looked at Patsy incredulously. "We could have been arrested as spies by the KGB," I said.

"But at least I have my watch," she replied. She still has it today.

To say that the Russians were not prepared for the freethinking American gay people is an understatement. AIDS was just beginning to rear its ugly head in the former Soviet Union and the organizers of the conference had smuggled in thousands of condoms. We handed them out to people at the conference who rushed to grab them. When we asked one guy why he wanted American condoms, he replied, "Soviet condoms taste like machine in factory." So we all grabbed bags of condoms and went back to the main street to give them out. Amazingly, even the police began to assist. Patsy took a great photo of me handing condoms to a peasant woman, who kept coming back for more. I believe she wanted to sell them on the black market. At least they'd find a user.

Though you couldn't even buy a bottle of soda that wasn't rusty, one evening Robin Tyler, the comedian and activist from Los Angeles, was somehow able to rent a white Cadillac limo, complete with a sunroof. She and I and another couple took off to a casino, which turned out to be a dingy little place without much gambling going on. Disappointed, we returned to our dilapidated hotel, but not before getting a bit drunk. We stood up and out of the sunroof and shouted at the tops of our lungs. Nobody seemed to notice these Americans on the prowl in their city.

Tyler went on to Moscow and performed her out lesbian humor for an audience of eight hundred astonished Russians. Earlier in her career she'd paired with her partner as the first lesbian comedy duo, Harrison and Tyler. Back in 1970 they had joined Jane Fonda's *Free the Army* tour at a time when Fonda was being labeled Hanoi Jane, and after their first appearance Fonda canned them. "I don't remember Jane yelling anything," Robin explained to me. "I do remember that she came over to our apartment in Hollywood and told Patty and me that we could no longer be in the *FTA* show because we had showed that kind of open affection onstage. In the 1980s she apologized. But when I met her almost a decade after that she pretended that she didn't know anything about the incident. Very strange. By then I believed her to be a born-again Christian or something like that."

When it was my turn to speak at the conference, I was awestruck looking out at gay and lesbian Russians. They were just beginning to find their sea legs in activism and it made me think of the humble start of LGBT media in the US, not only in our

struggle for equality, but in building community. I tossed my prepared remarks aside and spoke from the heart.

Through an interpreter I explained how oppression leads
to activism and how important communication is to any movement. I knew they cared deeply about these issues because they
took a major risk by being present. We hoped that they'd use
what they learned at the conference to foster an active Russian LGBT community. Never would I have expected that years
later the "democratic" government of Vladimir Putin would
oppress the LGBT community to the point where people were
comparing it to the country's historic subjugation of Jews. The
homophobia of the Putin government reached its pinnacle in
2014, as Russia geared up to host the Winter Olympics in Sochi.

Through my involvement with Comcast and NBCUniversal's
Joint Diversity Council, I had a front-row seat watching the
company mitigate the issue of homophobia at the Sochi Olympic Games. The company was getting flack for broadcasting an
event from a country with an egregious civil rights record. But
it was difficult to advise what steps could be taken to pressure
Russia since our television contract was with the International
Olympic Committee, not with the country of Russia. Strategically, the company made a brilliant move when they chose an
openly gay man, Thomas Roberts, to host the Miss Universe
pageant from Moscow, just weeks before the games. It was Comcast telling Putin and the world that it stood with the LGBT
community. Roberts bravely took on the task and spoke openly
about being gay and the restrictive laws in Russia, thereby sending a message to Putin: *You better not touch anyone during the
Olympics*. To make the message even clearer, NBC sent numerous LGBT staffers to cover the various sports, including one
flamingly out gay man, retired figure skater Johnny Weir. If he
had been a Russian citizen, I believe he would have been ar-

rested without question. He, like all other non-Russian citizens, was left untouched and the games went off with minimal issues. Brian Roberts, David L. Cohen, and the entire Comcast-NBCUniversal team were brave and brilliant, and made me proud.

The LGBT community applauded NBC for pushing the boundaries, yet noted that after the games, when the cameras were off, the oppressive homophobia inside Russia tightened. Putin and his team were taking Russia back to the days of the Soviet Union, with massive restrictions on the press and the alleged murder and imprisonment of many journalists. The opening we saw as a group in the nineties had long gone. I hope that the LGBT Russian community will someday regain a foothold in their country to advance their civil liberties.

At the 2008 Democratic National Convention in Denver, *Philadelphia Gay News* covered the events for many of the LGBT publications that were unable to send their own reporters. Each day we had a preproduced interview to be posted. Before we even boarded the plane we had interviews with Barney Frank, Tammy Baldwin, Howard Dean, and a host of others. We tweeted from many of the LGBT events and meetings, including the roll call of delegates, where the number of LGBT delegates was proudly shouted out for each state. We took polls on gay marriage from people at the convention, including notables like Spike Lee and Maria Shriver. We knew before all the other media about the "secret" set being built for Obama to accept the nomination at Invesco Field. But there was something else I knew and didn't report.

I wasn't surprised when in 2012 Vice President Biden made a very public gaffe preempting the president in support of marriage equality. Why did he do this then? I'd suspected his position for four years already. The morning after Joe Biden was nominated as Obama's vice president in 2008, his first speaking engagement was with the Pennsylvania delegation. It was fitting since he grew up in Scranton and spent his formative years in Pennsylvania.

After making a triumphant entrance at the 2008 convention, VP nominee Biden made his way to the platform to deliver a few remarks to an excited crowd. Jill Biden was standing on the side near us, and we spoke for a while. She knew I was from *Philadelphia Gay News* and I asked her a few questions, including one about gay marriage. She thought for a moment and then said, "Of course I support it."

Jill Biden is a delightful, personable, and brilliant woman, but I didn't do my job as a journalist and instead dispensed some advice: "Since Joe is the nominee, the two of you might want to mirror Obama's position." It was her first day on the job and I didn't want to taint it. I didn't ask the vice presidential nominee the same question. Was this a missed opportunity? I'm happy to say I have no regrets.

The second conversation I had that morning was with MSNBC pundit Chris Matthews, who was considering a run against Senator Arlen Specter, and that conversation was reported in the LGBT press. Here's the exchange:

Mark Segal: *You're running for Senate in Pennsylvania. As you know, there are some very important issues going on. We have a Republican in that seat, Specter, who voted two ways on the Defense of Marriage Act. So what would you be doing?*

Chris Matthews: *Well, first, I'm not going to answer it that way. I always start with freedom. That's where I start* *on every issue, whether it's reproductive rights or it's crime. There's a constitutional right that starts with freedom and inherent rights, exclusive rights to the Constitution. But I really do believe that we always as Americans start with that. Then we work our way through things. Do you understand? It's very important. Individual freedom has always been the way we start. First governments, sequestered governments like in England, always start with state power. This country has always started with individual freedom as the basis to work at what you allow the state to do. But obviously, this is an evolving thing; my thinking now is different from what it was ten years ago. [For] a lot of people it's been evolving, and for a lot of gay people it's been evolving. A lot of gay people didn't think marriage was going to be the issue. A lot of friends of mine didn't think it was going to be an issue, because it was too far out. A lot of people are changing on these issues. I think a lot of people are going to work our way through these things.*

MS: *Well, where are you on the issue?*

CM: *I have an open heart. I'll have to live with it.*

MS: *In other words, you won't answer the question.*

CM: *I can answer it the way I have, which is any fucking way I want. I can answer in my way even if it isn't your way.*

What's interesting here is the irritation Matthews had with the question. I'd like to believe he was in that "evolution" mode. Again, no regrets. Watching Matthews show his support of marriage equality now sometimes amazes me. He completely understands the history of the issue, and could give other pundits lessons in the proper journalistic approach to describing marriage equality. He has become passionate in his support of civil rights.

Chapter 11

Bringing Up Baby

In 1996, my nephew Jeffrey called me after years of my trying to reach him. He's one of three children born to my older brother. He and his two sisters, Jennifer and Stephanie, hadn't lived with their father since early childhood. My brother is not the most nurturing person alive and we've been estranged for many years. But his children are my parents' grandchildren, of course, and that led me to seek them out. At first their mother allowed both Jennifer and Stephanie to visit with my partner and me. That was usually around holidays or during the summer. The first time they arrived at the airport from Florida, I immediately saw how beautiful they were.

When I'd ask about their brother there was always a different story. I couldn't find out much about him. This game kept going for years. Once in a while, when I called their mother and asked, Jeffrey was put on the phone, but he spoke only briefly and with trepidation. When I got the call in 1996, he began with the words, "Uncle Mark, may I come to see you?" This time, his mother allowed him to visit for a weekend, or so I thought.

The minute he got off the plane I could see the family resemblance. We did touristy things around the city, and I treated him to dinner, but it took him awhile to warm up to us. As I'd say later, he came to us broken. By the end of the weekend he was trying to either con us (something which I found charming and amusing) or get us to adopt him. (It turned out that he was a ward of the Florida court.) The last night of that weekend visit, my partner went to sleep early to allow Jeffrey and me to have a heart-to-heart—though we had already decided to take him. After all, how hard could it be to have a teenage son?

That night Jeffrey told me his story. We both cried a lot. I'm sure that some of it was embellished to spur me to action, but regardless of what I thought at the time, I soon learned from the court that much of what Jeffrey said was true and much of it was not his doing. I promised then that we'd get him out of Florida. A promise I had no idea how I'd keep.

I also knew we had to act quickly. I called some political friends involved in the judiciary and requested that they contact their colleagues in the Florida court system to see what they could do to help me. Within two weeks I was on a plane to Florida to be interviewed by the court guardian, during which time Jeffrey was placed in a group home. The guardian, almost on sight of me, opened up about Jeffrey. She adored him and wanted him out of reach of his family. I spent two days in Florida, returned home, and almost overnight I had somehow been approved to be his new guardian. I don't believe his mother had any idea this was happening, and since I was never in any court in Florida, I don't even know how this was legally possible. Regardless, my teenage nephew-turned-adopted-son was about to arrive.

Our first thought of parenthood was to give him everything he had been denied. He went from being a rural, hardworking child laborer and ward of the state to a child of a successful gay publisher in an urban setting. My friends in the media were kind enough to ignore all the hijinks with Jeffrey, since many of them were parents and knew very well that I had taken on a challenge. They preferred to sit back and enjoy the show rather than report on it.

When Jeffrey arrived, we gave him twenty dollars and told him to walk around the city and enjoy himself. A few hours later he called in tears. Seems he felt he needed a more contemporary haircut than his Florida crew cut, and went into a fancier-than-he-realized spa. He thought the massage and shampoo were part of the haircut, but panicked when he was handed the bill for eighty dollars. No problem.

He had heard about my many trips to jail. By this time I thought that this part of my life was over. But along came Chris Bartlett, who had put together a demonstration against the local CBS affiliate after their news broadcast did an exposé of "gay men having sex in public restrooms." The real story was that in almost all cases they were married men. Chris explained something to the effect that it was my duty as an elder to show the younger generation the significance of the issue. In other words, he guilt-tripped me.

His plan was to toilet-paper the entire building. Jeffrey went along and wanted to be a part of the demonstration, but in my first parental protective gesture I told him to stay in the car and watch. The police were called, and he got to witness his uncle and new guardian being arrested, handcuffed, and hauled off to jail. (Perhaps it was a good civics lesson?)

Jeffrey and I had a chat one day about family boundaries. He still quotes to me my words: "Jeffrey, there will be times that you'll try to get something over on me, but believe me, I've pulled every stunt that has ever been pulled, and I'll catch you, so don't even try." That was my first mistake as a parent, since Jeffrey took it as a challenge. His first try came very quickly. He noted that we had numerous parties at the house and that it was a great way to get to know people. He got comfortable chatting with the mayor and other notable individuals. At sixteen he was living the life, but it was his uncle's life—and he would imitate it. One weekend, as we were about to leave for our shore house, Jeffrey asked if he could stay home. My partner and I agreed, since we thought he was doing well, adjusting to city life. We didn't really give it a second thought. Until we arrived home. When we got upstairs, the house was oddly clean. Not clean, immaculate. Something was wrong. While taking a walk, I noticed items that used to be in our house in public trash cans. On my way back into the house a neighbor saw me and said, "Quite a wild party you had last night." According to other neighbors, people were hanging off the balconies. Hey, at least we taught him how to socialize.

It was obviously time to have a sit-down with Jeffery. I must admit that I was almost proud of him, but he lost points since I had caught him. I told him he was grounded, and instead of an allowance, which I never understood anyway, he had to get a job. He found one and kept it, all the while dealing with the unforgiving Northeast winter. He was just happy to be out of Florida and with role models for the first time in his life. He had earned his GED, so we investigated getting him into a community college.

Jeffrey hadn't seen his father since he was a young child. He couldn't even remember him. One thing I suggested was that since his father lived in the same region, it might be good to meet him sometime, so at the very least he'd be able to form his own opinion. I handed him his father's phone number and reminded him that the only things he knew about his father were what he'd heard from his mother and me. It was important that he meet him and make his own judgment, then decide whether to continue the relationship. His attitude toward a father who he felt had abandoned him was quite negative. He snapped at me, saying that he didn't want to see him, but I insisted he take the number and call his father when he felt ready.

Having a child about to enter college was a shock for some-one who had never paid for school supplies before. Jeffrey made a list of all the things he needed, and I'd supply the cash or credit card. What I didn't know is that Jeffrey had indeed gotten in touch with his father and was asking him to pay for the same items. He was double-dipping. My brother's girlfriend called me out of the blue for the first time in years and asked a question about Jeffrey's school supplies, and I suddenly put two and two together. When Jeffrey came home, I called out to him in a stern voice. He came over to where I was sitting with a smile on his face. "Guess who I was just on the phone with." He knew I knew. "Jeffrey, I've got to hand it to you, that was a good one, but the gravy train just stopped." This was also the end of his new relationship with his father. Jeffrey does not like to talk about my brother, and neither do I, so we just don't. But I've always believed that it's good to know where you come from.

To my great pleasure, Jeffrey became a first-rate IT head-hunter, now living and working in New York. It will not surprise me when he opens his own firm. He's talented, sociable, and smart. His success and our relationship come with an added bo-nus for me. Whenever we chat on the phone, I get to say to him, in my best Jewish accent: "Jeffrey, when are you going to find a girl, settle down, and give me some grandkids to spoil?"

After Jeffrey moved to New York, I began to appreciate the empty-nest syndrome. I also began to ponder what it felt like to be really single. The emotional damage from my twenty-year relationship had filled me with 100 percent self-loathing and 0 percent self-esteem. As I detailed earlier, this breakup, aside from the deaths in my family, was the lowest point of my life. I survived with the help of prescription drugs, my physician Dr. Mounzer, a psychologist, and a pharmacologist. It took them and a team of friends to get me to the point where I'd even consider seeing someone again. And the first two dips into the water didn't work out so well. The first candidate and I weren't quite hitting it off, and on our third date one evening at Ruth's Chris Steak House, I told him we should stop seeing each other. He stood up and started waving his steak knife at me, yelling, "You're breaking up with me?" It took the staff to get him away and out of the restaurant. Then the second guy kept disappearing on various evenings. I later found out that he was picking up drugs from an unsavory guy. Maybe it was best to remain a bachelor.

But life wasn't *all* down at that time. My friends the Mezzaroba family and their matriarch Rita adopted me. At first, when I wouldn't leave the house, they brought over care packages, which were as delicious as any restaurant. They insisted that I spend the holidays with them. Christmas Eve, feast of the seven fishes, in their Italian home, was my particular favorite. Rita grew up in the heart of Italian South Philadelphia. Her husband owned a construction company and did very well. They still lived in a row home and shopped at the Italian market on a stretch of 9th Street where each grocery has stalls out front; it resembles New York's Lower East Side circa 1900. They had their favorite cheese shop, butcher, and pasta maker. Her husband even made his own wine. I'd joke with Rita about being a Mafia princess, and occasionally she'd almost make me believe it. She was elegant and a damn smart woman. I adored her. The warmth between her, her daughter Charlene, her son-in-law Jack, and their children allowed me to believe that decency, kindness, and love were possible for me.

Rita's favorite restaurant was an elegant wood-paneled downtown joint, stocked with antiques. A photo of Marlon Brando as the Godfather sat discreetly next to a tin slide photograph of Abraham Lincoln. It was reputed to be a mob hangout, but the food was incredible. One wintry night with an icy wind blowing, Rita was waiting for me at the bar when I walked in. She had a glass of wine in her hand, and as I dragged a heavy stool across the black-and-white-tiled floor to sit next to her, she shook her head sadly and said: "Things just don't fall off the truck the way they used to." She was serious. "There were fur coats and designer jeans, and the shoes! Now all we have is going to the shops." She sighed and finished, "I miss that kind of living."

Around this time Dad began a slow drift into loneliness. Mom was his world and he had lost her. My attempts at making him feel important were sometimes totally out of place. For his seventieth birthday I used my brand-new video camera to make a *This Is Your Life, Marty Segal* highlights film. Mayor Wilson Goode: "Marty, I have some news for you, hospital records have been found that prove that we are brothers." A hooker played by *Philadelphia Daily News* columnist Stu Bykofsky's former wife Maria Merlino (yes, of *that* Merlino family) telling Dad he's "one of her best customers." Then Philadelphia District Attorney Ron Castille, who went on to become a Supreme Court justice of the Commonwealth of Pennsylvania, explaining that he had just sworn out a warrant for Dad's arrest for using too many prostitutes. Then we took him to dinner where at the restaurant he was surprised to find the complete family waiting for him and applauding as he walked in.

At that time Dad only wore jeans and short-sleeve shirts. I wanted him to come to one of my political fundraising dinners, explaining that it required a suit and tie. He objected, but finally gave in and allowed me to have someone take him shopping to get the proper outfit. He not only picked out the suit, he sat for it to be tailored. He chose the shirt and tie and was very particular about the matching shoes. When he showed up at the fundraiser, he was in jeans, a short-sleeve buttoned shirt, and his old brown shoes. He saw my smile and shrugged. He never wore that suit and when he died it was not among his possessions. I have no idea what happened to it.

During the last couple of years of his life, until he succumbed to myasthenia gravis at age seventy-three in 1996, Dad lived with Aunt Rose, his sister. Her daughter Ilene remains to this day my favorite cousin. Rose's children grew up seeing their cousin Mark on the news being carted off to jail or interviewed on TV. Ilene knew of the various pressures on my time but she attempted to get me to attend as many family functions as possible. Her children went through puberty during the early years of HIV/AIDS. Through my work with doctors, she learned how to explain safe sex to her children as they came of age. And to the embarrassment of her children, when their friends visited them, Ilene occasionally felt compelled to offer safe-sex lessons. Sometimes the other parents did not appreciate this.

One time at her daughter Stacie's school, when they did show-and-tell, Stacie brought me in and told them about the fight for gay rights. But more than anything else, their home became a refuge for many of their young friends who were coming out of the closet. Ilene and family opened their home, and at times Ilene lectured parents who wouldn't accept their children. In a way she was able to show me how my work was used in real time . . . and she never let me feel left out. She has raised three incredible children. That closeness continues; one night her son Michael and his wife called and asked if they could name their first child after me.

When my twenty-year relationship ended my family was there

for me. So was my friend Rob Metzger. He told me of an e-mail he'd received from a young man, a journalism student at NYU. Rob had found the perfect man for me, or so he thought. The e-mail began with something like: *Your friend Rob Metzger suggested I write you since we have so much in common.*

This started a yearlong e-mail correspondence with Jason. No chat rooms and no phone calls, just e-mails. Somehow, after a while, I lost sight of the fact that he was a student. Our messages were intense, full of discussions on current events. He even began to offer advice on some my projects, and eventually the exchanges became emotional, though never sexual. Twice he invited me to New York, and twice I backed out at the last minute.

Then Mayor John Street won reelection and allowed me to create an official LGBT inaugural gala to benefit our LGBT community center. It was on Saturday, January 3, 2004.

At ten p.m. we did the check ceremony, announcing to the crowd that we had raised $110,000, and Patti LaBelle sang "Over the Rainbow" to me and I swooned. The party was jumping and we still had a couple hours to go. But something hit me: I wanted to go home and send an e-mail to Jason. He had worked with me on this project the entire time. Why hadn't I invited him? He should have been standing next to me in the glory of that evening.

By eleven p.m. we were e-mailing away. This lasted till the very late hours of the morning. It was decided that the following weekend he would come to Philadelphia so that we could finally meet in person. We decided on Philly so that I could not back out.

All week I prepared for that first date. I hadn't been on a real date in decades, so I thought it should be special. There was no way to contain my excitement, and this somehow took on the shape of a city project. After I mentioned the date to a friend in City Hall, word seemed to get around. Friends started calling with suggestions. What I didn't grasp was that everyone was working to get me back to my old self.

Jason arrived by train. At the station, I met him with yellow roses and I sang a Bette Midler song. He should have run then, or I should have, but instead we got in my car. The first stop was showing him the Philly skyline, which he'd never seen before. We drove to the top of the Philadelphia Museum of Art with its famous *Rocky* steps. The police had cleared out all cars and people for me, so we'd have that romantic view of the city all to ourselves. There I gave him a treasure trove of Philadelphia tchotchkes, donated to me by various city tourism organizations. Moving along, we went to RiverRink by the Delaware River to go ice-skating. The Delaware River Waterfront Corporation had a guard at the gate awaiting our arrival at Penn's Landing, and he escorted us to our parking spot next to a tent erected specifically for our use. Inside the warm tent were carpet, chairs, and a sofa. Candles flickered all around a bottle of champagne, fruit, and a chocolate fountain. It was a scene out of the *Arabian Nights*. My favorite part was a framed message on a little wooden table, *Enjoy Your Night, Mark and Jason. —Your friends at Penn's Landing*. We looked at each other, hugged, and yes, we had our first kiss. We chatted for a while, held each other, and finally we tried on the skates that were laid out for us in the tent.

When we emerged there were two escorts waiting to take us to the rink. Someone asked over the speaker system that everyone leave the rink temporarily, and we were brought onto the ice. They changed the music to Bette Midler and Jason and I began to skate. On our second lap around the rink, he took my hand and the crowd, who had been forced off the rink, actually applauded. I knew then that this was something special.

After skating, it was time for dinner. We had a reservation at Buddakan, a Stephen Starr restaurant with an Asian twist. Inside the restaurant, a long string of tables usually sits in front of a two-story golden Buddha statue. But not that night. Stephen had rearranged the tables so we had Buddha practically to ourselves. When dinner was done, a giant dessert arrived at the table. I didn't know it at the time, but Jason loved sweets and was delighted. And on top of all that, there was no bill.

Then and only then did we go home, and he saw the house for the first time. That was over a decade ago, and I thank God (a term I rarely use) for each and every day with him. Aside from my parents, he is the only person in the world who has ever truly understood me; he supports and encourages me, and wants nothing in return but my love. He's my best friend and soul mate.

I've left out some details from that first date, but I suppose I should come clean. When Jason arrived in Philadelphia and came up the train station escalator, I almost ran for the doors. Seeing him for the first time shocked me. I had somehow stopped thinking about how he was a student at NYU, i.e., young. In the previous year, his e-mails had made me feel like I was corresponding with someone of my age and maturity level. His knowledge and calmness were new to me. His youth scared me. To make matters worse, after three laps on the ice rink, I stopped. Translation: I was out of shape. He was the star of the NYU swim team, and earlier in his career had been on the Maryland state team with Michael Phelps. He was tall and slim, I was short and portly. His family was Catholic while mine was Jewish. He came from a conservative military family, and I was a left-wing pinko fag. But somehow we connected. He was and is one of the brightest people I know. I am truly turned on by brainpower.

Jason thinks I changed his life, but the reality is that he changed mine far more dramatically. The past decade has been among the happiest and most productive of my life. Like all couples, we have our problems, a primary one being everything that comes along with being me, that circus I call a life. Instead of complaining, he encourages me. He allows me to think big. When I do fail, he's there to suggest new projects to keep me busy and engaged.

Just a few months after Jason and I met, the organizing began for a big Elton John concert. I had somehow gotten engaged, and Jason accompanied me and several others on a related trip to Vienna and then to London for negotiations with the Elton John AIDS Foundation. This trip showed me what a partner should be and that in some ways our relationship was like a fairy tale. At the Hofburg Palace in Vienna on a private tour, when we arrived in the queen's bedroom, a band in the courtyard below started to play, and without a word he took my hand and we danced.

Being part of Elton's entourage was an experience that would scare even seasoned media veterans. Jason was not fazed at all. Motorcades, shopping trips, dinner with Elton—nothing rattled him. The one thing I noticed on that trip is that he challenged me without making me feel threatened. The numbers showed him to be young, the brain showed him to be Yoda.

Shortly after our return from London I hosted a meeting of the National Gay Newspaper Guild, an organization of LGBT publishers, and invited Jason along. On our first day of meetings I asked the mayor to say a few words to open the conference and he obliged. After welcoming the publishers to the city, Mayor Street got up and went around the table to shake hands. When he came to Jason he said, "I've certainly heard a lot about you."

Then he turned to me and said in a loud whisper that all could hear, "A little young, Mark." He patted me on the back with a warm smile and made his way out.

We've had so many special moments and have been through a lifetime of memories, including deeply challenging situations. We even separated for what now looks like the blink of an eye. I was so saddened that I wrote a column about it, and then equally joyful when I wrote another retracting it.

For a time, Jason lived in Japan as an English teacher, and he also worked for a national network news show in Washington. But we always made a point to keep in constant communication, for which our year of e-mailing had prepared us well. When he was in Washington, we only saw each other on weekends. As I expected, he rose through the ranks of the show remarkably quickly, to the point where he was actually assisting the executive producer with running a nightly newscast. And yet as well as he did there, I was delighted when he was able to return home to Philly to work as a producer for another big media company.

We complemented each other in ways that enhanced both of our lives. We couldn't have been happier. But our families were not so thrilled with this union. My first introduction to Jason's family was to one of his two older sisters. We were all visiting New York and a dinner meeting was arranged. It was early in our relationship and I was still recovering from the end of my long-term relationship. It felt like his sister hated me at first sight. In retrospect, she should have. She probably didn't expect an overweight older man who was from a culture totally different from theirs. I'm also sure that my appearance was not as neat as it could have been and my manners not impeccable. To make matters worse, when I get nervous I chat and chat, and often don't let anyone get a word in. I chatted.

Her true impression, she later told me, was of a man telling her how he would try to change the little brother she loved and had helped to raise. In hindsight, she was correct and I simply was not ready for prime time. The guy who had done thousands of interviews had failed this one.

Jason's parents were about as welcoming as his sister. By this I mean that I didn't meet them until we had been together for seven years. But Jason holds that he is really at fault here, since he gave up on trying to introduce us early on. Somehow I was not worried about meeting them and as I expected, at that first meeting, seven years after Jason and I had been together, we hit it off immediately. Jason was the most nervous person in the room. The other three of us got along famously. And I was able to see the love between Jason and his parents, and instantly realized where he had gotten all the qualities that I cherish about him. I adore Jason's parents and enjoy every visit with them.

As for my side of the family, my cousin, upon first meeting Jason, actually walked out of the restaurant and called me later to ask what I could possibly have in common with him. According to her, our age gap was too wide. My lifelong friend Barbara just didn't get it, but guess who did? On Jason's second trip to Philly I introduced him to Rita and Charlene. After we dropped Jason off at the train station, they just kept repeating, "He's a keeper."

Jason gets the credit for bringing me back. He has also taught me how to distance myself from negativity. It's a political tactic, one that I never embraced before. No longer is my time spent defending myself against false allegations or those trying to use me to raise their personal profile. Like me, Jason is passionate, in particular with his writing. On many nights we are both at home writing or reading or, if too exhausted, sitting in front of the television. We treasure our quiet evenings at home.

We've become an old and boring couple and we love our old and boring things.

One night during bedtime conversation I asked Jason, "Do you think I can raise nineteen or twenty million to build an affordable LGBT senior living facility?"

He looked me in the eye and said, "Of course."

Those two words of support were all I needed to start on my next project, the biggest one yet. But it had to wait until after my stint as a concert producer.

Chapter 12

Elton John and a Bag Full of Diamonds

Like many things in my life, the Elton saga began by accident. In the fall of 2003, in the midst of Mayor John Street's reelection bid, a story broke. The FBI had bugged Street's office as part of a federal investigation of political corruption in Philadelphia. The mayor, who at one time was considered one of the most homophobic elected officials in the city, had done a complete turnaround in his first term and was trying hard to correct his past. Any decent man believes in human rights, after all. Street had come to embrace the LGBT community and I endorsed him for reelection. But his history still gave people pause and my endorsement was not very popular in my community.

There was one thing that most people never understood about John Street: he wasn't about personal wealth. For him, politics was all about the power, specifically the power to bring on a progressive agenda. The FBI, as it turned out, taped our calls and many others. Not to leave any stone unturned, they also got the mayor's e-mails. This was discovered when the *Philadelphia Inquirer* successfully sued the government for access to information and materials related to the investigation. Those correspondences appeared on the front page of the paper. Marcia Gelbart wrote a story about the mayor's attempt to understand the LGBT community and published our e-mail dialogue.

It showed a side of John Street that most people never saw, a caring man from a devout background who was trying to accept that his religion, or those who taught it, might have gotten some things wrong.

As a result of the investigation, the campaign for mayor between Street and Republican rival Sam Katz was now a dead heat. Some polls had Katz ahead, even with a five-to-one advantage in Democratic voter registration. As a Street supporter, I tried to change the odds. About an hour after the FBI story broke, I asked myself, *Could a federal bugging of a mayor's office be used as a positive rather than a negative?* It sure could, if it was tied back to someone very unpopular in the city of Philadelphia, someone who nobody in their right mind would ever support. That would be the president of the United States, George W. Bush. So I ordered five thousand buttons that read: *Bug Bush! Reelect Street.*

I then turned my attention to the LGBT community, which, now a decisive political force in the city, was coveted by both parties and could make the difference in a tight election. Katz thought that given Street's antigay reputation our votes were attainable. But Street knew he had an ace in his pocket—me. Katz was somewhat popular in the community, while Street was still hated for rallying against domestic partnership legislation despite his increased support and actions over the past three years. But I knew how to turn the tide. By putting the focus on Katz, I could deflect the negativity away from Street.

The Katz campaign had an advisor, Brian Tierney, future publisher of the *Philadelphia Inquirer.* Tierney was, as some would say, close to the Catholic archdiocese, and a fierce, even vicious opponent who led attacks on Street for one major pro-gay position he had taken. The mayor had promised to combat discrimination in Philadelphia by evicting the Boy Scouts from a very well-situated city-owned property for which they were paying an annual rent of one dollar. The Boy Scouts, you might remember, had taken a strong antigay position, barring adult gays from serving as scoutmasters and young gays from participating in their programs. It was clearly in violation of Philly's nondiscrimination law, so the city began the legal process of bouncing them from their sweetheart deal. The question for the LGBT community became, simply, *Can we really trust Katz to toss the Boy Scouts out?* Katz, as I expected, wouldn't answer. We editorialized in *PGN* that anyone who would not support our community in the fight against discrimination, or even attempt to speak up on our behalf, did not deserve our votes. Since Katz would not support the gay community in our battle against the Boy Scouts, I wrote, no major gay leader could possibly endorse his candidacy. And indeed that is what happened.

Upon his reelection I could have asked Mayor Street for almost anything. I had tarnished my own reputation in the community by working so hard for a candidate who many still viewed as a homophobe, and whom I myself had fought against during his early unenlightened days. But supporting him was the right thing to do. The mayor called to thank me for my help and I asked for an LGBT inaugural gala at the William Way LGBT Community Center. It would be on the Saturday before his official swearing-in ceremony. He agreed. I was pretty elated until I realized I'd have to organize this inaugural gala in less than seven weeks. It was my first opportunity to become a producer.

First thing first, I needed some kind of entertainment. For years, I'd wanted to recognize Philadelphia's favorite hometown diva, Patti LaBelle. Patti was one of the first show-business personalities to support LGBT rights, including being one of the first to raise funds for HIV/AIDS, even before Elton John. She also was a supporter and friend of John Street. In short order, Patti agreed to be the star of the gala.

The next thing was food and drink. If I throw an event, there must be some good food. My ancestors would never forgive me if people went unfed. So we got ten of the leading restaurants in the city to agree to set up tables and bring their best samples: prime rib, oysters, shrimp, fois gras, champagne, and more. Liquor and soft drinks were donated by the LGBT clubs. At one hundred dollars a ticket, it would be the best party in town. Almost every item was donated, and almost every politician wanted a ticket.

On the big night, men arrived in black ties, women in beautiful gowns. It was standing-room only. The evening was going great. The community center ballroom was elegantly decorated and we made sure that every logistical detail not only made sense but would run smoothly. Or so we thought.

Patti wasn't feeling well on the night of the ball. She wasn't ready to acknowledge how serious her diabetes had become; only a few people knew of her illness. But that lady is a trouper, and she doesn't disappoint. Sitting in her limo, I explained that the ballroom was on the second floor, and that there was no elevator. She was concerned at first, but then we came up with a strategy that would allow her to climb the stairs to her dressing room and to the ballroom gracefully. We pushed through the crowd to the foot of the stairs. People pressed in, wildly applauding. We took deep breaths and went up the first five steps. At the first landing, Patti turned around to pose for pictures and receive even more applause. We continued and the applause got even louder. Every two or three steps she would turn, wave, and be photographed. It took many turns and many photographs, but ultimately Patti got up the steps and the crowd was delighted. This solution offered her fans the opportunity to give her the proper worship that she deserved. When she got to her dressing room, she fell into a chair and said with a big grin, "Mark Segal, I should kill you before you kill me! Get out of here so I can get ready."

The mayor took the stage. He thanked us profusely and told the crowd that he could not have won his reelection without the support of the LGBT community. This brought overwhelming applause from an audience who never thought they would hear that kind of appreciation from a purportedly homophobic man. Naturally, there were awards to thank the people who'd made the evening possible. I then had the pleasure of introducing my diva, Miss Patti LaBelle.

"Enough talk," said Patti, shooing me off the stage, "we need some singing!" She sang a couple of her most well-known songs accompanied by my friend Dennis Cook on the piano. Then I reappeared onstage. "You know, Patti," I said, "you don't have any background singers with you tonight, do you? How about we form a new group, Patti LaBelle and the City Hall Bells?" We coaxed both Mayor Street and Governor Ed Rendell to the stage, draped them in blue feather boas that we'd stashed in the wings, and the City Hall Bells rang out. At the end of the night, Patti invited me back on the stage and asked what song I wanted to hear. I told her and she performed a heartfelt rendition of "Over the Rainbow." I melted. I still shiver when I think of that moment.

The following morning the front page of the *Philadelphia Inquirer* carried a photo of the mayor and governor at the ball—looking good in their boas. On that night, January 3, 2004, we raised $110,000.

The Monday after, I received a call from Gary Yetter, a man I'd never heard of before. Gary helped run Lunch Around the World, an annual celebration of Elton John's birthday that raised funds for the Elton John AIDS Foundation (EJAF). He wanted to meet with me about supporting their event in some way. I'd just come off weeks of intensive labor to organize the gala and was whipped, so I tried to politely brush him off by saying that the only thing I'd consider doing was a concert with Elton. To my surprise, the idea excited Gary. Like me, Gary is very focused when he believes in a project. He was relentless about EJAF and putting him off was impossible. A few weeks later he and a guy named Michael Anzalone, who would later become pivotal to this venture, joined me for dinner at Judy's Restaurant in Queen Village. At the end of the evening I arrogantly repeated that I'd only be interested in doing an Elton John concert. I thought that would be the end of it. But a few days later Gary called again, asking for another dinner to further explore the idea of a concert. He said he had brought it up with EJAF headquarters in London and they didn't say no.

Soon Gary, his beautiful wife Maureen, Jason, and I were jetting off to Vienna to Life Ball, Europe's largest and most luxurious AIDS benefit. Thirty thousand revelers would contribute nearly a million euros to AIDS charities in the third world. Some four thousand VIP guests would pay 130 euros each for their tickets. And Sir Elton, seller of 200 million records, master of outrageous stagecraft and costuming, member of the Songwriters and Rock and Roll Halls of Fame, founder of the Elton John AIDS Foundation, and the most famous gay man on the planet, was to perform. Gary informed me that if we did a concert in Philadelphia, this would be an example of what the EJAF expected of us. The whirlwind tour was enhanced by the fact that Jason and I had just started dating five months before and everything felt dreamlike. After Vienna, we were to fly to London for meetings at EJAF's offices to firm up the plans.

Everything concerning Life Ball in Vienna was lavish. Held

on the grounds of Vienna city hall, the event is equal parts fashion show, casino, disco, banquet, costume party, and den of iniquity. Guests were dressed in outlandish and incredible costumes. The liquor and food flowed while celebrities and Eastern European porn stars strutted around or played up to the wealthy.

The day before the actual event, Robert Key, the executive director of EJAF, took Gary and me on a backstage tour. The dressing rooms for the fashion show were a swarming hive of people stitching garments, ironing dresses, models trying on outfits, rooms filled to capacity, racks and racks of haute couture clothes. We saw the stage area and the sound and light setups. We then went around the building to check out the different spaces. Each room had a corporate sponsor, and as we saw, each spent a lot of time and money to make their room the most extravagant at the event. One created a casino with people in animal costumes, while another presented a seventies pop culture room. It was a spectacle even before the main event. Finally, we visited the most important room, one of the main reasons we'd flown all the way to Vienna: Elton's dressing room. Right off the bat, I saw that it had been decked out with new furniture, a new carpet, and, to my amazement, material stretched around the room to cover the walls. Behind the material was diffuse lighting. In another room was a full bar and lavish food for guests. I was already overwhelmed, thinking about having to replicate everything.

Later that day we toured Vienna. We saw the palaces, took in the baroque architecture and the spectacular gardens all around the city. We had been given a specific time to meet at the hotel to go shopping with Elton, but when we returned, we found out that Mr. John had gone on without us! According to rumor, he was expected at a certain time to get something to wear that night at a jewelry store. Soon, with a very good-looking security guard in tow, he came back with a paper bag with a quarter-million dollars' worth of diamonds nestled inside. Not just your average, run-of-the-mill shopping trip, and certainly not one that could wait.

Next we all headed out to the cars. Four of us trailed the car behind Elton's. Inside our car were two women, one a high-powered agent and the other a member of a female rock band. We were explicitly told that when we pulled in to the portico of Vienna's magnificent palace-like neo-gothic city hall, we should get out before Elton did and assemble behind him en route to his dressing room.

As we rolled under the portico, the paparazzi pushed and elbowed to get in optimum position. Then the door opened of the first car in line. The scene exploded with flashes and even more pushing, shoving, and shouting. We had been prepared for this riotous scene by the expert security team, used to protecting the famous: keep your arms at your side, say nothing, nod, smile, and keep walking in tight formation behind our leader. Inside, it only got stranger and more elaborate. For a kid from South Philly, it was like suddenly finding myself in the middle of a Fellini movie. Models in appropriate regalia were posing and strutting in each of the themed rooms.

In Elton's guest room there was a very interesting mix of people. Pop stars, former pop stars, major contributors, the upper echelon of EJAF, some Eastern European porn stars, and the handsome security men. We enjoyed the comforts of his suite as the fashion show continued below, outside our window. We paid close attention to the stage and crowd. Gary and I had already decided that if we were to do this, it would be at the Philadelphia Museum of Art, a much better place to set a stage and on a much grander scale than Vienna city hall. I knew that if our event were to happen, it would have to be spectacular.

After the fashion show we made our way outside, just as it began to pour. Unlike in the US, where we prefer not to be electrocuted, the show continued on full-speed ahead. There seemed to be no worries about the large LCD screens, wires, and cables running around the stage and runway. Politicians and people from various political organizations gave speeches, which went on for some time. It was all in German, so we had no idea what was being said. Finally, they brought Elton on-stage. After a few words from the organizers (also in German), Elton spoke of how much this benefit meant to his foundation and to him personally. He did it in English while holding a live microphone in the pouring rain. He then—wisely, due to the hazard—lip-synched the song "Are You Ready for Love." Soaking wet, Elton gave a bravura performance. He left the stage to a standing ovation and we all headed to the dining hall.

After the show, four of us were scheduled to have dinner with Elton, but he was running a little late. We were told he wouldn't be around for at least an hour. We decided to use our all-access passes and leave the comfort of Elton's suite. Outside the suite was bedlam. People packed everywhere, many of them in costumes: aliens and all types of animals. But an equal number were quite simply not in costume. I remember one guy who wore nothing but a six-gun holster and a ten-gallon hat. Oh, and cowboy boots. There was no one way to dress—anything from white tie and tails to leather, latex, and fur.

Exhausted from the sensory overload, an hour or so later we returned to the dining hall. When we got there, Elton, now dry, embraced us. As we all posed for a photo, Elton whispered in my ear, "Don't worry, Mark, we'll do this." Then an idea sparked. One that I thought might really fascinate the star, whose song "Philadelphia Freedom" celebrated one of his favorite cities.

I had never done anything close to a megaconcert, but the

idea began building in my mind as we flew to London to close the deal with Elton's foundation. Except for Live Aid, nothing of this magnitude had ever been staged in Philadelphia. This wasn't Mickey and Judy putting on a show in somebody's father's barn. This was a very big deal. For some reason, I wasn't frightened by the job ahead.

Elton had already given me the okay in Vienna, so the meetings in London were working sessions to flesh out some of the details, though we still needed to iron out the contract. Elton arrived at one of the meetings with dogs in tow. As the plane took off from London, I looked at Jason, shook my head, and kept wondering what I'd gotten myself engaged in.

My father used to have a saying when he and Mom treated us to an all-you-can-eat buffet. I'd look at the array of food and begin putting every single thing I wanted onto my plate: mac and cheese, mashed potatoes, fried chicken, biscuits, and whatever else. The mound of food would be sky high. Dad would come over with his reasonably loaded plate, smile, and remark matter-of-factly: "Your eyes are too big for your stomach."

First the mayor explained that I'd have to work through the existing contracts with Welcome America, the city's quasi-government corporation that usually produced the July 4 celebration. Welcome America had contracts in place for events such as this. The most beneficial was with WPVI, the ABC affiliate that broadcast the Philadelphia July 4 concert every year. Another was with Sunoco, the oil company that had the naming rights to the events. Obviously, the concert needed to be dedicated to AIDS awareness, to connect us to the work of Elton's foundation. It also had to give our local organizations a chance to showcase themselves. The mayor had no problem with that, but it seemed this was the last concession that Sunoco, WPVI, or Welcome America would ever give us. They viewed us as competitors rather than partners. And fought us on everything including port-a-potties.

My two partners in this endeavor were my friends Dan Anders and Jeff Guaracino. Dan, a lawyer working at the law firm Pepper Hamilton LLP, provided us with pro-bono legal work, which otherwise would have cost us tens of thousands of dollars. Jeff worked for Greater Philadelphia Tourism and Marketing Corporation (now known as Visit Philadelphia), and was given to us by his boss, Meryl Levitz. Jeff had come up with Philadelphia's historic and award-winning LGBT tourism campaign, "Get your history straight and your nightlife gay." To complete the team, we brought on Nina Zucker to do the day-to-day public relations and Rita Mezzaroba to spearhead contributions and in-kind services. That was our team, along with Jason, who kept me calm no matter what situation reared its head.

The mayor, knowing that he had just handed me the key to the city's biggest day, realized his guidance might be needed. Thus began our weekly eight a.m. meetings in his cabinet room, every Wednesday. His reasons were twofold. Primarily, he would help mitigate the inevitable turf wars that would occur with an event of this magnitude. And secondly, he reveled in the fact that, as the most anti-morning person he knew, I had to drag myself to City Hall at that early hour. My reaction, as Dan tells it, was that I threatened to show up to the weekly meetings in pajamas as protest. To his great credit, Dan talked me out of it.

The first point of order was to have a firm contract with Elton. At this early juncture we still had only a loose agreement. Dan, EJAF, Elton's tour manager, one of his lawyers, and I all jumped on a conference call. I thought, logically, that we could save on costs by having Elton onstage solo with a piano.

"What's the projected audience?" the tour manager asked. Before I could finish my reply, he interrupted, "We're bringing the bloody band!" I tried in my best negotiator's drawl to get him to reconsider, but he knew his craft, and a single piano would not work for a huge crowd (expected to be as many as 500,000 people) out in the open. We relented with little fanfare. The band was in. Due to the various agencies and nonprofits involved, Elton had to be contracted by yours truly—a personal services contract. There was no way out now. I had to deliver.

Working with city agencies for a fifty-person block party can be a headache. Multiply that by tens of thousands and it's a nightmare. The agreement with the mayor was that we'd be given the budget that was usually set aside for stage production. (Even here, Welcome America tried to get a share.) All other expenses we'd have to come up with ourselves. We had thirteen months to put it all together; it was a daunting project no matter which way you looked at it. Fundraising, programs, production staff, concessions, souvenirs, everything down to street closings and traffic patterns.

On February 9, 2005, we held a press conference to announce the event, now titled Philadelphia Freedom Concert & Ball. The concept was to give the city a free concert and use it as a way to promote AIDS awareness. There would be a grand ball in the massive Philadelphia Museum of Art, as I'd envisioned in Vienna, which would pay for it all. We were holding the press conference from the mayor's reception room with the mayor and many other elected officials. The room was at maximum capacity and every official who had any connection to the production wanted to be up front and in camera range. Elton was to join us courtesy of the satellite hookup via WPVI from Las Vegas, where he was doing his regular show at Caesars Palace. We scheduled it for 12:05 p.m. so it could be carried live on all the TV channels' noon news programs. Everything was set.

The plan called for the mayor, EJAF president Robert Key, and Elton to speak, and then I would introduce Geno Vento from the famous South Philly Geno's Steaks who was donating $100,000. As we were about to begin, Key told me he'd never given a speech of this importance before. I looked at him and said that I didn't believe him. But it turns out he was telling the truth. Up to that point, EJAF had never accomplished something on this scale, although Vienna was grand and drew 100,000 people.

The foundation was made up of Elton's friends and exiled employees from the business side. It seemed a place for castoffs; even an ex-lover was on the organization's payroll. Key, aside from his EJAF duties, was, according to him, directing the construction of Elton's new French getaway home. (On a side note, let me state clearly that post-2005, EJAF has become a professionally run organization in which Elton can take much pride.)

At the first meeting with the general manager of WPVI, she had told us we could work together on finding mutual sponsors. I asked her what the financial split would be. She had no answer. I then asked her who they had already lined up. Again she wouldn't answer. When I asked how much money they would give us to produce a show that would be financially beneficial to them, her response was that they were helping *us* by broadcasting it in the first place. I understood that to mean we'd receive zero dollars from them and realized, on the spot, that they could be counted on for nothing. It saddened me, since up to that point, other GMs at WPVI had been supportive of the LGBT community and committed to fighting AIDS. They had been a major partner in the original AIDS awareness campaign in the 1980s, which was revolutionary for its time. This woman might have been good for the station's bottom line, but not its soul. And she made it very difficult for us when she proclaimed that no sponsor of the concert would get any airtime, including forbidding us to put our sponsors' logos on the stage unless they bought time on the broadcast from WPVI.

After this woman's departure from WPVI and promotion at ABC, the new general manager once again became a partner in promoting diversity. The current general manager, Bernie Prazenica, is a champion for diversity at every level at the corporation, and a friend.

Back to the broadcast. So, we were all ready for the press conference. The aforementioned general manager of WPVI came over and told me not to introduce Geno's when we were live, since they were not sponsoring the concert broadcast. After I declined her demand, she countered with a different issue: the satellite transmission seemed to have a problem, so they couldn't broadcast at all. It was now past noon. This went on for a while. I guess the tipping point came when she realized that the station needed the publicity too. We finally got clearance before the end of the noon newscast. I made it a point to have Geno on live. What the general manager hadn't realized was that the sponsors WPVI had lined up for the broadcast were calling me directly, expressing how proud they were to be contributing. They were mistaken on that front, since WPVI would be keeping any dollars made from broadcast advertising. But it was not in anyone's interest to let them know they were not actually helping combat HIV/AIDS. Jonathan Saidel, former city controller, told me years later that he stood at the back of the press conference and looked over the scene, saying to himself, *What is Segal doing up there with all those thieves? They'll eat him alive.*

When the conference was over, Dan, Jeff, and I had a meeting to discuss a budget. I took a napkin and a pen and we began to sew things together, stitch by stitch.

* * *

We began adding new acts to the lineup, which now consisted of Sir Elton John, Patti LaBelle, Rufus Wainwright, and Bryan Adams. Comedian Wayne Brady had come on to emcee the show with Bruce Vilanch. We now had our own orchestra with Peter Nero and the Philly Pops, our legendary ensemble made up of musicians who played orchestral versions of a variety of musical genres. And, of course, the fireworks finale! One treat that I was especially proud to have secured to start off the show was a video dedication to AIDS awareness from my friend Walter Cronkite. On the logistics side, we had redrawn the Parkway concession areas, gotten my old friend John Dougherty from the electrical union to agree to line the Parkway with bigger and better LCD screens than previous years, and we even found a more efficient way to reroute the traffic.

Little more than a month before the concert, I woke up one morning to a startling news headline: "Mayor Announces Live 8, a Mega-Concert Celebrating the Twentieth Anniversary of Live Aid." The date of the concert would be July 2, two days before our own megaconcert.

It's during times of crisis like this that you discover who your true friends really are. Many realized what was happening, and stepped up to the plate to help make it all work. We decided to simply accomplish what we'd set out to do: put on the best July 4 concert in city history, and the largest AIDS awareness event ever. In a way, Live 8 freed us. It finally made me realize we were our own bosses; we didn't have to answer to anyone. I stopped worrying about our competition and I didn't think twice about making decisions that I would have previously run by others first. Though I admit I took my newfound autonomy a step too far on one occasion.

We were advised that President George W. Bush might want

to be present and give a speech during the ceremony at Independence Hall, when Elton was getting his award. Citing Bush's homophobic reelection campaign and his generally unwelcome policies, I categorically and not so politely told his representatives that he was not welcome on our stage. Yes, that was a step too far, and I was admonished by the mayor, who politely explained that you never turn down a visit by the president of the United States. In any case, Bush did not end up coming.

One night over dinner, Dan, Jeff, Jason, and I were laughing about the absurdity of it all and recalling the mayor's gentle warning to me that the show had to be family-friendly. It was this advice that made us realize that there was nothing outwardly gay in the show, and we needed to fix that. Fortunately, Jason and I had a trip to New York planned, to see Bruce Vilanch. After watching him play Edna in *Hairspray*, we went backstage to chat about his hosting duties. He was getting out of his costume as we met. We asked him if he'd consider doing Betsy Ross, the woman credited with making the first American Flag, in drag. As two assistants were helping him out of all the padding he needed in his role, he said as only Bruce can, "Please note, I'm a big man, but even I need padding to pull off Edna. How do you think I can get a costume ready in a month?"

On Monday morning Bruce called to say it would be done. Seems the *Hairspray* dressers, wig makers, and costume designers wanted to contribute to our show, and creating a complete Betsy Ross costume from scratch was their way of giving back. How I love the Broadway community!

To assure that July 4 was as patriotic as possible, Congressman Bob Brady arranged for an Air Force flyover just as the show began; the police would sing "The Star-Spangled Banner"; and a color guard of the military would open the show.

Our Wednesday-morning meetings in the mayor's office

were now somewhat calmer since his staff was busy dealing with Live 8 and had to contend with an even more outlandish set of demands. It was fun to watch knowing that we had absolutely nothing to do with that chaos.

Two weeks before the concert, on Wednesday, June 15, 2005, the headline on the front page of the *Philadelphia Inquirer* read, "Caught on Tape: City Deal-Makers," then the subheading, "Lana Felton-Ghee Wanted More Action on City Contracts. The FBI Heard it All." At this point I believe the mayor understood the ongoing problems we were encountering and began to show compassion. While the *Inquirer* story was about the alleged corruption at the top of Welcome America, our concert was unrelated and above reproach. In fact, we seemed to be the only people connected to city government who were not called in to be interviewed in the investigation by the FBI and the federal prosecutor. When I later met the former federal prosecutor, Patrick Meehan, while he was campaigning for Congress, I asked him why we hadn't been called in and he said, "We knew you were clean and we didn't want to give you any more problems than what you already had." That was a kind remark. He went on to be elected congressman for the Seventh District.

In the days leading up to the event, the mayor had a request for me: "Mark, I want you to speak on the July 4 morning at Independence Hall." My response was that I would be too busy that day ushering Elton around; we'd agreed to give him an award at Independence Hall in the morning, then go to the William Way LGBT Community Center and name a portion of the Street "Elton's Way," then jet over to the Philadelphia Museum of Art for sound check.

The mayor insisted, and after each meeting Dan and I wondered why he was pressing so hard. Then it dawned on me: I would be the first openly gay person in history to make a speech on July 4 at Independence Hall. I called the mayor one morning and agreed to do it.

The morning of July 4, Jason and I dressed in our suits and walked to Independence Hall for the award ceremony. We'd done a walkthrough the day before. Elton's security was demanding that they be allowed to carry their guns onto the premises, to which the National Park Service guards firmly said no. I wasn't sure if that situation had resolved itself or not.

At Independence Hall, looking out over the platform in front of the building, a chill went down my back. Then my friends Robert Metzger and Barbara Lichtman came over to wish me luck. As I watched them return to their seats, I noticed a man next to Barbara in the front row. It was Barney Frank. When I approached and asked him what he was doing here, he said he knew this was an historic event and wanted to support me. I was so very honored. This also made me fully realize the magnitude of what I was about to do.

Elton was supposed to make an appearance for the morning program, which was being broadcast live. Our start time came and went and Elton hadn't arrived. The mayor quickly decided that enough was enough, and said we'd start the program and stall until Elton showed up. He made an introduction, and we all stood for the national anthem. I peered up at Independence Hall, marveling at what was happening, when suddenly we heard sirens. *Oh my god*, I thought, *something's wrong*. For a second, I thought it might be a terrorist incident. I turned around to see a black SUV with a police escort screeching to a halt in front of the stage. Out popped Elton and his armed guards. That's one way to avoid being searched by security. At the command of the mayor, I retrieved Elton and brought him into the building to wait until called to the stage.

The program continued, a band played some patriotic music, and finally the mayor introduced me. The boy from the Wilson Park projects at 25th and Ritner, the boy raised on the other side of the tracks, was about to address Independence Day from the nation's birthplace, Independence Hall. Approaching the podium I took out my speech and began:

"Mr. Mayor, Senator, Congressmen, Fannie Weinstein [she was still with me in spirit], ladies and gentlemen, what a wonderful exciting and historic July 4 this is in Philadelphia, and tonight will witness the brilliant musical talent of a legend and the man who gave our city its anthem, 'Philadelphia Freedom,' Sir Elton John. I'm on the stage for two reasons today. First, as a producer of the Philadelphia Freedom Concert & Ball with Sir Elton John, which will raise awareness for HIV/AIDS. That mission began over twenty years ago when Jane Shull and I created the first AIDS Awareness Day in Philadelphia in the early 1980s. Then, AIDS was a gay man's disease; today, more than half of all new cases in the US are not. In most parts of the world HIV is a heterosexually transmitted virus.

"There is another reason I'm here today. I am representing what up to now has been an almost invisible minority, the gay community. On this very spot in 1965, the first gay civil rights march in America was held. Last Friday we commemorated those brave souls with a historic marker which you could see over there on the northwest corner of 6th and Chestnut streets. Millions of patriotic gay and lesbian Americans have watched speeches in front of this magnificent building on July 4 and we've still remained invisible. But today, for the first time in 229 years, a member of their community, an openly gay American, has the opportunity to stand on this podium and say, God bless America."

When I made my way back to my seat, the mayor reached over and said, with a large smile, "Very well done."

Elton was given an award that we had created for him. He accepted with grace, and posed for a picture with the mayor and Barney, before getting back into his SUV. The ceremony now over, Jason and I got into a car and, before we could catch our breath, the motorcade was on its way to the William Way Community Center, our second stop of the day. Dolph Goldenburg, executive director of the community center, was awaiting Elton to unveil a new sign for a street renamed after the star.

In rapid-fire succession, Elton got out of his vehicle, made a few remarks, cut the ribbon, and posed for a few more photos. We then parted ways, Elton back to his hotel to prepare for the concert and me to the Parkway to see how sound check and other preparations were going.

As I walked down the Parkway, I glimpsed the stage. Mike Barnes and his stagehands from the union had erected what must have been the world's largest red ribbon as a backdrop. I was also delighted as I walked past every one of the ten giant LCD screens lining the Parkway. I had badgered my old friend John Dougherty from the Electrical Union to donate the additional $80,000 that we were short for the rental cost. It was beautiful. The sound system was top notch too.

The first words I heard coming out of the speakers were during Patti LaBelle's sound check. She was going off about Elton with more than a few choice words. I rushed up to the stage. Jerry Blavat, a legendary radio deejay known locally as the "Geator with the Heater," whom I had asked to keep an eye on his friend Patti, was standing off to the side. He shrugged as I got to the stage. Patti had just been informed that Elton, who had previously agreed to perform a duet with her, had changed his mind. When I went over to Elton's road manager to inquire about possibly of putting the duet back into the program, he told me that the star had made up his mind and it was final, no questions.

It was now up to me, the producer, to placate Patti. "How's my favorite yelling diva?" I said as I approached. She didn't laugh. She just kept shouting, letting it all out. I wasn't too up-set because I knew she wasn't mad at me, but at the situation. I explained how sorry I was but that there was nothing I could do. Being the professional that she is, Patti eventually concluded her sound check and then said, "I'm all done here now, what time should I arrive tonight?" I gave her the details and kissed her on the cheek, then she said to me sternly: "You owe me."

With that bullet dodged, I went inside the Philadelphia Mu-seum of Art to check on the rest of the Freedom Ball prepara-tions. Fred Stein, our party organizer, had created an atmosphere that was beyond elegant. Elton's signature was emblazoned in lasers atop the grand staircase. Members of the Philadelphia Boys Choir were lined up on each side of the magnificent stone staircase rehearsing the song "Circle of Life" from The Lion King. Food tables and bars were being erected with special buntings displaying our logo. It looked like something you'd expect from a White House event, and even at a thousand dollars a ticket it was still a bargain. For those who paid more, there would be a photo op with Elton that we had negotiated with his team.

Before the event commenced, Jason and I did one last check in-side the backstage production trailer. Bruce, our emcee, ever my friend but now in need of support, walked up to me and asked for his script. I just stared at him. My brain was overloaded. He shook his head and said, calmly and with a hint of a smile, "There is no script, is there?"

My reply was as timid as they come: "Thought you'd just wing it."

Bruce, the consummate professional and take-charge guy, said, "I'll write it. Ask Wayne Brady to come over to my trailer and we'll get it done. But Mark, did you know there is no mirror in my dressing room? Betsy Ross doesn't happen unless she has a mirror. The first lady of the flag must look proper." Even under stress, Bruce had a great sense of humor.

It was five p.m. and time for the ball to begin. Jason and I left the production area and ran up those famous *Rocky* steps. Midway up I tripped, and for an instant believed I was having a heart attack. Jason grabbed me, and as I lifted myself back up, I could hear the Philly Pops playing the overture to *Star Wars*. Enlivened by the music and happy Peter had honored my request, Jason and I walked hand in hand up the remainder of the steps.

For the first time I got a glimpse of the crowd. It was overwhelming. People were stretched far beyond what my eyes could see. With Jason still holding my hand and Peter's music inspiring the crowd, I knew the evening was going to be a success. Bill Fraser, with a long-range camera, somehow captured that moment on film. It is one of my favorite photographs of all time.

Jason and I quickly headed back into the museum and found an empty gallery in which I could change into a fresh suit. I was standing, if you please, next to a Renoir.

When we entered the party it was going very well. Sponsors and people who donated their time, money, or services to help us make the evening a success were mingling with politicos and corporate CEOs. Trumpeters stood at the top of the stairs that were lined by the Boys Choir in white pants and blazing red jackets. Jerry Blavat in his distinctive radio voice announced each of the dignitaries as they descended the steps. They came down in pairs with the trumpeters blaring away like they were Cinderella making an entrance at the ball. Somehow, in the middle of it all, I lost Jason. I didn't have time to look for him as it was my turn to accompany Robert Key of the EJAF, who was having the time of his life, down the magical steps. As the trumpeters blared, Blavat announced, "Ladies and gentlemen, please welcome the producer of our ball, Robert Key of the Elton John AIDS Foundation, and our own Mark Segal." The crowd went wild as we descended the stairs and the Boys Choir serenaded us with "Circle of Life." At the bottom I made a brief speech and then gathered the people who had paid extra money to have their photo op with Elton. We all made a mad dash down to the painstakingly appointed dressing room in the basement to get ready for the star.

Before we actually entered the dressing room, Robert Key said that Elton wanted to skip the photos. I finally snapped. "You call him right now and tell him that if he does not come here, it will be a violation of the contract and he will be fired." Robert, one of the most dignified and stiff-upper-lipped people I've ever known, looked very nervous. He asked what I'd do if Elton refused to come, and I replied: "I'll march onstage and announce that Sir Elton John did not honor his contract and has been fired."

Fortunately, Robert was able to restore the original plan, but as we walked to the photo area, another member of the EJAF pulled me aside. "Just wanted to let you know that Elton prefers to have good-looking guys in the front row. It helps him perform better." Dumbfounded, I glanced around and saw Bruce Yelk, who worked with Jeff Guaracino at the tourism agency, and who I thought might be able to fulfill the request. He took it all in stride and stepped away to make some phone calls. To this day I wonder if Robert was just attempting a joke.

When I paused for a moment to catch my breath, Jason reappeared and asked what he'd missed. I rolled my eyes, too tired to even laugh. We left the ball and went back down the steps to the production trailer. Bryan Adams and Rufus Wainwright had already performed, and Patti was next. As Jason and I opened the door to the trailer, we saw a man arguing with a group of svelte girls in black dresses. The man, a security guard in charge of keeping people off the stage, was refusing to let the girls up. "We are Patti LaBelle's singers!" one of them shouted. Jason recognized them from the earlier rehearsal, and told me they were fine. I ran up to the guard and demanded that he let them through, then apologized to the singers.

We sat in for Patti and her singers as they performed "Lady Marmalade" and then headed backstage again. The next time I saw Elton was just before my introduction. He was chatting with Bruce and said I reminded him of Nathan Lane. Then I was told that it was time for me to go onstage to thank all our sponsors. Yet in all the confusion, we had forgotten to print out our list of sponsors. Dan and Jason, from inside the trailer, wrote out a list and handed it to me just in time.

Walking onto that stage I was exhausted. But the applause, which seemed to go on forever, was humbling and lifted me up. My job was simple: read the list and introduce Elton. I was also there to pump the crowd up for the final act, the most grand performance that had ever graced the July 4 stage. (Afterward people told me that I sounded like a man at the end of a long and arduous ordeal and was simply glad to be rid of it all. Producing this concert was one of the most thrilling things I've ever done but I was never more relieved than when it was all over.)

It was now time for my introduction: "Ladies and gentlemen, it is my honor to introduce you to the man who gave us our city song and made tonight possible, Sir Elton John!" With that it was over for me, but not before one last interesting moment.

Apparently, Elton's band did not start playing on cue after my introduction, so when I returned to join Jason in the wings of the stage I heard Elton screaming, "Play! Play!" Finally they started, and Jason and I took our seats and watched as Elton mesmerized the crowd. He truly gave, in my estimation, and many of his longtime fans agree, one of his best performances ever. He even dedicated a song to me, which was a surprise. As Jason and I held each other toward the end of the performance, Jason said, "It's over, you did it! I knew you would."

When Elton and his police escort were leaving for the chartered plane, the fireworks began. Standing on the stage with Jason watching the fireworks, I let out a sigh of relief. Heading down the steps, we saw Dan passing by on the back of a police cart, waving goodbye. It dawned on us that we hadn't arranged for a ride home, and since the area was blocked from cars, including cabs, we had a nice long walk ahead of us.

Naturally, we still had one more highlight left in the day. As we were walking away from the Philadelphia Museum of Art, out of nowhere came the SUV limo that had just taken Elton to the airport. When the doors opened, it was full of what looked like a group of female hookers. Huh? We continued on, and as we hit Logan Fountain a man yelled out to us, asking if we wanted to buy an official T-shirt. It wasn't; he was a counterfeiter. I stepped up to him and started to call the police over, but once again Jason held me back. We'd been through enough already. We finally made it to Market Street and near City Hall we found a cab. We slept late the following morning.

Chapter 13

Meeting with Mr. President

had promised Jason a nice vacation after the concert. We went to Greece. With our friends Barbara Lichtman, Rita Mezzaroba, Dennis Cook, and Larry Furman, we rented a four-cabin catamaran out of Athens with Rob Metzger as our captain and set off to sail the Greek isles. The deal with my friends was that there would be no drama. Somehow, no one had told us about the infamous Etesian winds of the Aegean Sea that can whip up waves of fifteen feet or more and tear the sail off a boat.

We made it to two islands before we hit Mykonos where the harbormaster literally shut down the harbor and forbid any boats to sail. I could think of worse things than being stuck in Mykonos for a couple of days. We had a blast dancing on the rocks at Super Paradise beach and visiting the local discos and restaurants. Enjoying the beauty of the island was an additional treat.

Once we were allowed to leave Mykonos, we set sail to our last stop, a small island called Kythnos. As we were approaching we dropped our anchor and it got stuck on the bottom of the channel leading to the harbor. After numerous attempts to get the attention of the harbormaster, or anyone for that matter, it seemed we'd be stuck all night. To heck with it, we'd figure it out in the morning. Then we heard a blast. It was the horn of a 40,000-ton ferry headed directly toward us. Everyone started running around the boat in a panic. Rob was at the controls, and as I saw the ferry heading for a direct hit I yelled, "Just step on it!" He did, and the ferry passed by so close you could reach out and touch it. Later, after the night had gone and turned into early morning, we cut the anchor loose and headed to port in Athens. Drama seems to follow me.

On my return home, it was back to business. I needed a new passion, which became examining LGBT history. October is LGBT History Month and each year the *Philadelphia Gay News*, along with eighteen other LGBT newspapers and numerous websites, coordinates the National LGBT History Project.

Mark Horn informed me that a Gay Youth reunion was being planned for the fall of 2007 and I wanted to prepare myself. I began by doing some historical research of my own for the first time.

On November 3, 2007, the first-ever Gay Youth reunion was held at New York City's Lesbian, Gay, Bisexual & Transgender Community Center. While the organization had gone through many names and mission changes over the years, its doors were still open, making it the longest-serving LGBT organization in the city. Nearly one hundred of us met up that day. Five of the originals members showed up, including Mark Horn, my vice president.

When I arrived, people came up to chat, many of whom I didn't know. Then the chairperson welcomed everyone and said, "Without this guy, we wouldn't be here—the founder of Gay Youth, our papa, Mark Segal." As people got to their feet one by one and explained what the organization had done for them, it felt like an out-of-body experience.

Following the after-party, there was a special moment for the class of 1969. Mark Horn, Jeff Hochhauser, Michael Knowles, and I left the reunion, locked arms, and walked down Eighth Avenue chanting once again and for the first time since 1971, *"We are the Stonewall girls . . ."*

The bubble burst on the train home to Philly. Recalling everyone who had spoken, I sobbed uncontrollably, tears of pure pride. At fifty-six I was still a Gay Youth. My brain had a hard time taking in all that had happened, and it was also the first time my age truly registered with me. On the train, here's how I wrote about that day:

> *It only took thirty-eight years, but today in New York City, it was graduation day. Presiding over this day were members of Gay Youth, GLYNY, and all its other reincarnations through the years. The organizers were brilliant in hosting first a meeting, which served as our graduation, then an after-party which served as a prom, one that most of us never had.*

And Tom Approbato wrote in New York's *Gay City News:*

> *Gay Youth would over time emerge as the parent of every other gay and lesbian student group throughout the United States. From humble beginnings, with a handful of dedicated teenagers, Gay Youth left a legacy for LGBT youth in America.*
>
> *GLNY was in fact one name for an organization whose mast changed several times over the years—Gay Youth; Bisexual, Gay and Lesbian Youth of New York (BiGLYNY); and Bi, Gay, Lesbian, Transgender Youth of New York (Bi-GLTYNY) at different times were the words on the common banner . . .*
>
> *Eighty-nine alumni spanning the years 1969 through*

1994 traveled from their homes all across the country to answer a common call. Members came from New York, New Jersey, Pennsylvania, Florida, Illinois, Wisconsin, Arizona, California, and even the UK. There were men and women of all ethnicities, backgrounds, and even persuasions with one common bond—the feelings of friendship established during our teenage years.

We shared some of the toughest coming-of-age experiences with each other. In a peer-run support group, there was no place for false sympathy. Our bonds of friendship and support were earnest and heartfelt.

Mark Segal, one of the founders of Gay Youth from 1969, addressed the membership with a stirring speech. Although Mark now lives in Philadelphia, he made the trip into New York to see his contemporaries and his surrogate progeny. He spoke passionately about the lifelong friendships he established as well as the ongoing effect that this teen support group has had on his life.

"It's like the graduation I never had," Mark said. "I never went to my high school prom or my high school reunion. This is my prom. This is my reunion."

Many of us in the audience echoed those sentiments as we sat in a big circle and introduced ourselves.

Back home with a new sense of pride, several projects were moving forward, but one that had never been completed was building an elevator at the community center for those in wheelchairs. Councilman Kenney had lobbied the mayor to give the center a grant for the funds required to finally complete this task. A community center is a place where we should all feel free to gather, no matter what our political positions are, and like Switzerland be politically neutral.

Our community was in full preparation mode as we headed into the presidential primary year of 2008. By the time the Democrat wagon reached Pennsylvania in March of 2008 the field of nominees in the Democratic party had been narrowed down to Senator Hillary Clinton and Senator Barack Obama.

Throughout the primaries, in each state Senator Obama campaigned, his staff would often promise the local LGBT media an interview, then pull out at the last moment. As far as we at *Philadelphia Gay News* were concerned, that was not going to happen on our watch. We requested interviews with both Clinton and Obama. Due to Clinton's relationship with Governor Rendell, she quickly agreed. Obama agreed too, but kept putting it off. Finally, with only two weeks to go before the primary, we decided to wait no longer and to act.

On April 4, 2008, the front page of the *Philadelphia Gay News* was filled, on the right side, with the interview with Senator Hillary Clinton. The entire left half of the front page was a blank space, with the exception of a box in the middle that read, "It's been 1,522 days since Sen. Barack Obama has spoken with local gay press. See editorial, Page 11." The reaction was immediate. Every network took notice and newspapers around the nation wrote it up. It was a united and bold decision made by our entire staff. In her interview, Clinton had urged state legislative Democrats to vote no on the anti–gay marriage legislation, so we decided to continue our campaign to get an answer to this question from Senator Obama. The following day we put out a press release asking, "Day 2: What is Senator Obama's position on the antigay legislation in Pennsylvania?" The day after that: "Day 3: What is Senator Obama's position on . . ." This went on each day until a week before the primary, and almost every reporter in the state now wanted the answer. I finally received the following e-mail from Chris May at the local CBS affiliate:

Subject: Obama finally answers, thanks to our friends at Capitol Wire

Hi Mark,

Not sure if you saw it on Sunday, but we put the question about the gay marriage amendment to Barack Obama. In an interview after his town hall meeting in Reading he told us this:

"I have said before and continue to believe that a constitutional amendment banning gay marriage is unnecessary, it's divisive, and it's something I would oppose. I think that it is important for us to recognize that same-sex couples should be able to engage in civil unions, that their rights to transfer property or visit each other in the hospital—all those things are matters of law. Even those of us who may not believe in gay marriage should still be able to confer those benefits. And the problem with a constitutional amendment is—I'm not in favor of gay marriage but I certainly don't want to see a court suggesting that somehow we can't pass laws to make sure gays and lesbians aren't being discriminated against. So I think this is a distraction from a lot of issues we need to be tackling, and if I were in the state legislature I would oppose it."

Thought you would be interested.

A few days before the primary, the Philadelphia Democratic City Committee held its annual Jefferson Jackson Day dinner, where both Clinton and Obama would address a crowd of over a thousand party workers. My friend Congressman Bob Brady, who also served as the committee's chairman, erected a VIP tent outside the union hall for a few of the elite and somehow he managed to include me. Bob's wife Debbie and I watched the scene unfolding together. We were teasing the Secret Service agents; one looked at me and said, "I'm from San Francisco." We laughed, assuming that the guy had just come out to us. There was an air of excitement when Senator Obama entered the tent. He said a few words then went around the tent shaking hands.

City Council President Anna Verna wanted a picture of herself with the senator and shoved a camera in my hands as Obama made his way toward us. "Take our picture," she said. So I did. Then, in a polite gesture, Senator Obama reached out to shake my hand. I'd feared this introduction.

As my hand met his in that VIP tent while a thousand Democratic Party workers waited to hear his campaign speech, I said, "Senator, I'm Mark Segal."

His eyes opened wide. He stood even more upright and pulled me toward him, a serious look on his face. "So you're Mark Segal," he said. Then, with hurt in his eyes and sincerity in his voice, he added, "I really am good on LGBT issues. We have to talk further on this, but I have to go in the other room and speak." He then made a fist and wanted to fist bump. There is just something in me that must win every debate, or at least have the final word. Somehow, he recognized this and said, with that great broad smile of his, "Come on, Mark, give me a fist bump." I did. The man is charming.

That would have been enough drama for me in one evening, but a half hour before, Hillary Clinton had been in that same VIP room. After she spoke to our small group of elected officials, union leaders, and major contributors, Governor Rendell, a major force in her campaign, spotted me and brought her over to say hello. She gave me a warm hug and said, "You're more tenacious than me!" Coming from her, it was the ultimate compliment.

* * *

The following day, Steve Hildebrand, Obama's deputy national campaign manager, called me to follow up for the senator. During that call, Steve told me he was gay and I quickly realized that this in itself was a story. I asked if we could get an interview with him about being an openly gay deputy campaign manager in a presidential race, and Steve said he had to run it by David Axelrod and Obama first. Luckily, they approved. Then in August, in the middle of the race between Barack Obama and John McCain, I finally got that interview with the future president, and to make it sweeter, it was shared with all my fellow LGBT local publications as part of our National LGBT History Project. Here's an excerpt:

> **Mark Segal:** *You are the most GLBT-friendly candidate in history running for president. Are you concerned John Mc-Cain and the Republicans might use this as a divisive issue as they did in 2004?*
>
> **Barack Obama:** *No. I think they can try but I don't think it will work for a couple of reasons. Number one, I think that the American peoples' attitudes with respect to LGBT issues are continuing to evolve. I think people are becoming more and more aware of the need to treat all people equally regardless of sexual orientation. There are some people who disagree with that, but frankly those folks—many of them—probably have already made their minds up about this election earlier.*
>
> **MS:** *You've talked about your many gay friends. Would you and Michelle be comfortable attending their commitment ceremony?*

BO: *We would. But I'll be honest with you that, these days, I can't go anywhere.*

MS: *The current President Bush has used signing orders to change military rules and regulations. If White House counsel advised you that you could end "Don't Ask, Don't Tell" by attaching a signing order to a military appropriations bill, would you?*

BO: *I would not do it that way. The reason is because I want to make sure that when we revert "Don't Ask, Don't Tell," it's gone through a process and we've built a consensus or at least a clarity of that, of what my expectations are, so that it works. My first obligation as the president is to make sure that I keep the American people safe and that our military is functioning effectively. Although I have consistently said I would repeal "Don't Ask, Don't Tell," I believe that the way to do it is make sure that we are working through a process, getting the Joint Chiefs of Staff clear in terms of what our priorities are going to be. That's how we were able to integrate the armed services to get women more actively involved . . . At some point, you've got to make a decision that that's the right thing to do, but you always want to make sure that you are doing it in a way that maintains our core mission in our military.*

MS: *Many lawyers contend that the Defense of Marriage Act passed by Congress is unconstitutional. It takes away more than 1,100 rights, including IRS joint filings. If a suit is filed in federal court, would you expect or instruct your attorney general to join in that suit with an amicus brief questioning its legality?*

BO: *I would want to review carefully any lawsuit that was filed. This is probably my carryover from being a constitutional lawyer. Here's where I can tell you [what] my principle is: DOMA was an unnecessary encroachment by the federal government in an area traditionally reserved for the state. I think that it was primarily sent as a message to score political points instead of work through these difficult issues. I recognize why it was done. I'm sympathetic to the political pressures involved, but I think that we need to bring it to a close and my preference would be to work through a legislative solution. I would also point out that if it's going before this court, I'm not sure what chances it would have to be overturned. I think we're going to have to take a different approach, but I am absolutely committed to the concept it is not necessary.*

MS: *In the wake of the torture and murder of Matthew Shepard in 1998, Senator McCain voted against adding sexual orientation to the definition of hate crimes and says he'll vote against it again. Isn't this inconsistent for a man who knows torture?*

BO: *You'll have to ask Senator McCain that. Here's what I can say: There is no doubt that hate crimes based on sexual orientation are all too prevalent. It is something that we have to hit back hard against and identify these vicious crimes for what they are: hate crimes. This is something that I believe in and will continue to believe in when I am president.*

MS: *President Reagan, President Bush, and President Clinton, when meeting world leaders, have raised human rights* *questions. Amnesty International has documented countries that imprison, torture, and kill gay men, some of which are very close US allies. Would you be willing to raise that question when meeting with those leaders?*

BO: *I think that the treatment of gays, lesbians, and transgender persons is part of this broader human rights discussion. I think it is not acceptable that we would in any way carve out exceptions for our broader human rights advocacy to exclude violations of human rights based on sexual orientation. I think that has to be part and parcel of any conversations we have about human rights.*

At this point I personally had no doubts about how Obama would evolve on the issue of marriage equality. As he promised me, he has indeed been great on LGBT issues. Before he was even sworn in, he had appointed a host of LGBT people to high positions in his administration, including Shin Inouye, who had LGBT media in his portfolio as a deputy press secretary.

Once President Obama took office, he quickly stated that he would work to end "Don't Ask, Don't Tell," and his attorney general filed a brief before the Supreme Court opposing the Defense of Marriage Act. Any time a state introduced anti-LGBT legislation he publicly opposed it. But what he should get special credit for is that when Maryland was about to vote on marriage equality, he got personally involved and urged the citizens of Maryland to vote yes, and he urged the pillar of the African American community—the churches—to do likewise. This one act created a sea of change in the black community, not just in Maryland but across the nation. While African American leaders have supported LGBT rights in the past, this was the first black president asking them to stand with LGBT Americans in the struggle for equality.

And when the Supreme Court ruled in June 2015 that marriage equality was now the law of the land, President Obama made an impromptu emotional statement from the Rose Garden, and that night the White House was lit up in rainbow colors.

After the August 2008 interview, I wouldn't speak to Barack Obama again until 2010, when as president he made his first official trip back to Philadelphia and I was asked by Senator Bob Casey to be one of the official hosts. After the president delivered his speech that day, we were ushered into a small room with no windows. Obviously it was chosen for security. A group of us all gathered, chatting away until the president walked in the room and said, "Hi, everyone."

Silence fell and we all seemed overcome with stage fright, even the seasoned political folks. Since everyone else was standing still, I walked over and said, "Welcome to Philadelphia, Mr. President."

He smiled and said, "How you doing, Mark?"

Now I'm sure he didn't recognize me and someone had whispered my name in his ear, but hey, I have no complaints.

He asked, "What's on your mind?" to which I smiled and said, "Mr. President, I appreciate all the great points you've been making about LGBT equality, but what about LGBT funding?"

He asked if there was something in particular I was referring to, so I told him about our plans to build an affordable-living facility for LGBT seniors.

He said, "Send me the plans."

My reply was: "Yeah, like you have the time to look at them."

A big smile appeared on his face and he said to Reggie Love, his personal aide, "Give Mark your card," and to me he said, "I'll look them over and if they seem possible, I'll pass them on."

Then we did the photo op and others stepped forward for their moment.

That night the plans, everything I had on the project, were e-mailed. The only hint I had about whether the president actually looked at the plans came at the 2012 Democrat National Convention in Charlotte, North Carolina. I was at a Human Rights Campaign/Victory Fund lunch with my friend Klayton Fennell where the first lady was speaking. At the end of the speech I went over to the rope line to shake her hand. Giving her my name and my affiliation with the *Philadelphia Gay News*, she said, "The senior project." Then she leaned over to hug me. When the Secret Service got alarmed, she added with a delightful smile, "I forgot, the first lady is not supposed to hug."

This period of time was a whirlwind of activity. Publishing the paper, pushing full speed ahead with the senior building, the *Philadelphia Gay News* winning awards, and more.

Then, in late 2011, my life and history punched me right in the face. My friend David L. Cohen, now at Comcast, called to ask if I'd serve on something called the Joint Diversity Council. My initial thought was that this would just be a rubber-stamp group or show horse for the company. David assured me otherwise, then added what should have been obvious: "Mark, you of all people in the LGBT community should appreciate this opportunity to create change in the media."

On August 19, 2013, at 30 Rock, the NBC News world headquarters in New York City, presidents and producers from NBC News, MSNBC, CNBC, and the *Today* show were packed into a conference room. I was there in my role as an LGBT advisor and a member of NBC parent company Comcast's Joint Diversity Council. The Latino, Native American, and African American

representatives of the council had spoken. When I was introduced all eyes fell on me. Looking over the assembled crowd of
executives I knew what I had to say and it was unrelated to the
bullet points on the paper in front of me. I smiled at the NBC
news brass and simply uttered: "The last time I was in this building was forty years ago, and you had me arrested and taken out
in handcuffs." Silence swept over the room, but soon they all
began to laugh, and then they actually applauded. Phil Griffin,
president of MSNBC, was laughing the loudest. I had met him
at an earlier Comcast event so he'd had a taste of my humor.

At another Comcast Joint Diversity Council meeting, David asked me to talk about my appearances on the *Phil Donahue
Show* in the 1970s. I explained that the 1973 taping with my
parents was one of the first depictions of a gay family on television. I also said that when I ran across Phil Donahue years ago,
he told me that many of his tapes from that time were lost in a
fire. Since then I had searched television museums and private
collections, but a recording of that particular show remained
elusive. At this point they perked up. Klayton Fennell, who
had become my minder at Comcast, asked Beth Colleton at
NBCUniversal if, through their connections, they could help
track it down. They requested any information that I had on
the taping.

At home, I searched through boxes of memorabilia and
finally found the official letters from *Donahue*, and even the
TV release forms signed by my mother and father. A new hunt
through various television archives began. To see my friends at
Comcast and NBC commit the time and resources to search for
what would be a treasured piece of memorabilia for me was heart-
warming. Ultimately, they confirmed that the fire that Donahue
had mentioned had indeed destroyed all copies of that tape.

* * *

On a cold day in January 2013 I watched President Barack Obama give his second inauguration speech.

"We, the people, declare today that the most evident of truths—that all of us are created equal—is the star that guides us still; just as it guided our forebears through Seneca Falls, and Selma, and Stonewall; just as it guided all those men and women, sung and unsung, who left footprints along this great Mall, to hear a preacher say that we cannot walk alone; to hear a King proclaim that our individual freedom is inextricably bound to the freedom of every soul on earth."

My congressman had graciously invited me to the inauguration, but I'd decided to stay warm and watch it on television at home. As the president spoke those words, my mind tried to fully grasp the magnitude of what he was saying. Something came over me. I'm not sure how long I cried but I know that in the end the tears washed away a lot of the pain and hate that had been stored up in me for years—the pain of growing up and listening in fright as my relatives spoke in hushed tones about cousin Norman, the shame of looking at those men in the catalogs and worrying that I would forever cause anguish to my parents, and the belief that I would have no future due to who I was. It erased all the battles I'd witnessed and the battles I'd fought within the LGBT community as it grew and changed. In a flash, all of that was gone. I was still and at peace.

It was a moment that had to be shared with someone who had been there during the Stonewall period with me. I Skyped Jerry Hoose and we just looked at each other with tears running down our cheeks. While the president had compared our work to that of the founders of the nation, and those who fought for civil and women's rights, only we knew the toll it had taken on us, and the toll that it had taken on everyone involved. We had gone from the lowest class of fighters for human rights to equals.

To me, the kid from the projects, who was always the lower class in every category, it meant the world. I also recalled that first meeting with President Obama where he told me, "I'm good on LGBT issues." Yes, Mr. President, you are.

This inspired "We Are America," the following year's National LGBT History Project. The October series was devoted to LGBT people from the American Revolution through the Civil War who had helped build a nation.

Every year the local LGBT media collaborate in publishing articles pertaining to LGBT history. That year we had thirty publications with a combined print run of 650,000 dedicating numerous feature stories on those LGBT people who had helped create the USA. No longer could the far right wing say, *Our founding fathers did not have LGBT people in mind when they created this country.*

Chief among the features was a piece I offered for the project.

If it were not for this man, there would be no USA: Baron Frederich Wilhelm von Steuben . . . Von Steuben had a brilliant military mind . . . but he had one problem. He was on the run from several countries for having sex with men.

Luckily, the colonies had a representative in Paris who was there to win the French courts' financial support for our revolution and find professionals to boost Washington's failing continental army. His name was Ben Franklin.

Franklin interviewed Von Steuben in his home in Paris. Franklin—the Bill Gates of his day—was impressed with him but also knew of the rumors, and passed on the first interview. Several months went by and now Von Steuben was being hunted down by French clergy. At this point a second meeting took place in Franklin's home. This time Franklin, understanding the situation, arranged for Von Steuben to be whisked out of Paris on a boat full of armaments and with a letter of introduction to General Washington. I therefore bestowed the title on Franklin as the father of "Don't Ask, Don't Tell."

We also featured articles on Abraham Lincoln, a gay African American soldier who led a segregated troop in the American Revolution, President James Buchanan, Katharine Lee Bates (writer of "America the Beautiful"), and yes, our first president, George Washington. All had connections to the community, whether they were allies or gay/lesbian themselves.

To top the project off, I wound up being featured on the front cover of the *Philadelphia Daily News*, dressed in a Continental Army uniform. The project was a smashing success.

Chapter 14
An Army of Pink Hard Hats

That night in 2005 when I asked Jason, "Do you think I can raise nineteen or twenty million dollars to build an affordable LGBT senior living facility?" he looked me in the eye and said, "Of course." He might have believed so, but to me it was a pie-in-the-sky dream, and that's what the project became. Inspiration had begun in 1998, when we received a state grant to look at issues facing LGBT seniors.

We conducted a survey, the results of which surprised us all. The number-one issue facing LGBT seniors was housing. Not only the issue of affordability, which affected them like all communities, but the treatment of these seniors in existing low-income housing. Many people seemed to think that "gay" and "low income" could not be uttered in the same sentence. We were being stereotyped as typically childless, two-income households with lots of disposable funds. This was incorrect.

Significant credit was due to Mike O'Brien, my state representative who identified with the problem and was responsive to my interest in creating LGBT-friendly affordable housing for seniors. His advice was simple and something that nobody had told me in a long time: "Mark, you're not pushy enough." Mike, a proud, heavyset, blue-collar Irish Catholic member of our state legislature, sat me down along with his chief of staff, Mary Isaacson, to tell me the political facts of life as he saw them.

"Mark, you've supported the Democratic Party for forty years and you finally want something back. It may not be for yourself, but you want something and they owe it to you. It's about time you start demanding. Be pushy again."

Mike was correct, and that chat is what really put this project on the road to becoming a reality. Once again I was not knocking politely on doors—I was busting them down. But it started a little before those words of wisdom from Mike.

"Senator!" Every time I made a pilgrimage to State Senator Vince Fumo's office in South Philly, he knew the bite was coming. "If we're going to get this senior building off the ground, we'll need some seed funds."

"How much do you think you'll need?"

There's a personal rule in politics that has served me well. It's called the 50 percent rule: you ask for 50 percent more than you hope to get. "A million would work," I replied.

Now, if memory serves me well, his response was somewhere along the lines of, "What the fuck?" Then he continued: "We're talking about a first-of-its-kind, historic project—with a long road we'll have to maneuver." He just stared at me, half in disbelief and half in amusement. "No one would ever—"

"But Vince, you know this is needed and you know there's no other way."

As I left he said, "I'll see what I can do."

The project trudged along after that conversation, but a couple of years later I got a letter in the mail from the Department of Community and Economic Development saying that my organization had been awarded a grant for $500,000.

The funding gave us the ability to do what had become a pattern with each of my successful initiatives: find a partner who can look after the details. After all, I may have a strong vision but I sometimes lack skills in the small-details department.

From Mark Horn and Gay Youth, to Harry Langhorne with the Gay Raiders, Jane Shull with AIDS Awareness Day, Andrew Park and Andy Chirls with the domestic partnership crusade, Dan Anders and Jeff Guaracino and the Elton John concert, the incredible staff at *Philadelphia Gay News* who allow their publisher the time for other endeavors, and Klayton Fennell at Comcast-NBCUniversal—I always surrounded myself with top-notch and highly skilled professionals. Each one was an equal partner, keeping me on track and sometimes in order. And they all had something in common: they were much smarter and much more diplomatic than I am, and they paid attention to details.

Now I needed a partner for what would become the biggest project of my career—the $19.5 million facility would be the largest LGBT building project in the nation created entirely with government funds and tax credits. Enter Micah Mahjoubian.

As he tells the story: "I joined the project around October 2010. I remember being worried about paying the bills. It was after I had finished the Arlen Specter campaign. My only client was Ceisler Media and it wasn't enough. My dog needed surgery and I had no way of paying for it. I literally ran into you on the street with my dog after we got the news from the vet and I said that I didn't know how I was going to pay for it. I said I needed work, and I was interested in helping on the project. You immediately said that was a good idea. I've been thankful ever since."

Micah is a brilliant political operative; he had been an openly gay member of Mayor John Street's administration, as well as a cochair of the local LGBT Democratic Club. He's also very tech savvy. He entered the project as we were finalizing the concept of building the apartments on top of the existing LGBT Community Center, which was actually the second location that we explored. The original location, proposed by Senator Fumo, was an old army armory on South Broad Street that was then being used for once-a-week bingo games. The games were somehow sponsored by the archdiocese and run by a South Philly doctor. The building was in major disrepair, which made it a perfect candidate. We had to talk the archdiocese and the doctor into the deal. Things had been going well, but then the federal prosecutor raided Vince's offices and began to crack down on his staff and friends. While everything we had done was above board, I didn't want to get embroiled in the publicity circus. So I sent the money—that $500,000 grant—back to the state. Two months later, at my annual holiday party, Governor Ed Rendell walked in the door with an angry face. He grabbed me, took me into a corner, and snapped, "Mark, you *never* give money back to the state. Do you know how many nonprofits would kill for those funds?" As I explained that we didn't want to get caught in the middle of whatever investigation was going on, he began to calm down, and I recognized the look that now crossed his face. He had a solution to the problem. "I'll reissue the money from the governor's office." And he gave me one final piece of advice: "Use it correctly." We did. It was the seed money that kept us moving.

A couple of years later I was in the governor's office asking for more. So began an endless procession of meetings with public officials and department heads to find the right formula for the funding. "Equality" was now a key word, and we ran with it, arguing that we were pursuing this project in the same way that Catholic charities and Jewish federations do their senior homes. All we wanted was equality, to be able to build our project in the same way. The first group to understand this was the team at the US Department of Housing and Urban Development. With the assistance of HUD Secretary Shaun Donovan, and his able deputies Dr. Raphael Bostric and my longtime friend Estelle Richman, we became the first federally designated project with the acceptable designation "LGBT-friendly." That in turn allowed us to apply for funding.

Sometimes when you're so involved with numerous meetings to secure funding, gain community support, and round up corporations to partner with, you lose sight of why you're even doing the project.

I remember Veronica, a women in her late sixties, who told me that as she and her partner of thirty years neared retirement age, they faced the real possibility of homelessness. Both women had worked their entire lives, but never earned enough to save for retirement. Both volunteered their time caring for those in shelters and hospices, and now they were in need of the very care that they provided—but where would they turn?

Donald, sixty-two, was a former teacher and longtime activist in the LGBT community. Surviving on Social Security disability for the past twenty years, his arthritis and neuropathy made living alone in a third-floor walk-up—his only affordable option—more difficult with each passing day. Why shouldn't he be able to live with dignity in his golden years among the LGBT community to which he belonged?

Then there were my Gay Liberation Front brothers and sisters. Due to age and illness, some were left isolated, far from the community that they had helped create. There were also those who lived in religious-based low-income homes and were being mistreated by the staff and shunned by the other residents.

This is the first out generation. The way we treat the needs of our pioneers will define our community, just as the call to help our gay youth and trans communities did in the early days of the movement.

And we as a community were failing. Gay rights pioneer

Frank Kameny, for many years and up to his death in 2011, had to constantly call friends to request money. In 1957, Kameny was the first US government employee to fight being fired because of his "homosexuality," thereby launching his activism. He lived long enough to get an apology from the president of the United States, Barack Obama.

Shame on us! Near his death, Frank still lived in his mother's home (he actually owned it), but to generate the funds to live and be an activist, it was mortgaged to the hilt. Frank's friends, including Bob Witeck, Charles Francis, Rick Rosendall, and Marvin Carter, took over his finances and attempted to put him on a budget, but somehow Frank, who for years begged, couldn't or wouldn't conform.

The year before Frank died, my friend Jeff Guaracino, who at that time was working to generate tourism in Philadelphia, asked me to help arrange the honoring of some of our early pioneers. So in a parade on July 4, 2010, Frank Kameny rode past Independence Hall in a convertible car with a banner in front stating, *Early Gay Rights Pioneers*. Forty-six years before to the day, he had been picketing at that same historic building. As always, Frank wore a suit and tie on that hot, humid July 4, but the suit was old and worn. Frank wasn't begging for funds any longer, but he couldn't get used to the changes that came late in life. At lunch after the parade, he asked if he was allowed to order anything on the menu.

No senior, much less a pioneer, should find him or herself at an advanced age with little resources from our community. For a long time, seniors were, literally and figuratively, the last issue to be considered.

Frank is a good example of our pioneers who live in poverty. We need systems and assurances in place similar to what we now have for gay youth.

So what does the future hold for our elder community? To answer this question, we should first ask: how much do we know about them? We know much about youth and bullying issues, much about our LGBT citizens in military uniforms, much about those couples who wish to marry and have children. Even those interested in playing professional sports. But what about the elders? We know very little, and that is a sign that our community's agenda has, for the most part, left them behind.

Financing for the $19.5 million project would have to come from federal, state, and city funds. It would give seniors a safe, accepting place to call home. Los Angeles was one of the few places helping elders in this way, and a facility in Chicago would open about a year after our ribbon-cutting—but there remained an entire country full of LGBT seniors facing serious housing issues. Success in Philly would be a step in the right direction.

There were zero LGBT senior advocacy programs in our region when we began. We started by funding the Delaware Valley Legacy Fund, which resulted in the creation of the LGBT Elder Initiative spearheaded by a man named Heshie Zinman. We met with every mainstream senior service organization in the region and requested their help and lobbied for their inclusion of LGBT seniors. We asked for seats on governmental senior boards and commissions. And we helped fund another study on the concerns of LGBT seniors, this time by the Philadelphia Health Management Corporation, and once again found that housing was a major issue.

The next step in the process was to decide where to build. I was out looking at buildings on Spruce Street one day and bumped into Dolph Goldenburg, then the executive director of the community center. He asked what I was doing. When I told him in confidence, he said why not build it on top of the center?

Dolph is a man courageous enough to think big, and it was a good idea. We could build our space while doing much-needed repairs to the community center. Dolph's timing could not have been better. The week before, I had met with Richard Barnhart from Pennrose, who would become a codeveloper of the building. The community center gave us a site but not the magic words *site control*. Without that you cannot apply for low-income tax credits. Up to this point, only a few people knew of the dream, namely our board, consultants, the elected officials who had agreed to fund us, and our development partner, Pennrose. But in order for Pennrose to draw up plans, they needed to know the full and true condition of the community center and we needed the center's board to give us a document that included those two words. We enlisted the support of the center's cochairs and asked them not to tell anyone what we were planning, including their own board. They nervously and bravely shepherded the project, up until it was time to get the paper with the words *site control*. In order for us to receive the tax credits needed for the project we had to present that document to the Pennsylvania Housing Finance Agency, which was headed by Brian Hudson. We staged an all-out lobbying campaign to get those tax credits and he, poor guy, was on the receiving end. But instead of asking us to stop, he actually encouraged us, realizing that we might be needed later for public support. It must also be stated here that the staff at PHFA, a state agency then controlled by a Republican governor, gave us every bit of support requested. They treated us as equals. Which is all that we asked.

When we went to the full community center board for approval, it was the first time they had heard of the project; we had successfully kept it quiet. Yet there was one additional hurdle: Dolph was about to leave the center to move to Atlanta. Enter the new executive director with no knowledge of the project,

Chris Bartlett, one of the most affable members of the community. He too was a bit shocked by our news. He knew it would be controversial, but he also understood the difficulties faced by low-income seniors. It was a gutsy move for him to take on the job.

As expected, once we made it public, the project irked some in the gay community. The community center called a public meeting to discuss the proposal. While we were ultimately given a yellow light to proceed with caution, my takeaway from that meeting was the image of a young man standing up and screaming at the top of his lungs, "If you build this old person's home on top of the community center, no young people will ever come here again!" After forty long years of fighting, I couldn't resist yelling, "Ageist!" back at him.

That young man soon left the city to go to school out of state. But there were others in the community who felt the clientele for an LGBT-friendly low-income building would be, in their words, "drug addicts, drag queens, and prostitutes." My response was that people selling drugs would be in violation of their lease and tossed out. Who would be calling a sixty-two-year-old prostitute? As for the drag queens, bring them on, we want them!

Another element of resistance came from my personal detractors, who met with our major supporters, Governor Rendell and Senator Casey, requesting that they drop their support of the project. We also had some contentious negotiations with the board of the community center over the repairs that would need to occur if we were to build on top of it.

We were simultaneously negotiating with the community center, designing the building with the architects, working with Jacob Fisher of Pennrose to finalize the paperwork that would be submitted to the Pennsylvania Housing Finance Agency

(PHFA) for funding, and explaining to city and state officials that the federal government would accept the term "LGBT-friendly" and that it was not discriminatory in any way. Micah and I were trying to organize an advisory board from the community to ease any problems with the neighborhood associations, and all along keep our eyes out for any new objections that surfaced. We were in heavy negotiations over our contract with Pennrose regarding ownership, property management, and the responsibilities of each party. We also had to work out agreements with unions, since we wanted to have LGBT contractors involved with the construction. It was an incredible juggling act.

Our negotiations with the community center fell through along the way due to differing expectations related to repairs and operating expenses. We parted on good terms, though, and Chris Bartlett managed to keep the line of communication open, so the center could help out as needed.

When we entered discussions with the city for a parcel of land on 13th Street, Mayor Michael Nutter pushed his administration along with record speed. It was a choice parcel, and some people really didn't want to give it up. The mayor deserves tremendous credit, along with the Redevelopment Authority's board chair James Cuorato, for making it happen. With the new location secure, Jacob Fisher pulled all the strings together and completed a new plan. From the time we parted ways with the community center, came up with that property on 13th Street, and drew up the new plans, a mere ninety days had passed—we were rushing to make the filing deadline with PHFA.

Meanwhile, Republican Tom Corbett was elected governor—and we discovered that Ed Rendell hadn't been able to complete the state's part of the project. So I had to go begging a new Republican governor to finalize the state funding. Pennrose had a good relationship with the Corbett administration, but to ensure our success, I began to make myself known within the governor's circle. Soon I was told that if it was a good project, they'd fund it. They not only did this, but when various issues stymied us, as they usually do on a project of this magnitude, the administration was always fair and helpful. They helped calm the waters. Then, in April of 2012, we were approved for tax credits. This is how I wrote about it that week:

> On Monday we announced that the pie-in-the-sky project, which was made public about two years ago, is now a reality. For many of us, it's the most ambitious project we've ever undertaken. To find a home, a safe place to give our LGBT seniors to live; to bring them a home to thrive in their very own community—that's the goal. I have no illusions that the proposal has many more milestones to meet. It is not a done deal yet. And it will take the support and input of the entire community and our elected officials who have committed to follow through on this dream.
>
> Last Thursday, the Pennsylvania Housing Finance Agency met to decide which projects would be awarded tax credits this year. I'm happy to report that the pie-in-the-sky project was awarded credit in that very competitive field.
>
> The project is now fully funded at $19 million. It is, as the mayor said during the announcement, the largest LGBT-friendly capital building project in the United States. The White House and HUD spotlighted the project as "pioneering innovation in US housing solutions for low-income LGBT seniors."

Good things kept coming our way. When our board decided to name the building after John C. Anderson, a former city council member who was both African American and gay, and who had died from AIDS, we had no idea of the impact it would have. At the groundbreaking for the building, State Senator Tony Williams spoke with great emotion: "You may have bridged the gap between the African American and LGBT community with this building, since it is to my knowledge the first building in America purposefully named after an LGBT African American public official."

When Mayor Nutter cut the ribbon, he was joined by former governor Ed Rendell, US Senator Bob Casey, the entire Philadelphia congressional delegation led by my old friend Bob Brady, Brian Hudson, who was president of the National Council of State Housing Agencies, various other state representatives and senators, and members of the city council—headed by Council President Darrell Clarke—along with District Councilman Mark Squilla. The council had suspended rules in order to pass our zoning changes, unanimously.

By the time we started to build, the vision had grown. We understood that we had to nurture a broader LGBT senior advocacy movement. We knew we couldn't do it alone and we wanted this project embraced by the community and dearly wanted them to have a feeling of ownership. So we went back to the community center and suggested that once we opened, they could take charge of the activities and social services. We asked the Mazzoni Center to create courses on law and safe sex. ActionAIDS was chosen as the HIV/AIDS services agency in the building. We even built an office on the first floor for outside organizations to work from.

Joe Salerno became our architect; he was a gay man who wound up, in a way, coming out during the process. My instructions to him were simple. We were building in an upscale area, and the concept must give our residents dignity. I wanted them to feel that "wow" factor when they walked through the front door. Joe and I came to a quick agreement, though Pennrose didn't like how much our vision would cost them. I had learned that a good partnership always involves compromise, so with every change they'd explain how much it would cost, and we'd attempt to find savings in another area.

The vision: Enter the building into a spacious open area with staff offices and resident mailboxes. Walk a little farther and you'll discover the lobby and library, complete with etched glass and fireplace. Sitting by the fireplace, you can peer out through glass windows that reveal a five-thousand-square-foot private courtyard with paths, benches, and even a fountain. There's a community room with an eighty-inch flat screen and seating for sixty. Farther down the hall is a computer lab station for the residents with five computers hooked up to the Internet. On the fifth floor there's a sundeck with sweeping views of the city's skyline.

Negotiating all of those areas, especially my request for glass walls, was a constant battle with Pennrose, with Jacob Fisher in the middle. But they were eventually completed and, in my opinion, completely worth the cost. The one item that most surprises people actually happened by mistake.

At our first meeting with the full construction team, many of whom were men employed by our general contractor, Domus, we all gathered around a table in one of Pennrose's conference rooms. Joe, who was reviewing the architectural drawings, noted that due to the shape of the building and the configuration of our courtyard, four apartments would have larger closets and a smaller bedroom than the others. I explained, "That's not a problem for our proposed clientele. We'll call them 'drag queen closets.' In fact, can we do the same in all the apartments?" The look on their faces was priceless as they all began to smile. Those closets are one of the most popular features of the building.

Residents must be sixty-two and above and earn no less than $8,000 a year and no more than $33,000. Surprisingly or not, there are lots of LGBT people with low incomes, especially those seniors about whom we know so little. Consider, as just one example, a trans person in 1969. What kind of job could they keep, and what savings, Social Security, or pension do you think they would accrue thirty or forty years later? Think of those stereotyped and shunned individuals in the 1960s who had to receive welfare in order to survive.

During the construction, we'd offer tours of the site to those who had taken part or those we wanted to get involved in the project. My friend Klayton Fennell from Comcast sent me a box of pink hard hats to give out on tours, and soon it became fashionable for a public figure to be photographed wearing one while touring the site. Those hard hats with our logo have become collectors' items.

The project was going in so many directions at once and often kept us guessing where we were actually headed. But behind the scenes was my board of directors, each with her or his own specialty. Irene Benedetti, the longest-serving member of the board, worked with the women's community, while Tyrone Smith, a pioneer in black gay rights, did the same with the African American community. Jane Shull coordinated with the HIV/AIDS community, while my good friend Rob Metzger handled small LGBT contractor firms. Larry Felzer was our liaison to the regional senior organizations. Jeff Guaracino dealt with government affairs and public relations and Judith Applebaum connected to the neighborhood organizations. Rick Lombardo worked on security issues while Judge Dan Anders was the guy I'd call and say, "What would *you* do?" No project of this size gets done without the support of its board. I have never been so honored to work with a board in my life. And, of course, there was Micah, who was by my side seven days a week, keeping me on track.

The Department of Housing and Urban Development asked us to showcase the project at their first conference on LGBT senior housing. Webcast live from their headquarters in Washington, DC, they and the White House hailed the project. From that meeting with President Obama in 2012 to the day we took in our first resident, only three years and nine months had passed. Yes, that was record timing for a project like this. Since opening, we have been deluged with requests to both tour the building and assist those wishing to replicate our success.

As I was driving myself to the state capital one day, my phone rang and I had to pull over to the side of the road. The call was from Openhouse, a group planning a similar senior project in San Francisco. They had finally gotten their seed money, found a developer, had site control, and were planning a forty-unit rehab facility. They asked, "How did you do the marketing to get the desired population?" San Francisco was asking *us* how to get members of the LGBT community into their building—the enormity of that question spelled out for me a job well done.

At the ribbon cutting on February 24, 2014, I took the microphone to welcome the large crowd. I pulled out a letter I had recently received and began to read it:

> *I send my warm regards on the opening of the John C. Anderson Apartments. For generations, courageous lesbian, gay, bisexual, and transgender Americans spoke up, came out, and fought injustice, blazing trails for others and pushing us closer to our founding ideals of equality for all. In the*

face of impossible odds, these leaders and committed allies demonstrated that change is possible and helped our nation become not only more accepting, but also more loving. And across America today communities are tackling challenges that remain and writing bold new chapters in this story of progress.

By working together as advocates, business leaders, and officials throughout government, we can address the problems of LGBT discrimination in housing. Offering security and affordability for Philadelphia's LGBT seniors, this apartment community is an example of how we can create a more hopeful world when we better care for one another. My administration stands with all those in the fight to ensure every American has equal access to housing—no matter who they are or whom they love. May this effort inspire us to continue striving for equality for all people in our time.

As the John C. Anderson Apartments opens its doors, I hope it provides warmth and comfort to all who call it home. I wish you all the best for years ahead.
—*Barack Obama*

The audience stood and applauded, and for an instant in the emotion of that moment I saw an image of my cousin Norman— who had never gotten the chance to live among people who treated him with decency and respect.

Chapter 15

And Then We Danced

In June 2014, I drove for an hour and a half in the rain to Harrisburg on the boring Pennsylvania Turnpike for a meeting at the Pennsylvania NewsMedia Association, one of the nation's oldest journalistic organizations, of which I now serve on the board of directors. It was the same organization that had refused me membership for fifteen years. The meeting would be held at a grand Georgian mansion overlooking the Susquehanna River, the organization's headquarters.

Pennsylvania NewsMedia Association is just a few blocks from the governor's official residence, where six months before I had met with our Republican governor, Tom Corbett, after he'd made a very public gaffe that caught national media fire. When asked about same sex-marriage in an October 2013 TV interview he'd compared it to incest. Shortly after that show, I received a call from one of the governor's staff members, asking if I'd come to Harrisburg and meet with the governor privately at his residence. The meeting would include Ted Martin, executive director of Equality Pennsylvania, Chris Labonte of consultant firm Sellers Dorsey, gay lawyer Tom Paese who was a codirector of Corbett's transition team, and Betty Hill, executive director of the Persad Center in Pittsburgh. The governor's chief of staff would also be present. This was a high-level meeting with people who meant business on LGBT issues. In a premeeting we had decided to focus on the nondiscrimination legislation currently sitting before the legislature. Martin would bring a slew of data and polling information. Hill would provide the personal stories of her clients and the negative effects caused by the absence of such legislation. Labonte knew how to stage a campaign, and Paese already worked closely with the governor.

In order to move the meeting forward quickly, the governor started out with an apology, which we all accepted. But when we got down to the basics, the governor was concerned that if he did anything now it would just look like a political move since he was about to enter a reelection campaign. That was my cue.

"Governor, as a member of the media, with all due respect, we see a man with a loose tongue. Someone will, in the near future, try to get you to make another statement on marriage. If I can humbly suggest that next time that happens—and it will—turn it around on that reporter. Turn directly to that reporter and say, *Why haven't you asked me about nondiscrimination?*"

And that is exactly what happened. This time the governor kept to the script. On December 18, 2013, the progressive blog *Think Progress* reported:

> *Pennsylvania Gov. Tom Corbett (R) announced Tuesday that he was "coming out in support" of a bill that would create nondiscrimination protections based on sexual orientation and gender identity. In his statement, Corbett claimed that he did not previously realize that the LGBT community was not protected by federal laws.*

The Human Rights Campaign in DC quickly put out a national press release that included the following passage:

In a surprise move today, Pennsylvania governor Tom Cor-bett announced his support for a bill banning discrimination based on sexual orientation. The governor joins other Re-publicans in the state who are in support of such legislation, including State Senator Pat Browne. Congressman Dent and Senator Pat Toomey are supportive of the federal Em-ployment Non-Discrimination Act which passed the Senate in early November and now heads to the House for consid-eration. Their position on the state legislation is unknown.

The governor not only followed the script, he improved on it. At that meeting, all of us present had suggested that we would be more than willing to stand by his side and help field any negativity, particularly from our own communities.

The governor had one more pleasant surprise in store, as well as at least one disappointment along the way. In Febru-ary 2014, when we had been finally ready to cut the ribbon on the John C. Anderson Apartments, we were hoping that Vice President Biden would do the honors. Mayor Nutter and Sena-tor Bob Casey, along with our congressional delegation, wrote a letter of invitation. When we discovered the VP could not join us, we quickly set another date, which unfortunately came at the same time as the National Governors Association Winter Meeting. Governor Corbett would be unable to attend.

But he made up for it when the marriage-equality issue found its way to Pennsylvania. I began a very private lobbying campaign with my friends in the governor's office. After all, they had now worked with me for three years on the John C. Anderson senior housing project. We expected that Judge John E. Jones III, a Republican appointed by George W. Bush who was handling the case, would rule in our favor, but we never expected how strong his ruling would be.

My campaign was only known by my most trusted friends and of course the governor's office. This was a highly controversial issue for a man who many thought was a Tea Party Republican, and my friends thought it was crazy that I believed Corbett would allow the state to accept the judge's ruling, should he strike down anti–gay marriage laws in Pennsylvania. The judge stated that he would not hear debate, choosing instead to rule from the briefs each side provided to him. During my conversations with Corbett's staff, I became aware of the timing of Judge Jones's expected ruling, which led me to suggest various options to the governor's legal team.

Option 1: explain that the judge had overruled a law that the legislature had passed and toss it back to them to start anew, but don't request a stay.

Option 2: explain that your hands are tied, since the attorney general should appeal this. AG Kathleen Kane had previously stated that based on the Constitution as well as her personal beliefs, she would not defend anti–gay marriage laws.

Option 3: pass it over to the state treasurer, who would have to handle the effect of the new marriage law on taxes. State Treasurer Rob McCord had also stated that he personally believed in marriage equality.

Option 4, the hardest and bravest option: do what Governor Chris Christie of New Jersey did. State that while you have personal objections, you won't get in the way of the judge's ruling, and allow marriage equality in Pennsylvania.

While attending the New York Tech Expo to help my nephew Jeffrey launch his new company, my cell phone rang. It was the governor's chief legal counsel, Jim Schultz.

"Mark, I promised to give this to you first. We're doing the Christie."

After everything I'd been through in politics, Jim was giving me a political surprise I hadn't seen in years. All I could think to do was offer my assistance if the governor needed some cover. Jim declined; they were good. I also knew that it was Jim who'd fought the hardest for this.

Soon after that call, the governor issued a statement: "Given the high legal threshold set forth by Judge Jones in this case, the case is extremely unlikely to succeed on appeal." Corbett went on to say that he still believed that marriage should be between one man and one woman, and that his faith had not wavered. That line was somewhat understandable, as he was running for reelection and needed to preserve his electoral base.

And as would be expected, *PGN* was the first to have the governor's decision up online.

Philadelphia County began issuing marriage licenses to couples on May 20, 2014. Ron Donatucci, the man in charge of this process, deputized me that day and allowed me to work with the applicants and issue licenses myself. It was the ultimate joy to sit down in a cubicle and have two happy people ushered toward me.

As Jason was helping me deal with all of this, our friend City Councilman Jim Kenney appeared and said he just wanted to be present to observe this historic time. Then he asked, "What about you two?" Jason and I looked at each other and said, after ten years together, why not?

We had just agreed to get married. That fact alone was overwhelming enough. But a problem arose as Jason and I walked up to the register. "That'll be eighty dollars in cash, please."

We stared at each other, dumbfounded. Neither of us had any cash on us. We turned to Jim, who, along with Ron, was chuckling. The two of them fished out their wallets and split the fee, forty dollars each—an engagement gift. We posed for some celebratory pictures and then joined the massive celebration outside City Hall.

When we got home that evening, Jason noticed a line in small print at the bottom of the marriage license. "Do you realize we have sixty days before the license expires?" We had two months, basically amounting to zero time, to make wedding plans. My head was spinning.

A few weeks later, back in Harrisburg for the meeting with the Pennsylvania NewsMedia Association, it dawned on me to take a close look at my calendar for the immediate future. Each day was filled with appointments, fundraisers, events, or meetings with developers. The John C. Anderson project was so successful that developers were lining themselves up at my door, pitching similar projects in New York, Washington, DC, and other cities.

Looking at that full calendar and the numerous opportunities ahead, a wave of memories came rolling back, and suddenly I'm standing outside Stonewall again, a boy who didn't know who he was or where he was going, living at the YMCA with no money and no prospects. The reality is that I had feared becoming one of those homeless kids that Gay Youth helped.

I noticed that I had two upcoming visits to Washington scheduled. The following Friday, I'd go with *Philadelphia Gay News* staff to the annual banquet of the Society of Professional Journalists at the National Press Club to accept the 2014 Investigative Journalist Award along with the *Wall Street Journal*. Then, on the last Friday of June, it was back to the White House for the president's reception in honor of Gay Pride Month.

The John C. Anderson project had taken me to the White House and Executive Office Building a number of times in the last few years, but there are two visits that stand out. The first was at the White House after a long day of meetings on Capitol Hill and the Department of Housing and Urban Development. I was joined by Richard Barnhart, one of the owners of Pennrose Management Company. Richard is a very successful man; he's the Ted Turner style of executive, impeccably dressed and often escaping to his retreat out West. At times, he presents a bit of a waspy, holier-than-thou attitude. He was doing that routine as we entered the White House, so I turned and asked him if he'd ever been there before on business. He looked around in amazement and said he hadn't. I replied, "You mean it took a pushy Jew faggot to get you in the White House?" He simply smiled.

The other visit that stands out was when I had the opportunity to introduce Jason to the president and Mrs. Obama. We were at one of the president's holiday parties. As is tradition, the president and first lady pose for pictures with their guests. When it was our turn, the immaculately uniformed Marine introduced us: "Mr. President, may I present Mark Segal and his guest, Jason Villemez."

The protocol is for the invited guest to stand next to the president and their spouse or guest to stand next to the first lady. Me being Mark Segal, I said, "Mr. President, I have enough pictures of us together, but I have none with the beautiful first lady, so I hope you don't mind if I stand next to her."

Laughter came from behind the camera. It was Reggie Love, the president's personal aide who had helped usher the plans for the Anderson project. He gave a thumbs-up.

That was the only time I've ever witnessed Jason in total awe. Nothing, and I mean nothing—with the exception of my driving skills—had ever fazed him before. To see that side of him was a joy.

With all my memorable trips to the White House, I was almost dreading another visit to Washington. But surprises—

delightful ones at that—seem to always pop up if I simply keep my eye on the target.

At the gay pride reception at the White House in June 2014, Jason and I stood near the back of the East Room with the photographers and journalists, giving others a chance to be close to the president. Midway through the president's speech, I thought I heard him say, "We must do more with affordable housing for our LGBT seniors." I did a double take, thinking I might be imagining things. But after the speech, one of the president's assistants, Gautam Raghavan, came over and said with a big grin, "Did you notice we got your line in?"

Later, Jason and I headed to the portico entrance, where the Marine band was playing, and we danced in the White House. The following Saturday, July 5, we got married in a private ceremony with Jason's sisters as best women and my nephew Jeffrey as best man, and my friend Judge Dan Anders presiding over the ceremony. Jason's parents were there too; in our pockets we each had a piece of his mother's wedding veil which she had given us for the ceremony.

Mom, I'm now sixty-four years old, and I finally have a response to that concern you expressed when I first told you I was gay. Rest assured, I'm not lonely. When people ask me, "Mr. Segal, what was the happiest day of your life?" I get to say, "The day Jason and I married."

It has been a long road from 2333 South Bambrey Terrace, from that lonely guy who escaped to New York with seemingly no future. While I haven't accomplished my father's dream of getting a degree, there is no doubt that he would feel very good about what I've done in lieu of that.

At the ribbon cutting of the John C. Anderson Apartments,

each and every public official spoke about how I was a pain in the ass to deal with. What's nice is that they all said it with pride. That's a compliment I welcome.